Books by Parker Tyler

THE METAPHOR IN THE JUNGLE

YESTERDAY'S CHILDREN, *with Pavel Tchelitchew*

THE HOLLYWOOD HALLUCINATION

THE GRANITE BUTTERFLY

MAGIC AND MYTH OF THE MOVIES

CHAPLIN

THE THREE FACES OF THE FILM

THE YOUNG AND EVIL, *with Charles Henri Ford*

CONRAD MARCA-RELLI

CLASSICS OF THE FOREIGN FILM

FLORINE STETTHEIMER: A LIFE IN ART

EVERY ARTIST HIS OWN SCANDAL

THE THREE FACES OF THE FILM: *New and revised
    edition*

THE DIVINE COMEDY OF PAVEL TCHELITCHEW

World Art Series: VAN GOGH

                RENOIR

                CÉZANNE, GAUGUIN

                DEGAS, LAUTREC

SEX, PSYCHE, ETCETERA IN THE FILM

UNDERGROUND FILM: A CRITICAL HISTORY

SCREENING THE SEXES: HOMOSEXUALITY IN THE
    MOVIES

THE WILL OF EROS: SELECTED POEMS 1930–1970

THE SHADOW
OF AN AIRPLANE
CLIMBS
THE EMPIRE
STATE BUILDING

Parker Tyler

THE SHADOW OF AN AIRPLANE CLIMBS THE EMPIRE STATE BUILDING

A WORLD THEORY OF FILM

Published in
1973

ANCHOR BOOKS
ANCHOR PRESS/DOUBLEDAY
GARDEN CITY, NEW YORK
1973

The Shadow of an Airplane Climbs the Empire State Building was originally published in hardcover by Doubleday & Company, Inc.

ANCHOR BOOKS EDITION: 1973

ISBN 0-385-01141-5

ACKNOWLEDGMENTS

During the three years of research and composition occupied by this book, I found myself restricted to studying not the whole body of conspicuous film criticism but only those ideas and attitudes (creative and critical) that had theoretical bearing or that formulated express theories; necessarily then, a great deal of sometimes astute and readable criticism did not fall within my purview. I wished the book to proceed steadily toward a goal of theoretical consciousness no less than aesthetic awareness. In this case my acknowledgments also must be particular and limited. To Charles Boultenhouse I owe much thanks for half a dozen conversations (all of them taped) in which he sought to test my views by providing a dialectic opposition. There remains only to mention my gratitude to William G. Whitehead for his faith in this project and his wise and patient editorship.

P.T.

CONTENTS

INTRODUCTORY

A world theory of film must be as much about the world as about film; else it is only a stab at a theory, a shadow of one. We cannot aim at a perfectly secure, a really satisfying and broadly based theory of film, therefore, without taking into account all our problems as a human society today, especially that aspect that involves the value and limits of the aesthetic position as such. Film, as so widely useful a medium (TV is also film), one so often involved with elements only journalistic, carries an immense technical burden and a corresponding moral responsibility. Obviously, then, it is impossible to propose a theory of film without examining a number of historical quantities.

A theory, in its own way, is very solid and very large. At its high level best, it is metaphysics; that is, it embodies the delight and glory of mankind known as the function of pure mind. Yet, really, metaphysics—even when concerned with its most practical function, reli-

gion (or divine observances)—is nothing in itself but the
space food of the mind. It is a subtle scientific conversion of mental nutriment for certain exquisite yet vast
purposes. Yes! And it is also quite like the food prepared
for astronauts, who must live under drastically sublime
conditions. So we may ask just what the composition of
actual space food is. It may have all the necessary vita-
mins, minerals and calories; thus it may perfectly sustain
life. Still it is not the product of the best cuisine; in
short, it is not *the experience of eating*. In the same way,
metaphysics, no matter how refined or intellectually
thrilling as a pure activity, is not *the experience of living*.
Film, like other arts, has or should have a philosophy
of form, but it is not a true and whole experience (no
matter how greatly regarded) till it be related to a philosophy of content . . . till we see just what it does, *all*
that it does; and furthermore, in full justice, all that can
be done with it.

So far, the process of human life—familiarly known,
linguistically, as history—is a matter of approved accumulation, a "body" of knowledge, more or less theoretical;
it is a vast dossier of actions interpreted according to
certain theories of knowledge. We even go so far in
optimism as to call this process and its conscious ingredients of thought, its living language along with its
library of documents, progress—by which we mean, specifically, civilized progress. We mean, necessarily, progress toward the *ideals* of civilization. Here, if most
delicately, we touch on metaphysics and its sober ecstasy
of magic. We touch it, we somehow involve it; we do not
easily or immediately systematize it with what we "know"
because, as knowledge, metaphysics is semantically suspect. Theory, as great as it is, must be kept separate from
practice, from actions, from experience.

Theory is a very civilized product, and so is magic as

a rather more distant phase of civilized aspiration. Moreover we see at a glance that metaphysics, however useful, is still accounted a standard academic virtue. It is itself (unlike magic) a phase of philosophy. It is something taught the young in order that they be "educated." But physics too is part of the high curriculum; physics is likewise a very complicated and difficult subject, requiring long study to be mastered: a fund of mental energy as well as moral dedication. Much the same is true of the many branches of medicine. So far as the world goes, *physics* need be no more practical than *metaphysics*; physics also may be a formal science only, a matter of mastering logical forms that supposedly correspond to the life processes of matter, and account even, on technical grounds, for metaphysics. All this is to recommend that we assess and criticize theory *through experience*.

It is when we come to the realm of empiric activity, the question of society living with itself, and "at peace" with itself, that the study and mastery of difficult forms (such as physics and metaphysics) receive their inevitable tests. As to the testable truth of philosophy, since this study really exists in the plural, that is, as philosophies; and since, under democratic systems of academic administration, different or even opposed philosophies can theoretically live together, the truth or truths of philosophy are really in perpetual suspense as representing an admittedly pluralist world—that is, "worlds"—subject to applied rules of civilized etiquette; by which is really meant, as to philosophic discourse, a domain of free and open propaganda. However, it is when the propaganda is *political*, and the academy is not concerned directly, that the pluralism of philosophic truth has to be limited and shaped by the political aims of a given state. It is now that *theories* must themselves be disciplined, their growth and character directed by non-theorists—that is, by politicians, diplomats, military experts, etc.—now that theories definitely take second place to what is known to science as "instrumentation" or, to put it quite simply, "practice."

Thus, the division between theoretic or "pure" science and practical or "instrumented" science can be gravely moral and even sometimes—so palpably different are they from one another—as black is to white. On the other hand, conceivably, theory and practice can be brought together, can become the same thing, can be unilateral and monolithic. For example, we find that the Soviet school, blossoming in the 1920s and controlling film practice in Russia, was the strict instrumentation of a political philosophy, Marxism, which itself had been founded on a dialectical philosophy that had been developed chiefly by Hegel from the model of the classic philosophic dialogue of ancient Greece, as practiced by Socrates and the Sophists. This aspect of Marxism has grown feeble, almost meaningless, in the Soviet Union today. But whatever its practical status, the formula of Marxist dialectics sounds disarmingly simple. If, as Hegel says, progress—or, to grant his term, life itself—depends on a "thesis" which is then conditioned by an "antithesis" so that a "synthesis" is the inevitable outcome of their friction, it would seem obvious and logical that the thesis of capitalism, the prevailing system, opposed by the revolutionary antithesis of Marxism, would eventually issue in the future ideal "socialist" society; that is, in a material synthesis. When this new society is perfected, Hegel's philosophy of dialectic as a progressive march toward a summit of ultimate perfection would cease to be "ideal," merely formal, and turn into a tangible reality; it would be proven; in short, it would be successfully instrumented.

Let us forget about the rate at which the social theory is being proven. What of the film theory? It produced some impressive films and talented directors, though the latter seem to have no successors. Theories are whimsical and so are fashions. Theories—those floating ideas which may mean a new dress style or an important scientific invention—tend to be swallowed up by—just by life itself, by time, by ineluctable changes of taste. Surely the working theories of Sergei Eisenstein and Vsevolod Pudovkin are still on book shelves and—like Hegel—included in college courses. Scholars, historians, even theorists of film still, presumably, have the old "teaching" function. However, categories themselves are not so distinct, less so nowadays than in previous decades; often, I daresay, scholar-historian-theorists (if the truth were known) are as confused in their functional capacity, these days, as they used to be, more or less, fused. Such confusion must be the responsibility of the educational systems, wherever they are in our teeming world. To speak in the most academic and scholastic sense, one must observe that film as a study course has less of a recognized working tradition behind it than does any other academic subject. The emphasis is thrown decidedly, even a little flat-footedly and stodgily, toward the history and technique of practice. Film study is the shibboleth of a naïvely technological age. The causes for this paucity of theoretic richness should not be overlooked; in a way, the causes are obvious, but they ought not, for that reason, to be taken for granted or slurred over.

One should bear in mind the curiously urgent empiric temper of our times and that the film, as a world industry, is the more saturated with commercialism because, as a popular entertainment, it must make huge profits in order to survive. The most detached regard for filmic values is not free of this overhanging bugaboo: the prestige of historic examples, historic "successes" and (alas!) "classics." For example, film is the last of the arts, so to speak, to win slices of the vast moneys the big Foundations have been dispensing for decades to education, science and the arts in the United States. The present book, surely, is not to be limited to *American* experience. At the same time, the American film industry is one of the world's largest, and its relation to general culture and the nation's philanthropic establishments is to be regarded, therefore, as a world prototype.

At this date, film museums and archives are more numerous, and better endowed, than they used to be. Moreover, the small industry, as represented by independent film-making (sometimes termed the Underground), is livelier, more self-supporting and has more public prestige than ever before. Still, it is seldom recognized that this same popularity—evincing itself in more and more students wishing to enroll for film courses and thereby gain college credits—is not so much due to "film culture," though this term has a flattering currency, as to the growth of public awareness of the film as a compelling communication medium: the original "pop art."

Some observers, particularly Marshall McLuhan, believe the energized interest in film as a distinct medium is owed to the historic shift of public sensitivity from the literary or "print" phase of optical communication to the pure image phase; and not to the latter as painting, of course, or even still photography, but rather as motion pictures. And even more significantly, as television. There's a theory for you! But is it really true? Perhaps other theories of visual communication, gauged at somewhat higher levels of intelligence, can refute McLuhan's —and incidentally the two or three others that have appeared since the elementary montage theory of Eisenstein. There are astoundingly few to have followed that neat step from political theory into film theory. But there are some. The urgent point is that these few are unfortunately far too much post-facto rationalizations: the servants of humble achievements falsely glorified into portentous platforms for the future of mankind and the "visual arts." These theories must be carefully examined and methodically scuttled by something that really deserves, historically and artistically, the label of theory. I mean: there must be a *new* theory. For this, the world itself must be evoked.

part i

CREATIVE GROWTH

HISTORY AS FILM MONTAGE

When sound and talking were added to the commercial film by scientific progress in developing this medium, a school of film purists appeared with the thesis that the technology of sound, even though it made film a direct competitor with the legitimate stage, was undesirable to the "film art" because that art was thus rendered impure. Art! Whenever broad discussions of film engage us, it almost instantly becomes evident that the category of "aesthetic" is less relevant to the issue at hand than is the case in any other medium. All "art" to one side, and according to the theory of history as the record of accumulation (or, tacitly, aggrandizement), it was inevitable for film to add heard speech, or audible dialogue, to its technique as it was for the stage to add *film* to *its* established techniques. Both were extra shows of strength by a given medium.

We cannot historically and universally consider the theory of film, then, without conceding a certain dynamic trend in the social-economic process—what I mean, in a phrase, is the medium's synthetic aggrandizement; and I mean history not as the mere accumulation of records, but as a motivating force of a civilization designed logically and constantly to better itself, to *produce* more and *be* more . . . more, of course, that is *good*. Hence the word *progress* necessarily appears to us, from the philosophic standpoint, as essentially Hegelian, whatever else it might be, since Hegel's dialectic, detecting in society a ceaseless play of movement by contradiction, posited an equally constant "aggrandizement." This was to be understood in terms (however strictly materialistic) of gradual improvement, a spiral getting nearer and nearer to a desirable goal; a goal Hegel felt it proper, as I have noted, to call perfection.

Nevertheless I doubt we have to think of film as having a necessary debt to dialectic philosophy through the Soviet school of Eisenstein, Pudovkin and other Russians, even though palpably what is known as the Russian school of film-making *does* display this historic debt. To be sure, Eisenstein and Pudovkin are still honored constituents of Soviet history, as are Lenin and Stalin in the Soviet Union's political hall of fame. One wonders, however, since Stalin's precepts and modus vivendi as a leader have been discarded and formally repudiated by the current Soviet regime, and Lenin's leadership retained only as he looks like an old-fashioned national hero—a companion of Alexander Nevsky and even Ivan the Terrible—one wonders, accordingly, if an outmoded superstition, a sort of magic fetishism, has not more force in the Soviet Union than scientific Marxism would nominally pretend.

It is a very old habit of civilized society, through the technical survival of its religious instincts, not to demolish its old gods and ritual forms, but somehow to make use of them by reconversion—by creating a mausoleum that is a museum, a thing large, ornamental, prestigious, enduring . . . For example, there is the strong survival in modern Russia of the old court ballet tradition which now the Soviet Union proudly shows the world. The tradition is so strong, indeed, that defections of high-ranking dancers to other nations (though much feared) can safely be sustained. Soviet politicians, including the guardian-bureaucrats of culture, might be surprised to be confronted with the argument that a logical contradiction is involved with the mere survival of the Tsarist court ballet in Russia: everyone there has gotten so used to converting the universe into the domestic dialectic. The old dance tradition, thus, serves, and served, as a mere thesis for the antithesis of the Marxist Revolution, with its emphasis on the uprising of an oppressed people against their tyrannic masters, a process to which, embarrassingly enough, there seems never to be an end.

A Russian proponent could call to witness ballets such as *Spartacus*, which gets away from ballet steps as school formalism by shifting much emphasis to miming, reinforced as this is by the theme of *Spartacus*: a historic revolution by Roman gladiators. Along the same lines, Shakespeare, as a universal cultural property, could theoretically be revived with the Dmitri Shostakovich opera *Lady Macbeth of Minsk* (now called *Katerina Ismailova*), which however displeased Stalin and was instantly banned. A system based on mutation through dialectics can always rationalize drama itself as the portrait of historical contradictions, for which Communism is seen as the "inevitable" remedy. Yet, blind to all independent artistic standards, the overall bureaucracy thus created (even when it deposed its own tyrants) was based on the quicksands of inconsistency, lack of taste, and of course abysmal vulgarity.

If the court ballet tradition uniquely survived as a sort of Communist establishment, it was not until after a struggle that had started with the innovations of the gifted Sergei Diaghilev and the dancer-choreographer Michel Fokine long before the Revolution of 1917. The Russian ballet and its stars roamed the world before and after that revolution. As it turned out, "Imperialist" ballet was still strongest on its home ground! Valiantly, by rote, the totalitarian regime tried to sovietize the theatrical dance toward revolutionary themes and the folk, but balletomanes in Russia were bored by the stage spectacles offered them in a week's crash Festival, anticlimactically standing up to applaud and cheer a concluding students' presentation of the Imperial ballet *Swan Lake*, staged by Agrippina Vaganova. There had to be a frantic reappraisal: what was the dialectic moral?

The display value of the old steps, rife with athletic glitter, stood out as an applause machine and actually reflected the desire of the Russian élite under Communism to nurture a luxury article. Besides, the old plots could be freely twisted to reverse the classic transformation of peasant into prince (the archaic fairy-tale motif) by turning prince into peasant. Eventually even *Le Sacre du Printemps* could be presented because at the end the "heroine" (the ritual victim of Stravinsky's ballet) is rescued from her fate by a "hero." Psychology: Any sacrilege upon anything is justified by the Communist Revolution. All this starkly demonstrates the abstractness of the dialectic pattern (its "formalism") when it comes to administrative problems. The art of literature could not be thus manipulated if only because, for Soviet culture, words did not possess the naked naïveté of sheer theatrical glamour. Besides, all drastic thumbs-down decisions on styles of art could appear as virtuous "self-criticism." That today the high arbiters of the Soviet state are the sole judges of the "necessary" right of self-criticism was proven after the death of Stalin and the ultimate deposition of his successor, the late Nikita Khrushchev. Here was the state, safe beyond judgment by foreigners, indulging in self-criticism. The pattern of amnesty (however nominal rather than actual) was facilely borrowed from Christian forgiveness-and-reclamation through solemn confession of fault by individuals. In the U.S.S.R. the whole dialectic process was being brutally state-controlled.

Easily one sees, then, why *theories* may tend to look like books with old dates on their front page, thus texts hazy in the mind; without qualms, one can leave them to gather dust on the shelf. They don't have to be burnt —these theories in book form—they are just not read and hence not believed. Moreover, they may retain an ornamental value, especially so if they increase that department of propaganda known as international prestige. After three decades, it was found that the old Imperial dance idea could be thus implemented abroad. But the court ballet was not retained at all as a relevant form of life, a life style, but utterly, naïvely as a great gymnastic spectacle.

At this stage of world politics, cultural heritage is held to be a bargaining value at conference tables which actually have in view issues and stakes which the participating nations hold more important than the arts. Nowadays, space programs and their successful execution are very much up in international prestige despite the tendency in some quarters to oppose them. Of course, the space program involves new and very actual machines: it employs a science, not an art. If we look closely at such things as embodied in practical science, we see that the spectacular successes of a space program are, first, another *show of power*—that is, potentially destructive power. As destructive, it is the opposite of what is meant by constructive cultural ententes, however dialectic in structure these same ententes be. It is the stamp of excess that always betrays political showoff: the rhetoric of propaganda. I recall being reminded of Nazi architecture, its absurd multiplication of everything, when I saw a Russian film (I think it was the Khrushchev era) in which troops returning from the front were being welcomed to their home town; the scene was simply the spaces adjoining an old-fashioned railway station but there appeared so many people, carrying so many bouquets, and such enormous ones, that it looked as if all the flower shops of Moscow had been raided at once and utterly depleted. Space itself is "enormous."

As yet, however, achievements in space evoke no image of purely moral prestige, like a Nobel Prize for a physicist or a mathematician. Thus what we may call "space might" is in no sense of theoretical importance; it has no necessary status as scientific or historic theory, simply because as practice it is altogether self-sufficient, self-vindicating. Way out there, where civilization isn't, dialectic materialism seems to behave very much like capitalist exploitation. Such events could be added to the Olympic Games but not to the world of theory. Dramatically accomplished, self-evidently completed acts of might have no need of "theory." So it comes about that theories, all kinds, are destined to end up in the realm of archaeology—in a kind of abstract museum that has certain still existent, if much neglected, rooms.

It may be that there is a theory about theories that is built into some of them: they are no good unless capable of more or less instant ratification by life itself, by actuality. Let us cite the stratification aspect of history; for example, history as defined by deeply immerged layers of earth that tell stories of whole tribes and communities of prehistory, even of whole civilizations that have scarcely existed above ground for many centuries until they were excavated. These "natural museums," constructed simply by digging up and clearing away the earth, are composed of artifacts and skeletal remnants that symbolize a whole way of life, indeed a "life style," even a distinct if long dormant aesthetics. A vivid such reclamation of history and culture is the island of Crete, where a high court flourished at Knossos; where we see the origin of the modern bullfight and early examples of plumbing. In what ways does the historic existence of Crete reach us through a space other than the pathos of temporal distance?—as the museum which the partly reconstructed palace and the myths associated with it already reach tourists and scholars?

Certainly, history has its purely accumulative aspect, its dormant or semidormant library of records, which to some may look, like all monuments, most imposing, even refreshing. But history also has its vital or active aspect, which means (dialectically if we go to Hegel) that history is the present and continuing result of a long series of assimilations, co-extant with certain necessary eliminations. Ezra Pound's lifework became his verse project known as *The Cantos,* a modern, quite independent effort to present history as poetry—to expand the epic poem into a version of history commensurate with the vast complexity of civilization in the twentieth century.

Such was Pound's proud intention and hope. He believed he knew the truth because he believed he knew the truth of history, just where men and societies had gone wrong and just where they might go right through reconsideration and revaluing the "good" points of the past. For Pound, one may grow lyric not only over the emotions—say, the prime emotion of love—but over precepts of wisdom that can be historically located. *The Cantos* would sing, even as Homer had, men's "deeds of valor," but not necessarily those of the field of battle itself, physical battle, but those of the battle of wits, the field of accumulative wisdom: the realm of the lawgiver who first was prince and patron of arts, and only second a commander of the state's "armed forces."

Essentially, *The Cantos* were a rewriting of Homer, and to some extent a rewriting of history by reinflecting its more obvious emphases on what is "heroic." Yet Pound did not have a single historic episode, one general story, to make into an epic as Homer had in *The Odyssey* and *The Iliad*. If Pound, viewing the whole of civilization and the past, quickly placed his viewpoint in Italy, it was because he was an expatriate American living in a country he regarded as inheriting the most important civilized virtues, the virtues (he believed) of classical Western times, which virtues he centered in the figure of the enlightened Renaissance prince, the patron of the arts who understood the artist and ordered public works in the interests of human culture; the prince who represented a true élite and who brought to cultural ideals both the faith and the strategies of a tribal chief engaged in a mortal feud. Thus, in lighting upon Sigismundo Malatesta as "art patron" hero of *The Cantos* (Confucius and certain early American politicians also are heroes), Pound gave notice that his attitude toward crime and violence was extremely sophisticated. He rather took the bloodiness of human struggle as inevitable because, politically, mankind was engaged in a struggle with stupidity (a low order of culture) whose victorious outcome was not in sight. "Fear God and the stupidity of the people" is an aphorism attributed to Malatesta. But even now, as hundreds of years ago, the "outcome" still hangs in the balance. The distance between the tribal chief of old and the gang boss of this century was less than Pound romantically gauged it to be, and Benito Mussolini himself closer in dictator psychology to the gang boss than Pound, as a political analyst, decided he was. Explicitly, Pound thought of the contemporary Mussolini as Malatesta's direct descendant.

In reading *The Cantos* and admiring their word magic (for unquestionably Pound's literary gift was great), I frequently felt that *The Cantos'* method of reconstructing history according to certain valual formulas (for instance, Pound was an enemy of usury and espoused a modern economic plan called Social Credit) was far from being logically reasoned and completely responsible; rather, it was based on something that the theorists of film were then bringing out concerning the new medium; namely, montage, or the building of concepts as well as emotions through juxtaposition and manipulation of the optical image. As these theorists of film (primarily, Sergei Eisenstein) well knew, the concept had a linguistic counterpart, the ideogram, especially as found in written characters of the Far East.

Pound in *The Cantos* was making up (I almost wrote "mocking up") a hieroglyphics of history by a method of montage editing; strictly, that is, through certain juxtaposition and wily aesthetic processing, by word glamour and sound glamour. It was the encyclopaedic method, considerably slanted, and it depended far more on plastic dynamics (take "The Unwobbling Pivot" for instance) than on moral values and political ideas as such. It is well to remark that the world was hit during one decade with the Russian Revolution (1912–22), Cubism, Proust, Pound, Eliot, Joyce, Surrealism, Futurism, Eisenstein and montage in film, *Caligari* and expressionism in film. These produced very sensible changes in aesthetic logic and implicitly in moral attitudes.

Yet it never occurred to Pound that Mussolini, for all his favor toward beautifying Italy and sponsoring the arts, might also be stupid and brutal, and was in any case to be a conspirator with one of the arch-villains of human history, Adolf Hitler. Does it matter that today the Italian Fascist renovation in the arts (chiefly, of course, architecture) has left no mark whatever and is as ugly and almost as inflated as the Nazi style? Not all connoisseurs admire, for example, the survival of the Cretan style, yet there is little chance, I think, that the Fascist style will emerge in future museums, except as a statistical curiosity or by mistaken identity. It grew out of and has been absorbed by some of the worst modern taste in the way of public monuments.

Pound in the 1920s had no intuition of such a catastrophe. He resorted to the most refined and adept plastic values, transmissable by the word, to associate Mussolini not merely with the virtues of Malatesta, but with the virtues of poetry. Nor, if we wish to be rational, can we view this as a *new* ploy in literature. Many heroes of epic and tragedy have been the bloodiest of conquerors and granted as such by poets in the very act of giving their villainy the scale of grandeur and evoking that curious empathy audiences have for a great fighting man (whatever his character and motives) who eventually goes under. One need mention, among actual figures of the ancient past who have been thus "heroized," Tamburlaine and Alexander the Great.

The heroic villain of myth is a key case in the study of good and evil (take, for example, Racine's Nero or Camus' Caligula) as well as the study of relating art to ethics. As to modern hero-villains of history, if "aesthetically" Mussolini has that stature in *The Cantos*,

Hitler acquired that stature in the Nazi-made film *The Triumph of the Will*. No matter how one judges Germany's guilt, and Hitler's, in the Second World War, that film remains memorable as an inspired tribute to the grandeur of human leadership. In the movement of cinema, the masking off of individual shots and constant change, the anonymous massive weight of Nazi architecture as background is broken up and lightened, becomes a series of grand, rather abstract planes and ceases to be an architectural entity to be judged in itself.

The Triumph of the Will truthfully portrays the way that mass emotions, epic and lyric, may be organized, built up and glorified by a single mass energy. When, for instance, we have seen black savages doing a tribal dance on film, shaking their spears, musical instruments or fetishes, and leaping as if possessed by demons, an ecstasy of the heartbeat and a glory of the dance are equally conveyed to us, although (perhaps indeed *because*) we may not have stopped to think that this tribe might be working itself up for a foray against its enemies, whose dead flesh they will proceed to eat, whose heads they will mummify. However much, in our own historic times, black tribal dancers have obligingly performed "just for the camera," it is incontestable that whatever aesthetic feelings be aroused by their dance, the forms of that dance are inextricably associated (now as ever before) with the acts of killing and torturing human kind and animal kind. This would be true whether the dances were being filmed for a fiction film or a documentary.

I am, you say, speaking now of *morals*? I am confusing moral with artistic standards when, in truth, they are quite separate? I know that this criticism may be argued with much force and cogency. But what is it that prevents morals needing the assistance of art except the peculiar illusion, growing up with modern civilization, that there is a power still higher than the "good of the tribe," the value by which antiquity lived, and by which tribal values (as close to us as those treated in classic Greek times by Aeschylus) always prevailed? Good and evil, at one time in human history, were not an independent value-system at all, not the product of "reason," or the much later religious shibboleths of "good will toward all men" or "justice for all." "Good" simply meant one's own side, "evil" the enemy's side; just so, one's own ruler was virtually God, the enemy's ruler the Devil.

That was primitive man's way. Nowadays we are familiar with the struggles of philosophic benevolence and Christian benevolence to try to unite what might be called post-primitive man. The old Athenian state, for instance, felt it wise to unite itself politically by suppressing the family and clan vendettas—that "law" of justice reflected into biblical times by the adage of "an eye for an eye, a tooth for a tooth." The theme was worked out with much eloquence and pointedness by Aeschylus in the *Orestes* trilogy, where supreme divinity, supposedly, laid to rest the inferior "furies" of vengeance, who were actually the tribal gods themselves. It is illuminating to be reminded that Pound, as much as he speaks out in *The Cantos* for universal enlightenment through an élite wisdom, speaks out there also for clan solidarity— for hiding a criminal if he belongs to your family, for not giving him up to "justice." This exposes the true ambiguity of Aeschylus' academic conclusion in the Orestes plays. Pardon by a court, divinely or humanly appointed, does *not* necessarily suppress the Furies, who represent not just the persecution of a criminal's private conscience but also the vengeance of living members of the family he has mortally offended.

Let us, for the moment, forget film and the desirability

for an enlightened theory of it, possibly a grand aesthetic theory, and consider humanity, its achievements and its goals, from the strictly moral standpoint. Instantly we would become aware that civilized ideals once produced a world organization called the United Nations, whose prime duty was to "keep the peace" and meanwhile preserve the integrity of nations; the latter, if necessary, by force, or at least a show of force . . . It's strange how we come back, in this discussion, to "shows" of force, power, strength, as if mankind had no instinctive moral goodness, as if only its highest levels, its internationally- and intellectually-minded élites, really loved justice and peace and believed in moral goodness per se as a controlling force. But let us persevere if only for the sake of film theory.

Since self-evidently, in our world of today, all manner of crime exists in each nation, on multiple levels and among a broad range of economic classes, we continue to witness the kind of political force that Athens exerted when it began to interdict ordinary clan vengeance for the sake of supertribal unity. On a still higher level, in accordance with the present complexity of world society, that is what, theoretically, the United Nations is supposed to do internationally: exactly what the Areopagus did nationally at Athens, as once connoted by Aeschylus. One might even perceive, in this light, a spirit of super-justice working today in the expanding moral condemnation of capital punishment. This feature of contemporary human mercy is important because apparently it too bypasses that eye-for-an-eye, tooth-for-a-tooth form of retributive justice and situates its main point in the contention that capital punishment seems not to have proven, through the centuries, that it is a crime-preventive force. Therefore, *etc., etc.*

Is it obvious, furthermore, to assert that we cannot

expect any art, either film or stage or novel, to perform the function of moral sermons and homilies, to present the potentially guilty with so horrible an image of retribution that crime will thereby soon be eliminated? If, for example, capital punishment be entirely eliminated by nations everywhere, that would not mean, as I have just noted, that the murderer would be liberated from his own conscience or from vengeance by the friends or family of the one he had killed. In fact, it is silly, is it not, even to suggest that the withdrawal of capital punishment would or could do anything but flatter the already hypocritically held "mercy complex" of christianized modern man. Think of the immense, unwaning popularity of violence in films! Far from being discouraged by the threat of human extinction posed by the atom bomb, film-makers (those Geiger counters of the collective Id!) seek out the most esoteric ways of displaying violence, both in sex and war, in crime and natural catastrophe. As there is no letup in life, there is no letup in screen fiction.

Violence! Violence, you say, is inescapable? It is built into life and the struggle to survive? Yes, indeed. And so on! For example: the violence of cosmic accidents, for which only blind, senseless fate, or some (I suppose inscrutable) God, can be held accountable. Not yet made into a film, a certain science-fiction story by Arthur C. Clarke has demonstrated how even the worst that could happen to us Earth dwellers not only can be circumvented by enough scientific wit but converted into the superspectacular of all TV spectaculars. Far out? Exactly. Far out in space, we are asked to envision thousands of futuristic spaceships, filled with the former inhabitants of our planet, loath to leave it but forced to because of an imminent space collision diagnosed by scientists. Still, not only have all these ships been built to waft us (hopefully) toward other inhabitable universes, but great television antennae have been erected to convey to the triumphant escapists aloft the spectacle of their world destroyed, which they (I mean "we"), safe and comfortably seated, will behold on great TV screens.

The thought, from the viewpoint of film history, is not so far out. The visionary art critic, Élie Faure, wrote a pioneer essay on the cinema (1920)* in which he imagined some super-camera that would be able to photograph both past and future—in which case, he argued with disarming *élan*, we would acquire a perfectly true record of the life of Jesus; Jesus, one might add, among others. But willy-nilly, I have caught myself in the toils of a dual theory which I think quite worthless. This is that the great and the true, the only *precise*, theory of film is that it provides man with an objective record of nature and his own place in nature. It is the theory that Siegfried Kracauer rather needlessly but elaborately formulated in 1960. Thus a film camera, like a computer, would be programmed merely to report whatever happened, no matter what it was, so that its "greatness" would be its usefulness in accumulating a vast, endless body of post-facto and perhaps prophetic evidence. Its role as composer, I mean its *imaginative* and *artistic* role, would, by this canon, be quite secondary. Film could indeed report all man's inventions—as these fascinating events continue to materialize—but should it seek to invent anything of its own, anything such as a fiction, a truly created object, which is what every art does, that would then be presumptuous . . . not to say also redundant . . .

Just suppose, for the sake of a reprise, there existed a

---

* "The Art of Cineplastics." Reprinted in *Film: An Anthology* (Talbot).

film that could illustrate, "provide evidence for," all the considerations, moral and otherwise, which I have brought up and discussed regarding film and human history and the latter's reflection in art works. Well, I think such a film does exist. And happily it is Sergei Eisenstein's *Ivan the Terrible,* Parts I and II. Here was a figment simulating actual history, supplying a humanly vulnerable yet (especially to the Soviet State) superhuman hero who had performed the luminous historic act of attempting to unite Russia in the sixteenth century—an act which, as Eisenstein, educated in Marxist ideology, could well appreciate, since Stalin at that moment, in theory, was dialectically completing and perfecting it. Neither Joseph Stalin and his fellow bureaucrats nor Eisenstein could be unaware that the Soviet government, even so, was being criticized abroad by both democracies and dissident Marxists for being a fascist dictatorship, and Stalin himself (regarded thus alienly) for being a hero villain; indeed, from some intensely partisan views, Stalin was an arch-villain of socialism who had betrayed the Revolution.

Ivan the Terrible had been a ruler whose historic cognomen alone evoked the image of a man both majestic and cruel, but particularly a man illustrating an essential paradox of the modern dialectic—a man who, in emotional/dramatic terms, had been "cruel" only to be "kind." If Alexander Nevsky, Eisenstein's previous sovietized hero, had defeated the chief enemies from without, Ivan had defeated the chief enemies from without and within. When *Ivan,* Part I, was made (1946) the World War had taken place and Stalin was reputed to have exterminated the Kulak caste as ruthlessly as Hitler had exterminated the German Jews. Yet supposedly Stalin was "good," Hitler "evil." As Eisenstein's film clearly shows, Ivan's assumption of tsardom as a form of auto-

cratic personal rule was an irregular act, a deliberate
arrogation acutely resented by the Boyars, Russia's old
caste of ruling princes. Ivan, succeeding by his father's
death to the title of Grand Duke of Moscow, had himself crowned Tsar and proclaimed absolute ruler. It was
the classic military coup that worked without noticeable
violence. If Russian history revered Ivan IV, it revered
him with awe, it paid tribute to his genius for the "show
of power," for he was a bloody monarch who did "good"
to Russia by steadily crushing Boyar prestige and at one
point executing the Boyar leaders. He had to accomplish this, moreover, by defying the authority of the Russian Church and making its archpriest his bitter enemy.
This is what we see, posed very dramatically and plas-
tically, in Eisenstein's film.

The point is that Ivan, played by the veteran actor
Nikolai Cherkassov, is on the old heroic model of drama
and tragedy: a dynamo of a man, a born leader and ruler.
However much such a ruler be "lovable" and "good"
seems a minor moral issue; significantly minor, that is,
to the aesthetic issue, which boldly exalts him as the Man
of Destiny, the Man of Power. What Genghis Khan,
Alexander the Great and Napoleon have in common
with Ivan is the driving power of the conqueror type. It
happens that moral ambiguity, as built into Ivan's private
personality and his political role, was not, in the case of
Eisenstein's film, simply ready-made history. Actually, the
film director had been compelled to make a revision of
personal judgment—if it *was* personal judgment—since
previously he had expressed the view that this historic
ruler of Russia was taboo as a film subject. Ivan, it appeared, was the type of hero who belonged to Edgar
Allan Poe and therefore, in Eisenstein's own words, he
"would hardly interest the young Soviet worker." More
explicitly, according to Eisenstein, Ivan was "a Mephisto-

felean figure, a Tsar who was a wild beast." Yet this same wild beast and Mephistofeles Eisenstein abruptly consented to project as a distinguished precursor of Stalin, a man who had fought "alone" in order to "save Russia." This was the only possible meaning of the commission he had graciously been given to make the film and he could not turn down the honor. It was to be a version of Ivan specifically flattering to Stalin, humanizing his modern successor and according him a vindicative precedent, making Stalin a man wrongly criticized for being a brutal dictator because he too had been animated by a passion to save his country by uniting it. Such have been the moral conventions supporting such aesthetic structures as Eisenstein's films.

Yet what really happened when Part I of *Ivan the Terrible* was awarded the Stalin Prize, First Class, and Part II had reached the editing stage? Eisenstein's art was in crisis and so was Ivan as an illustrious antecedent of Stalin. But before further examining Eisenstein's art, its meaning in the filmic Ivan, and the grievous portent of this meaning for Eisenstein, let us note that the Ivan-figure in general perspective represents not only Stalin but also Mussolini; that is, he represents a historic tradition in heroes who, whatever judgments historians may render on them, enjoy the peculiar privileges traditionally allowed "national heroes." These men who strive "to save their country," these "great conquerors," are placed, aesthetically, beyond good and evil. The deeds of Napoleon, who belongs among them, aroused great passions, especially on the part of those who either desired or abhorred the "united" Europe he visualized.

Surely, the high heroes of history must have enemies, real or illusive, both inside and outside their own states; these enemies, logically, must be suppressed or exterminated. The only really safe, efficient way—usually found to be the chosen course—has been to exterminate them. This means some sort of war, international or civil, and in conspicuous modern instances of national leaders in the formal hero category, it has also meant, in recent times, mass executions. However much all killing be deplorable from certain humanistic and moralistic standpoints, war itself, as a nation's climactic moral weapon, has yet to be universally outlawed—*even in theory*. War is the very last resort, supposedly, and recently a category of "war crimes" has arisen. Still, no formal interdiction upon armed force as such has come about.

The only opposition to the amoral permissiveness allowed national heroes by tradition—especially art tradition—has come, of course, from modern democracies, principally the United States of America. One can hardly imagine a bloody-minded dictator in the American President's chair, can one? Yet ephemeral threats have arisen, notably the quasi-fascist personality of Huey Long, about whom the novel and film titled *All the King's Men* was rather too transparently built. Why too "transparently"? Well, the movie had to make the novelist Robert Penn Warren's fictional surrogate for Long into more of a gangland boss, even, than the novel had made him! A whole *March of Time* newsreel gimmick was used to make the fascistic threat look real in this country—as real as it had indeed seemed to the Democratic Party. Yet the existence of both novel and movie points to how inflammable the public imagination is, or at least is assumed to be. And the peculiar optical susceptibility of that imagination is what the new "McLuhanish" media seem all about. But let us continue to ride with the filmic tradition.

We must inspect exactly what Pound did with Mussolini in *The Cantos*, for it is fundamentally what Eisenstein did with Stalin in *Ivan the Terrible*. Mussolini appears mythologically in Pound's epic as "Duccio"— thus, an idealized leader, a hero superhuman enough, in his appointed capacity as protector of culture, to be pardoned mere human errors and weaknesses, mere private blemishes, and to be the eternal scapegoat—poor "Ben" as the poet intimately calls him at the beginning of the *Pisan Cantos*. Pound's strategy was to provide his epic with a moral inflection, yes, but inveterately and before anything else, it would favor the interests of *culture*. The heroic scapegoat (Jesus too was one!) is as natural a part of culture—even in Pound's ironic version of it, "kulchur"—as anything else. This is why Pound stresses the violent and headstrong Sigismundo, Mussolini's antecedent, as deeply clannish and deeply dedicated, as a patron prince, to preserving art treasures and promoting cultural works in the public domain. Sigismundo, it seems, had an eye for beauty no less than a mind for tactics. Pound could not think of a better formula for a powerful prince or a leader of the state. It is a Renaissance formula and so it is duly Machiavellian. And archetypally it carries a built-in amnesty for every "evil" deed by an art-loving hero/prince.

Behind all such paradoxes, ingeniously to be woven with a theory such as Marxist-Hegelian dialectics, is a certain inert acceptance of violence: violence as necessary, as morally proper, because one assumes that, the world being unchangeably made in a certain way, wrong no less than right must call might to its aid so as to prevail. And right, it is further assumed, resides in the pre-eminence of a people, a nation, a state—on a broad modern conception of a state as a union of interrelated tribes. The world's economic development in the nineteenth century brought a sharp change into the "tribally" motivated national situation through the welcome given by the United States of America to foreign-speaking immigrants whose ranks swelled its industrial power in terms of purely material prestige. One particular American show of strength was the fleet sent to a Japanese harbor to overawe a foreign people: the show certainly overawed the foreigners but it also inspired them to the most energetic emulation; thus "today" we have modern industries in Japan and "yesterday" we had the fearful show of strength that took place at Pearl Harbor.

Historically, religion has been the normal superstructure of a nation as a union of tribes, and thus religion has been usually the "natural" and unquestioned motivation of wars. We need only point to the Crusades in medieval Europe against the Infidels occupying Jerusalem. At this very moment, that same part of the earth's geography is in serious dispute because of ancient tribal hatreds (however presently inflected by the ambitions of political élites) originating in basically primitive emotions concerning "foreigners" as "enemies," and thus "evil" in relation to the "good" represented by one's "own side." In juxtaposition to such deeply embedded layers of human passion, the social ideal embodied by the United Nations has the aspect of a superstructural *theory* technically beyond religions, races or nations.

Great religious leaders, such as Mahatma Gandhi, who have loved peace and could recognize no formula of violence more positive than passive resistance or civil disobedience, would seem to agree with the proponents of pure rationalism, by which peace is preferable to war as constructiveness is preferable to destructiveness, life to death, pleasure to pain, and so on. Yet not only political ambition (after all, the very *instinct* of great conquerors!) but also broad material factors such as population increase, shrinkage of living space and the unequal distribution of wealth have all embarrassingly asserted themselves and today appear as objective deterrents to the aims and ideals of, alike, rational and religious lovers of peace.

For the present purpose, we must face the statistical relationship between violence of all kinds and the violence of the creative passion. Conquerors such as Napoleon and Alexander the Great looked upon violence as a means toward liberating "good" human forces and raising them to a higher plane, in which the principle of unification would play a part in dialectically reconciling certain natural, or at least traditional, differences among national peoples. The Hegelian idea of a higher or improved state achieved by synthesis persists, apparently, in all aspects of historical development on the planet. The generic term for this, as I noticed above, is aggrandizement. The point is that aggrandizement achieved by synthesis allows for violence, for "force" of some kind; indeed, the concept allots to force an indispensable function in all development toward higher good. Still, I was genuinely amazed when I came to the "Section Rock Drill" of Pound's *Cantos* (85–95) and found that this metaphor, used to describe education by force, actually corresponds to the sinister modern term —quite irrational and a strong arm of modern violence— namely: brainwashing. The rock drill, as a machine, is used to penetrate the ultimate passive resistance of matter, that residing in the hardest rock: here for Pound a figure of speech for the brains of those who oppose his ideas. It could only be the metaphor of a poet who was a hysteric, who viewed politics, actually, from the standpoint of a Machiavellian aesthete and viewed political heroes as but "agents" appointed by destiny to lead mankind out of the wilderness of stupidity while making flourish the truest flowers of civilization, the arts. Thus the mythical Duccio of *The Cantos* becomes Pound's version of Mussolini.

Nor must we lose sight of Malatesta as a historic prototype of the modern Duce or Duccio. Beyond any personal wish or aim of his own, beyond the arguable validity of historical contexts, Malatesta is a surviving remnant of time put into brisk service, in *The Cantos*, as a symbol. The same thing happened to Ivan the Terrible in his office as the prototype-antecedent of Stalin in Eisenstein's film—that is, the same thing happened to him analogically and in terms of structure, not in terms of the creative artist's private motive. For Eisenstein set out to trick Stalin, whose established procedure was to brainwash the artists of the Soviet Union by bureaucratic edict and surveillance. Eisenstein had far too strong an intellect, too pure an artistic inspiration, to submit to doing a portrait of Ivan that figuratively could be set beside one of Stalin on a wall of the Kremlin. What speaks eloquently to us at this point is the value of the technical factor: the film. We arrive—not too abruptly— at a mutual formula that covers the case of Pound and Eisenstein. This is our ostensible—and, let me hastily add, tentative—theory: FILM MONTAGE = HISTORY.

And yet how can this be, when we stop to think, since I have just maintained that both Pound and Eisenstein respectively had, actually, the most personal and prejudiced motives?—that, in effect, they were not the humble, mimetic reporters of history but its aggressive and special interpreters?—so that they were, as well as artists, rewriters of history. Hence this must really be our thesis: *Slanted history is best DISGUISED by film montage.* Documentary film montage (history unreeling before our eyes) has a revised-notebook technique: a flashy way of putting together selected surface events.

Film montage would be, then, a purely technical principle and equivalent to the mere parade of history as a series of actions and reactions, mechanically transcribable, leading to this, that or the other notable climax and a consequent temporary stasis, void of any dialectic violence. By this theory, a history of World War II could be made up from newsreel shots. Let us turn again to Élie Faure as an authority that the film camera does not even have to choose a method of presentation, does not have the obligation to invent, to visualize out of nothing, but is a machine merely to be pointed toward the future or the past for outstanding events to be mechanically, passively recorded, just as they happened or will happen. Their *meaning*? Any moral judgments of the *fait accompli* in majestic array? All that, ostensibly, does not matter. We must conclude that film montage, in its humility toward reality, is a very deep bow (all theory squeezed out of it) toward the fatality of the *fait accompli*. The necessary implication is that the same is true of events seen in time passing under our eyes: present-tense time. This is particularly the tacit theory of telecasts of day by day events—no matter what they are, they're "history": facts seen in process like "events" seen through a laboratory microscope. The television camera would seem the one sacred thing judged as a fetish, self-sufficient and uncriticizable as a phenomenon. It is the NEWS. If men wish to do something about it, they can (theoretically)—but as the god of Journalism, it has eternal human rights. Editorial comments by the networks, nowadays rather boldly independent, simply come along with these rights and are instantly submerged. Film montage might be conceived "in theory" as only the continuous image of history in the making.

A special emphasis appears in Eisenstein's theoretic

concepts, which he constantly and earnestly put to work in filmic practice. It is something that connotes the violence of contending forces: his term "collision." The medical theory of action and reaction, to restore order and balance, is convenient to cite here. Medicine, like legal reform, is one of the righters of wrongs. When a disease appears, its antidote is theoretically predicated and, if developed and successful, restores the sufferer to health. It is the physical world's paradigm of the Hegelian trio, thesis, antithesis and synthesis. However, the semantic character of Eisenstein's term to describe film montage, collision, is further determinative: it has a definite *abstract* nature. For instance, moving objects such as automobiles, perhaps people, may accidentally run into each other, bump each other harmfully or harmlessly, entirely without intention; in fact, collision happens to be the accepted expression for railroad and highway accidents involving vehicles. Its semantic importance in films vividly comes into play when we know that Eisenstein's rival, Pudovkin, while also recognizing the supreme value of montage in film-making, preferred designating this technical principle as "linkage." First, the character of the word, linkage, meaning merely the physical principle of joining one thing to another, suggests that even collision is not altogether violent, nor necessarily bad in character. Players in sports such as football and hockey collide, usually without harm, or else but casual harm; it is when automobiles collide head-on, or a locomotive hits an auto, that the resultant injuries are apt to be mortal or permanently disfiguring to occupants and machines.

So we must move to a still larger aspect of the argument, one that perhaps indicates Pudovkin wished to underplay the violence inhering in the dialectic struggle whose theory was embedded in the Russian Marxist concept of film montage. This larger aspect is the flexibility of Hegel's dialectic concept as affording a complete gamut of locked opposition from *violent* and *injurious* —even *deadly*—to *mild* and *pacific*; from persuasiveness (like an orator's rhetoric) to pugnacity (like the threats and preparatory acts of a war-maker). Eisenstein has said that the joined screen images of an empty plate and a mouth, whether or not juxtaposed in the same film frame, express the idea of hunger; just so, an opened mouth and a running stream express thirst. Possibly because Eisenstein had in mind single elements in separate (though successive, possibly alternating) frames, he lit upon the dialectically vivid term, collision. The principle thus achieved a form that could be termed hieroglyphic, as in the Oriental ideogram. In effect, Eisenstein decided for the bold visual metaphor just where Pudovkin, preferring the less vivid term linkage, plumped for the same idea by image association, something—as to Marxist dialectic—that would be more realistic, less formal and ideological, in visual character. Ultimately, Eisenstein was maneuvered by his opponents (including Pudovkin) into a position where he could be accused of "formalism," a thing turning out to be, paradoxically, a calendar sin in Communist Russia. I say paradoxically because what could be more formalist than the danse d'école that has come down in the ballet theater from Tsarist times to the present?

This suggests something pivotal to any concern such as the present one: the search for a true theory, an adequate theory. Yet just what is *a* theory? In the loosest, easiest sense, it is the brief, convenient statement of a general truth, always mental (in that it goes behind optical surfaces and grasps structure) and in its stricter form is a *theorem*, a proposition whose truth, or group of verifiable constituents, is not self-evident (that is, in appearance); as a theorem, it may function in mathematics as something to be proved by a demonstration or argument. Yet a mere theory may be only a slanted or prejudiced view of something put forward to account for it or justify it, in which case, as a post-facto rationalization, it is a mere dummy for our old friend, the *fait accompli*. Siegfried Kracauer boldly asserted that all the important and unique validity of film lay in his theory that film provided a "redemption of physical reality." His English publisher felt that "theory" was not a forceful enough, maybe accurate enough, term to risk on such a radical assumption and preferred the term nature. Hence we find in his book that it is the *nature* of film to *redeem physical reality*. If this be so—and whether or not we have a "nature" or a "theory"—the implications of Kracauer's proposition about motion pictures are, to my notion, very, very strange or totally without significance.

In any case the charge of formalism which I have been discussing would seem ruled out by Kracauer's theoretic proposition. For, according to this proposition, truth in the camera lens is merely accumulative and, as either neutral or tendentious, regards human and natural truths as its definitive subject matter or content: whatever it happens to report. Yet what are the criteria for deciding the *relative* truth, the *relative* value, of what is reported? A true theory of film, obviously, would have to be a set of rules for manipulating its expressive techniques toward given ends, for impregnating its methods with certain messages. In that case, formalism would be a necessary ingredient of all considerations of the film and its values, what it *can* say, *does* say, *might* say. It could then be viewed as it has been, not as a "theory" or "nature," but as a grammar, a rhetoric and even an aesthetic. This is to consider method, no matter how inspired, a purely representational problem, in short, a means without a necessary or given end. That, indeed, would seem to be pure formalism.

In Eisenstein's quarrel with the Soviet bureaucracy, the hostility of his critics would of course be oriented theoretically to the undesirability of the familiar art-for-art's-sake position. This supposes that his care was merely for exploiting methods and devices regardless of the general content or particular message. But transparently (as I have already suggested) this reasoning of the bureaucracy embodies an artificial dichotomy that is a strategy for criticizing and banning undesirable content. Certain laboratory devices—such as multiple exposure, varieties of transition, manipulation of plastic values (like polarization: the loss of the normal presence of chiaroscuro and an insistent abstraction of form away from normal appearances)—may indeed be exploited by film independently of reality or any human "representational" theme. There is already a school of film-making devoted to such abstract kinetic plasticism: a school that technically could be classified as "pure formalism." One young American critic, P. Adams Sitney, has dubbed it "structural film." Yet such, actually, is not the formalism meant by Soviet critics as the charge against Eisenstein.

No hostility existed against his theory per se, despite the fact that the theory was exactly one of formal composition rooted in a dialectics whose image values were technically aligned with the moral values of the emergent society of revolutionized Russia. The true objection to Eisenstein's tactics lay in his perfect awareness—a "theory" that could easily be "demonstrated"—that filmic methods, whatever they might be, had a technical independence of their messages, of the nature of their content, but not that they existed in a vacuum divorced from *any and all content!* Indeed, as his banned film *Bezhin Meadow* so beautifully and clearly proved, his "collision"—or whatever he chose to call this or some other feature of his structural procedures—was just as serviceable to the religious theme of primitive mysticism, a kind of pantheism attached to Christianity, as it was to the dialectics of an emergent socialist state. In *Bezhin Meadow*, decisive ideological links between the naïve religiosity of the Russian peasant and his consciousness of his new economic role were conspicuously missing.

Thus Eisenstein was promptly stripped of a film that he had managed to complete independently, then was put under strict surveillance when allowed to make another. *Alexander Nevsky*, an antique hero tale exalting a great liberator of Russia, redeemed his reputation. And now again, although *Ivan the Terrible*, Part I, portrayed a similar role (a lone Tsar's struggle against the Boyars as reactionary opponents of change and progress), Part II of the same film too clearly revealed the victorious Tsar's cruelly, perversely vengeful nature; moreover, it showed him, after being widowed by the poisoning of his Tsarina, absorbed in the militaristic cult of his private bodyguard (an all-male revel, including a transvestite act, is the anticlimax of Part II) and egotistically contemptuous of all other authority. He is seen as a towering sinister lone-wolf figure, which did not suit the public image of benevolent paternalism and brotherliness Stalin wished to create for himself.

Dénouement: Eisenstein's physical and mental tension caused a heart attack at the very moment of his triumph and he was recuperating from it in the hospital when the press announcement was made that the second part of *Ivan* had displeased high authority and his whole career (as well as, it turned out, his very life) was again in jeopardy. Soviet internal propaganda never let up in providing the "correct" ideological ambience for its arts as for its science and journalism. This ambience of course had its bureau of watchdogs. Yet nobody in modern Russia but those of the most exceptional surviving intelligence could have imagined that the whole of *Ivan the Terrible* referred quite as much to its author, Eisenstein, as it did to its patron and mythological model, Stalin. At the same time, all good Stalinists could see that certain glaring Ivanesque traits were not Stalinesque or creditably Marxist-Leninist. The filmmaker had used the freedom of a myth-maker by supplying a roomy and flexible spectrum of metaphor in *Ivan*. If its hero, singlehanded (with the help of a few collaborators), meant to overcome the collective conspiracy of the Boyars, Eisenstein, singlehanded (with the help of a few collaborators), meant to overcome the conspiracy of the Soviet bureaucracy. Moreover, for good eyes and minds, there are several private symbols in the film: among them the young Ivan as played by a girl rather than a boy, and the homosexuality implied in Ivan's relation to the captain of his bodyguard, the attractive young man who masquerades as a female dancer in the revel scene.

As for the facts of history (poor Élie Faure!), these became of no consideration to Stalin and the bureaucrats who hated Eisenstein and rightly suspected him not only of being a pure artist, but also of moral duplicity. Empirically, both "charges" were true! What was not true was the specific charge of formalism as meaning divorce from the interests of content. Eisenstein had more than once simply elected the *wrong* content to illustrate his method, his theory. Meanwhile, the Soviet ballet, loyally asserting the traditional technique of the old court ballet, could be manipulated (however incongruously) to accommodate certain revolutionary, proletarian and peasant themes. One naïve and (as one might expect) stupendous effort, titled *The Flames of Paris*, was a ballet having for its theme the French Revolution of 1789. With quite pointless irony, the theme involved the very overthrow of king and court aristocracy which had been responsible for the whole establishment of high formal dance in the West. But to organized nonformalists, mere formal contradictions are very puny, even chimerical, matters.

Would that *The Flames of Paris* and *Spartacus*, no matter what the styles of their choreography, had been better ballets! Somehow their creators did not take the sins of formalism seriously enough to invent good excuses for them—"excuses" as good as Gautier and Adam, collaborators on the fairy-tale ballet *Giselle*, invented for nineteenth-century ballet. The great trouble with the Soviet art bureaucracies is, and has been for decades, that, incapable of Pound's true formalist finesse in *The Cantos*, they have had no genuine eye for beauty. Their true artists, in whatever creative field, have had to survive without enlightened patronage. After all, Pound was an individual artist, not a bureaucracy or the nephew of a bureaucracy. Eisenstein tried to be both artist and bureaucrat, even as Pound, fatally, tried to be, besides a poet, a political propagandist with the artificial aid of his wonderful eye and ear. Pound's story became different when he had to transpose his propaganda and his mood to "free radio speech." In a way, Eisenstein brought off his art coup with *Ivan*, only to live long enough to see its climax backfire. For another, fatal heart attack ended it all.

The curiously montage-like, collage-like technique of *The Cantos*, where everything associable with great myths or perceiving beauty in nature—"And the sunset like a grasshopper" or "The ant's a centaur in his dragon world"—is integral and yet, at times, is put to the service of fuzzy and debatable political and economic ideas and personages; this technique is an example of autocratically, arbitrarily applied formalism. Consider that Pound's gift for the *leitmotif* metaphor, the extended, constantly reappearing literary trope, is a deeply personal, subjective and graceful trait of his own—much as if he were a great *danseur noble*—and that the leisure conferred upon him to continue using this gift—after Italy was vanquished in World War II, Mussolini was killed and himself arrested—was his detainment by the American Army in a makeshift cage and then a tent at Pisa. Oh, Pound was brave! And he was true! But not all brave and true and talented men can render a reasonable and adequate account of their total behaviors to what is known as a court of justice. There are bound to be ambiguities, uneliminated moral entanglements, if only because governments have never, precisely, known what to do with politically offending artists; that is, neither artists nor governments have adopted Plato's wisdom and stayed away from articulate political commitments in art forms. Such commitments seem not to be immunized because they are stated from a private citizen's armchair. We have but to shift our focus over to the Soviet Union to perceive what trouble they have had with their writers and the international embarrassments resulting therefrom in recent years.

If you can piece out the patterns of the fragmentary anecdotes conveyed in *The Cantos* (especially the Pisan Cantos) by sudden, fleeting allusion, Pound veritably wrote in this "endless" work the best, most highly polished and meaningful gossip column in the world— super super-*New Yorker*. Of course, it tends to be a historically reminiscent gossip column, not just the happenings and indications of the past twenty-four hours or the past few weeks. Looking at all the Cantos with a cinematic eye, one cannot but conclude that they are much like a privately edited newscast (so visually vivid at times that they're better than television) with Poundian plugs for dubiously valuable persons and politics functioning not as the *program*, but as the *commercials* interrupting it. The point here is that the power of Pound's medium, his own "great great show" is precisely one of those formalist affairs that make an artist seem, to certain governments, offensive and guilty of punishable crime exactly because of the supremacy of his technical attainment and the personal prestige he has won with it. At least, Pound's prestige won his case a vast amount of publicity that a treason charge against an ordinary citizen would not have evoked.

Insofar as we are tempted to relate these phenomena with film and with theory, we find that the evidence does not always focus on personal attainment and the owner's abuse of it, but on principles themselves, on a group interest such as modern journalism, where the principle or theory of "the freedom of the press" is put at issue. *The Cantos* point to a historical-type journalism, a rewriting of history to "make it new." Even as I write, the American government is at loggerheads with the news media (re the Pentagon Papers) over the issue of how much "right" political secrets (especially those bearing on the conduct of war preparations) have to be "secret." All this merely accentuates the fact that the daily continuous programs of the television networks exist within the Kracauerian conception of film theory as "flow of time" and "open end" and that "physical reality" has indeed been "redeemed." Not morally, assuredly —and let us omit the name of art—because "freedom" of the media as well as special government agencies themselves only *expose*, they do not *solve*, moral dilemmas.

Besides, dissident interests constantly accuse the news media, particularly television, of slanting the news, of being unobjective; they might as well be accused of being "poetic."

Reading *The Cantos* with as much attention as possible, we find that, while it is very easy to grasp Pound's gift for metaphor, language and rhythm, the hardest thing is to establish in the mind the continuity of his ideas, leaping about as they do in time and space. From the outset, this manner establishes—no matter how much special effort makes his ideas cohere with each other—a basic dichotomy between the form of *The Cantos* and their content. We get used to a *leitmotif* of politics as of image and myth, but that of the former is controversial, inconclusive, that of the latter (the aesthetic form) conclusive and tacitly acceptable. The flow of beautiful sensuous surfaces—simultaneous gratification for eye and ear, startlingly deft if often oblique evocations of human experience—begins to hypnotize the reader, lull rather than quicken his intelligence, his ability to receive and judge ideas: what the Cantos "mean" at this or that point, the whole continuous arc of their argument.

At times, the choleric tone of the poet rises to the level of an inspired sermon—as in the Usury Canto with its splendid images—but someone not obsessed with usury or the ironies of the Bible can equally well appreciate the hypnotic and beautifully wrought rhetoric of a John Donne sermon. Many passages of the Cantos would be utterly senseless, for instance, without knowledge of their cultural context. One such case is simple and conclusive: When Pound makes a passing allusion to "the possum," one must be aware that this is his particular nickname for T. S. Eliot or the sense of the reference is totally lost, and only sound and vague sense-associations remain. The genius of *The Cantos* is largely musical—

it is like the genius of Stravinsky for instrumental timbre, that of Mahler for the sustained variation of melody. Yet *The Cantos* are heavily charged with ideational and moral content; they are fraught with fleeting, curiously personal and prejudiced, major and minor, judgments of this, that and the other.

This is why—though there is great seriousness in Pound's mind and a totally committed morality of purpose—I define this work as a variety of historically imbued gossip column that includes some incomparably witty anecdotes. And yet why did Pound choose thus sharply inflected a medium?—why the dialectic between classic hero story and the lovely images of myth on one side, and on the other, cursive moral censures, witty but dubious slams and quips, platform invective and naïvely crude political and economic propaganda? I have mentioned a sort of hysteria as one explanation for Pound's style. But however well grounded, such a hypothesis does not answer the basic question. Perhaps, I hazard further, Pound made a decision that anticipated the later-advanced theory of one of his admirers, Marshall McLuhan, whose "critical" emphasis on the moral power of the communication media has had such wide success in terms of recognition in the press (even the academic press) and in book sales.

Only technically, only formalistically, is Pound advocating Mussolini or even Malatesta, anti-Semitism and anti-usury, systematic art patronage and Social Credit . . . He is against or for this or that as one is against or for a current political candidate, a proposed legal reform bearing on an immediate social issue, even a current movie by a famous director that may be below his established standard. The enduring importance is behind the passing semblance. Behind Mussolini and Malatesta in *The Cantos* stand Dionysos and Confucius—before them, speculatively and regardless of one poet's favorites, stand Senator James Buckley, Eugene McCarthy or Ralph Nader. Each represents something "in the running," something perhaps high-powered, destined to "succeed." Art should not exaggerate the importance of such chameleonism. The abiding fact betrayed by *The Cantos* is that, primarily, it is *poetry* that is being treated as "political" and "technological" and it was to *poetry* that Pound elected to bring the montage feeling of a day's television broadcast. But poetry did the converting, not vice versa.

And we have the secret: one branch, one dazzling impression, of our desired world theory of film. The true sensibility for a medium rescues a beleaguered artist from his worst internal and external dilemmas, which represent a rift in his creative genius. With Pound it was internal: the schizoid manias of a man obsessed with high cultural values and compelled to expatriate himself from his country of birth because of its low intellectual and artistic levels, its crudely exploitive economic mechanisms. With Eisenstein, the pressure was altogether from outside: he was never a free agent, was like a trapped animal that, to survive and grow and operate, had to resort to the subtlest strategies imparted to him secretly by his muse.

Film montage is greatly broadened, theoretically broadened, by contemplating and understanding these two artists so desperately compromised in their true functions. History? At no matter what tense we find it in their work, it was only a pawn in their life-and-death game. Eisenstein at last was killed, Pound driven to a rule-of-the-game treason. One man's film-like practice of poetry, the other's poetry-like practice of film, became a *theory of survival*. If film can be thus dynamically and dialectically meshed with the tactic of élite human survival, it already has great stature as a theory: it has peculiar universality, peculiar modernity. It is not just a grammar or a rhetoric; it is not just a slavish instrument of "physical reality." It is the high human status of that physical reality. Both Pound and Eisenstein were enmeshed with history's gossip columns. But they escaped.

2

STILL TO MOVING
The Roots of Photographic Subjectivity

I have mentioned the "search" for a film theory. Film theory has really, all this while, been searching for itself . . . for a real, not a reel, identity. The theory of a thing is not the thing itself, just as a series of blueprints is not a building or a complete anatomic chart a man— and yet they necessarily correspond with each other. Now you, the reader, may have concluded from the preceding pages that I am primarily engaged not with film, but with a general and speculative aesthetics, possibly even moral propaganda, possibly philosophy itself, and am using film merely as a convenient pretext. Not so! Quite the opposite: Film is my sole *central* concern here. And yet part of this concern is my feeling that all too easily, in its relatively short life, film has been too much taken for granted as a leading communication medium, suited for a variety of practical purposes, or else regarded as a highly specialized technique, virtually an isolated science such as chemistry or physics or botany. Either view seems to me both inaccurate and belittling; in fact, fatally misleading. I say this because of discernible results in critical opinion and in film-making.

Previously I have pointed to the false emphasis given film by considering it a series of laboratory procedures from camera and blank film to the projecting machine; that is, film = a showy domain of technological achievement. A thousand times NO! Structuralism in film is like fundamentalism in Biblical interpretation: it makes a creed out of an empty form, it imagines an arm or a leg equals a man. Since photography was first still, cinema when it came could be nothing, of course, except a new set of "laboratory procedures." Even still photography was concerned with utilizing certain scientific traits of the physical world—the action of light on certain sensitized material, the capacity of certain physical elements and conditions (like the smooth surface of water) to reflect images like a mirror. Truly, that was the very beginning of cinema, but this happening was far more complex than it may seem, since it was the product of a vast preparation of the past as concerned with the craft of image-making.

We must indeed go to basics here, and these must be filmic basics. From emphasizing and investigating contemporary values relating to advanced cinematography (as I've done in the foregoing section) I turn now to pre-technical fundamentals; in particular, to the function of the mirrored image (primarily the mirrored human image) as historically so long in evidence. Lifelike images produced in stone and other hard materials (primeval sculpture) sought to be anything but "photographic" in the modern sense, the sense which—despite all fantasy—predominates today in cinema, whether as film art or film reportage. The aim of ancient sculpture was to provide a simulacrum that would represent a human image in apotheosis as a god, or else, if we cannot assume a deistic psychology for very remote times, a great natural principle (a kind of demon) or simply the principle, and perhaps also the fact, of immortality.

Through examining mummies of the dead—royal persons or not, and let us conveniently take the Egyptian, which shows high aptitude in mummification—we find that the ideal of the created image was, in all its concreteness, anything but "photographic." As a result of death, the human being visibly disintegrated and remained, at last, only as a skeleton. Such at least was the initial observation, from which flowed, consistently with the primitive impulse toward immortality, the techniques of preservation with their physical base. Primitive peoples had only vague ideas of an afterlife. In any case, these ideas were poetic projections, not even systematic philosophic speculations (partly based on astronomy) such as Plato's. Hence only the more sophisticated civilizations, developing a powerful sense of individualism, sought definite ways and means toward personal immortality. Very ancient peoples, as far away as megalithic times, buried their dead respectfully, one presumes also fervidly, and provided the graves of chiefs with due architectural dignity and signs, or fetishes, indicating their importance; they also built godlike monuments with enough human signification on their pillarlike forms to identify them as modeled on human figures.

Yet men, not only as kings and divine surrogates, but as the race itself, feared death and abhorred the prospect of the individual's absolute dissolution. Before the techniques of mummification were known, evidence exists that artisans, able to manipulate plaster, modeled human features over skulls in what may be the earliest effort (more than eight thousand years ago)* to extend indefinitely the life of a human individual. One may call such a technique, together with mummification and painted depictions, the climactic form taken by purely magical methods to maintain the life of an individual who had died, from whatever cause, a natural—that is, physical—death. There seems little use in arguing that such efforts were anything more than what Frazer serviceably termed imitative magic. For instance, the funerary procedures of the Egyptian embalmers—the whole concept of a king's tomb as an emulation of his palace while alive—were not only elaborate and ingenious, structurally speaking, but utilized attainments in the science of physical preservation: the temple priests formed both an artists' and a scientists' guild, where every possible resource, medical and artistic, was used to make a surviving corpse lifelike—fit, as it were, for the continuance of his former life.

In all this, a power higher than kingship was recognized, but a power that could be successfully wooed, psychologically (as it were) seduced. The dead king, it was supposed, came before divine powers as a pleader for his own survival. If it were not for the paleolithic cave paintings of animals, it would be possible to say that the origin of the visual arts lay in the effort to imitate and/or reproduce the features of a dead queen or king. As conventionalized as it is, the so-called Mask of Agamemnon, found in the royal tomb at Mycenae, surely follows the lineaments of a given individual's face. Was it actual eyesight, inadequacy of technical skill or the principle of fetishistic psychology that makes the gold Agamemnon mask look, today, cursively formalized?

---

* Plates 1 and 2 in *The Realm of the Great Goddess* by Sibylle von Cles-Reden (Englewood Cliffs, N.J.: Prentice-Hall, 1962).

Note that the question of formal beauty as such is not involved here; I refer only to photographic or naturalistic reproduction.

In the cases of the great Egyptian effigies, we have to deal with an art style that was based on a life style; that is, the Egyptian face and figure (though in some periods statues, for example, were remarkably realistic, like the famous *Seated Scribe*) were stylized by makeup accentuating and setting off their natural molds. This is especially true of eyes, and of course for magical reasons: the eyes guided the footsteps and identified objects after life, presumably, as during it, so that they were set off by heavy makeup, and in pictorial representation of the profile, were drawn as if in frontal view. This may have been partly because the eyes themselves were long and extended *around* either cheek; Egyptian eyes, rather like those of animals, tended to be panoramic. In later times, we find representations of the eye attaining independent life—something with wings as in L. B. Alberti's personal symbol—and denoting God's all-seeing eye. These are actually the progenitors of the film camera's eye.

Inspecting the Egyptian mummies, we observe that a system of signs, basically magical, constituted the "art" of representing the human. Originally it was a utilitarian, pseudo-scientific art because its chief aim was either to proclaim the quasi-divinity of a king or else to ensure his immortality. We must note in passing—because eventually it will prove important here—how anthropomorphic was the more advanced version of decorative or fetishistic representations of the world. Man himself, the human figure, became increasingly the "center" of man's cosmic consciousness. The destiny of the eye as a symbol, a quasi-independent organism, confirms this trend as a way of apostrophizing human nature as superhuman nature. The ground plan of the cathedral and the temple, as well as the shapes of all grave monuments, descend from the shapes of underground megalithic graves: the basis is human anatomy. Man was typified as the chieftain-hero, involved with the task of learning the secret of immortality (take the epic of Gilgamesh) before the idea of an independent, overall divine force, anthropomorphic or not, entered human consciousness. When this concept did enter human consciousness, it was an abstract sublimation of man's physical identity. Eventually, the plan of the heavens themselves became a reflection of earth's plan and correspondingly man's image was "found" in the anatomy of the cosmos.

It would be hard to deny, with any persuasiveness, that the eye is man's most important sense organ in that it is vision of the earth's structure that best guides him bodily through space and most helps him to control it. This has been demonstrated in ways as microcosmically inward as macrocosmically outward. Among the lower animals, of course, smell and hearing are senses as important as sight, but this difference is determined by environmental/physiological factors: the nose and the ear of animals give crucial warning of the unseen; the usefulness of the olfactory and the auditory to man, of course, is just as obvious while not so great in practical ways. On the other hand, according to man's higher constitution as an intelligence devoted to knowledge for its own sake, eyesight has no rival in conveying important information to the human individual who not only needs it but also desires it ("for its own sake") as a *purely imaginary layout*. Now these imaginary layouts may not have had a very practical purpose. The visual concept of the map is historic proof of this purpose. The map eventuated through man's spatial quest that recently has been climaxed by his conquest of superplanetary space.

In very primitive times, the only reason for the tribe's envisioning "invisible" spaces was the negative one of escaping human enemies or natural calamities (flood, earthquake, an age of rain or ice) and the positive one of seeking a herd's or a human enemy's terrain, grounds with greater food supplies and pleasanter living conditions.

One does not need, however, to argue that the optical function acquired for man more than a utilitarian purpose. The fact is historically self-evident in the transition from the fetish image of man, supposed necessary to his "immortality," to the art image of man, his place in a visionary world apart from the real world. True, one may say that the latter derived from the former, just as one tacitly assumes that historically art arose from religious fetishes. But derivation, implying priority through causation, is not our problem in this place, morally or psychologically. The only true problem is how film came to be as connected with the values it has today and what its potential values are. As the reader knows, I suppose film to have a special identity and that this identity is yet, in its true specialty, undefined; hence a "search" for it so as to have a proper basis for filmic values. The first point to be settled re cinema, or film, is the problematically situated motive behind the invention of *still* photography and then of *moving* photography.

Usually it is maintained that this original motivation was scientific in that man was at his old and serious occupation of making a conquest of "reality," that is, the true conditions of the world he inhabits. Under the classification of reality, of course, would come all the physical sciences invented by man: anatomy, medicine, biology, physics, chemistry, astronomy, and so on. Now the lens of the photographic machine, the camera, is an artificial eye, and so was the magnifying glass that came before it and was incorporated in purely scientific machines, the microscope and the telescope. The issue of visual accuracy, near and far, should be reserved for opticians and optometrists. Beyond that, true vision, clear vision, is a speculative thing relating to all preconditions, such as the specific field at which eyesight be directed, the motives of the viewer, both his conscious and unconscious psychology, and especially the degree of his attention.

To the scientist who wishes to investigate worlds too small for the naked human eye to see, the quality of the motive and its identity are not disputable. Nor is anyone's desire to have maximum scope of ordinary vision to be questioned. But note that in this respect optical science is exclusively a means, it has (aside from specialization in medical fields needing microscopy or in professional astronomy requiring telescopes) no slightest relation to *what is seen* or any particular identity to be searched for. Thus, I think we must acquiesce to the assumption that, at the very root, the impulse behind the invention of still photography (which may make a record of anything large or small) was, on the one hand, interest in creating a mechanical toy, and on the other, a different method for producing the effects of painting, chiefly in the domain of human portraiture.

Here we naturally pause, I should say, to reflect on the popular or collective human aspect. Consider that the greatest sensation created by early photography was the relatively easy way a family portrait or a portrait of a celebrity could be made and duplicated. Painting, of course, was a very skilled craft that required devotion, training and determination. Nineteenth-century painters themselves, as men of taste, may have become bored with academic portraiture and the idealization of the court portrait, whose purpose was to flatter, and so they sought to change the standards of portraiture in accordance with creative impulses. But this connoisseurship was not true of the great public, whose highest wish was to have (mainly for putting up in the home) reasonable likenesses of self and family members that were, besides, politely flattering. Still photography was not only an amusing novelty, therefore, but made a most convenient historic transition from the court portrait to the drawing room portrait of the rich bourgeois and his family. If the wealth and power of emperors had been able to memorialize and "immortalize" themselves (think of David's much upscaled vision of Napoleon being crowned: a work appropriately hanging at the Louvre), now a simple bourgeois, with some extra cash, could acquire similarly enhancing mementoes.

Science as an exhaustive investigatory technique (of which the special lens is a symbol) must be distinguished from what may be called the "science" of memory and its material mementoes. The aging process is one of the well-known enemies of man, especially of those members of the race who place a moralized value on youth and beauty. What the eyes of a person looking regularly into a mirror can tell him or her about the physical literalness, the science, of the inevitable aging process typically becomes, year after year, a repugnant habit. Commonly this sort of person wants a photograph or painting of himself to preserve him—not for immortality necessarily (although in Japan photographs adorn funeral altars and even graves in modern times), but for the duration of earthly life, throughout which a portrait is presumed to show him always "at his best."

Quickly, from this popular aspect—from the family album of snapshots to the studio portrait on the wall, the desk or the piano—photography leapt to be the optical division of recorded history. Journalism was reinforced by the celebrity portrait and spotportraits of important events. For what better could there be to place next to a headline or a news story? Meanwhile photographers were inspired to make independent records of places in their daily, literal, rather than painted and select, aspects. Parisian painters have surely left us, especially in the latter nineteenth century, a wonderful record of the way their beloved Paris once looked, but the ardor of the Impressionists and a twentieth-century lover of Paris such as Utrillo was duplicated in the way the photographer Atget methodically, and with poetic feeling, excelled all such painters' zeal by reporting Parisian scenes in the early twentieth century.

If, even today, there persists the old-fashioned school of deadpan academic painting, without the slightest worth as art, it is solely because of luxury psychology, the status delusion of the moneyed classes. It costs much, much more, that is to say, to have an artist do your bust or sitting portrait three or four feet high in oils than to have the most expensive photographer make a studio portrait large enough to look imposing in an expensive frame. The oil portrait will remain—this is another luxury factor—unique; the portrait photograph can be reproduced hundreds of times from an original negative. As a matter of fact—something known only, of course, to connoisseurs—certain fine photographic portraits of the late-nineteenth century easily excel in beauty the portraits done contemporaneously by competent but indifferently talented oil painters.

As always, the status aspirations of the masses once more proved here a delusion and a snare. If we observe the oil portraiture of the American, Thomas Eakins, we do see something rivaling, maybe even excelling, the best photographic portraits of his time, and thus we see something much beyond what could be called the work of someone "indifferently talented." For one thing, the early technical limitations of photography gave even the most ambitious portraits a keepsake size, which could not be expected to impress as much as the life scale, or near, essayed by nineteenth-century portrait painters. Even Eakins, however, remains a dated painter of portraits that belong to social history as much as to art—I doubt any of these portraits could be termed great art—and it would be safe to say that, on the whole, the eminence of the middling academic oil portrait was slain by the invention of photography.

Part of the portrait painter's art, we must be careful to note, is to produce a sort of synthesis, something more various, richer, than even an astute photographer (now or yesterday) can catch by snapping a shutter in a camera. The portrait painter must be skilled in human observation, he must actually be moved by his subject as well as by his profession. True, an ambitious photographer might spend as much clock time as a painter in "studying" his subject, looking for the right shade of mood and the right chiaroscuro to articulate it. Yet this method, the photographic one, must necessarily rely too much on the subject's timed cooperation, since, materially speaking, all the photographer can record is a single moment, no matter how tactically approached and psychologically prepared that moment be. A painter, on the other hand, can actually, through protracted observation of his subject, literally synthesize a whole series of time aspects by a flick of his brush—by the very special line and shadow given a mouth, the encyclopaedic gleam imparted to an eye, the subtle droop given eyelids.

Moreover, simply by his genius for plastic design—this is seen in Renaissance portraits as well as in portraits by Edgar Degas—a painter can as it were "assemble" a look of pathos or importance, even drama, on face, bust or half figure which a photographer could pretend to imitate only with the most excruciating care; then, even so, the result might look strained and self-important instead of natural and grand. Here another factor is not to be neglected: grandeur is as much a sensibility as it is an architectural plan, a pictorial design. Three or four centuries ago, regardless of the medium in which persons were portrayed, there was more reason for one to feel "naturally grand" than there is (even in the cases of Very Important Persons) today. One thing to remember about Very Important Persons is that our time's enormous cult of journalistic photography tends to catch them on the run, at informal and unexpected moments, as much as when they pause and, posing, smilingly consent to be portrayed. The journalistically casual sort of personal image is the opposite of the studio portrait and could be called, in fact, the disportrait.

Years ago, someone compiled a volume of journalistic photographs called *The Breathless Moment*. Virtually all its hundreds of items came from newspaper archives and concentrated on natural and human catastrophes: the moment a building collapsed, the winner of a footrace dropped dead on breaking the tape, a man jumped to death from a bridge or a building. In other words, every page showed forth one high function of the journalistic photograph: the cultivation of sensationalism, the precious memoranda of death and disaster. What struck people as an exciting book to leaf through was actually a testament to that strange avidity of the human being visually to seize the moment of general misfortune—misfortune which he, the beholder, has escaped but which befalls, engulfs, others not so lucky as he, perhaps not so worthy or wisely cautious. These photographs provided a certain kind of theater, therefore, a pseudotragic theater of natural or lunatic accident. The book was one huge clot of *mementi mori*, a source of the vulgar aesthetic thrill of witnessing the fatalities built into the daily patterns of human life.

Is the above paragraph really banal, a rehearsal of the obvious? It is no less inevitable than is the world's recurrent daily sum of accidents. And here such material is essential to the psychology out of which the passion for cinema arose. *The Breathless Moment* enshrined, by an act of anthology, something typical and long surviving: still photographs of the same category continue to be part of a newspaper reader's joy, and if they failed to appear, their loss would occasion feelings of letdown, frustration and, doubtless, protest. The moral argument for their revival would be the modern citizen's right to be told "the truth" and to witness it as if it were documentary evidence in a court of law. One assumes that news stories—especially the dreadful ones—are by and large factual, but there's nothing like a photograph to underline their authenticity by allaying all possible doubts.

One relevant thing—it came up in regard to films taken by American cameramen of the fighting in World War I—is whether the photograph is "genuine"—that is, whether it is what it purports to be; for it may have been staged in good faith as an approximate simulation or faked in bad faith as an invention pretending to be real. During the French cinema's earliest days, news stories such as revolutions and gruesome conditions of prison life were studio-staged and offered forthrightly as information films: what later were termed newsreels or *réalités*. After all, in a legal inquiry, fake photography can provide fraudulent evidence; genuine photography, on the other hand, may help convict a suspected murderer. A film by Michelangelo Antonioni, *Blow-Up* (1966), pivoted its fictional plot on a case of photographed murder although the photograph was destroyed before it could function as evidence. However, for the present purpose, it is only the truth-telling faculty of the photograph that matters.

What sort of truth it tells—not what sort of life—is what matters most. Remember that newspapers and TV studios alike have quite an assortment of events to "report" and that so-called "slanting the news" depends to some extent on mere selectivity. On the art side, a few modern photographers of high accomplishment and style sensibility have appeared in recent decades. Among them, surely, is Henri Cartier-Bresson. And it is significant that the most compendious volume made of his photographs should bear a title similar to that mentioned above: *The Decisive Moment*. The difference of the adjective serves accurately the reshift of photographic values illustrated by Cartier-Bresson's work. While his photographs have often appeared in magazines and been given exhibitions, he was only incidentally and commercially a journalistic photographer. He made a documentary film about the repatriation of French inmates freed from German concentration camps after World War II and used to accept important commissions to do field photography. But his personal motivation was typically aesthetic in that he wished to bring into the open, onto the streets, something of the "studio" care of the subject and the "right moment" that Atget, not long before him, brought into photography and that was also cultivated by American photographers such as Berenice Abbott and the late Margaret Bourke-White.

Of course, between Henri Cartier-Bresson and his predecessor, Eugène Atget, there was an important difference that leads us directly toward the psychology that produced the film sensibility. Indeed, when Cartier-

Bresson began working, cinema had long been invented and had produced the genres of its first three decades. Not chronology, however, but psychology and sensibility are our concern at the moment. There are a few street scenes in Atget—scenes, that is, with groups of pedestrians or bystanders—but mostly he loved to photograph human types—a bakery boy, a flower seller, a pair of organ-grinders, halted in their activities to pose for him; and above all, he loved the contents of shops and markets as a version of a painting genre, the still life. These did not have to pause to be photographed, they were as if patiently waiting for him. Views of the Seine, of factories, of ornamental façades, of gardens in general and Versailles in particular, or just a doorway or an alley, engaged Atget, but always through the still-life sensibility. There is the reposeful sense of Jan Vermeer painting Amsterdam or some still serene Chardin when we see a common doorway by Atget with a loaded wheelbarrow beside it. He loved misty effects, impressions of quietness and emptiness: emptiness as of abandonment. So when we come upon deserted street vistas, street frontage with shops and signs but only a single person, or the palace at Versailles almost overwhelmed by the shadows of clouds, we are as if stilled ourselves, a little shadowed and breathless.

Cartier-Bresson's shift was to people, a lively pursuit of the "exotica" of types and their multiplicity and everywhereness rather than their rarity and particularity; at the same time, his images had an air of being caught in the midst of an action, at a moment of privacy "exposed," yet not posed or public. When Atget photographs a family of rag-pickers by their horse-drawn home, it is like a Pre-Raphaelite painting of a family of vagrants; that is, it looks back toward anecdotal and genre painting; it is natural enough yet not naturalistic, not quick with a special "decisive moment." However, when Cartier-Bresson photographs a Mexican peasant family, the layout suggests more the sort of intimacy of presence to be found in film, as if the shot were one of several such showing the same group; moreover, the view, looking "cropped" because of the camera's closeness, makes us more aware of the scene's invisible extensions—as if it were only a momentary pause both of the spectator and the spectacle—as well as of the abstractness of its still design. The more a scene in front of human eyes be artificially reduced by framing off special areas, the more the recognizable shapes therein tend to seem abstract volumes, abstract patterns of light and shade: the sort of abstract dynamics to be found in a simply designed painting of purely abstract torsions. Futuristic painting did this to physical movement and then blew up the scene (as Umberto Boccioni did) to mural dimensions suiting the violence of military combat or a football game.

The style sensibility of Atget was well interpreted by a brief tasteful film made of his photographs and having very few glimpses of human beings. The feeling was nature-morte, a feeling momentarily swept of human association. The tenderly shadowed, magically still, rather melancholy views of Paris streets and Versailles vistas are faded in and out to the rhythms of Satie's sweetly hypnotic *Gymnopédies*. The momentary duration of the still photograph on the film screen is an imitation of the time devoted to looking at photographs reproduced in a book or turned over from a stack; however, the "changefulness" produced by an action independent of the spectator's agency—the fade-in-and-out movement obtained by the film camera—perfectly creates the passive nostalgic mood of recall that Atget tried to build up as the image of his collection, as his "style." It is the regulated, soothing action of pleasuring memory; in other words, it is a visualized psychology of feeling.

Many capable still photographers have sought splendor and softness of chiaroscuro texture, sumptuous design deriving from sumptuous architecture and landscape, a general style of beautiful and varied plasticity, and have succeeded in making additions to the world archive of beautiful images (mostly in black and white), beautiful images which, nevertheless, fall into the decorative, less meaningful class, held in common with a great deal of valid abstract painting of this century. Our later photographic age is notable, in fact, for displaying the resources of the plastic sensibility for creating dramatic abstract effects by angled and framed-off shots of classic Greek architecture. This pursuit of forms symbolizes a single enduring facet of the film sensibility itself. While, conventionally, it must be called architectural photography (I think of the work of Roloff Beny and George Hoyningen-Huene) it nevertheless treats *as montage* the abstract chiaroscuric elements to be found in inert objects defined by light and shade; objects that, of course, are in themselves (in the case of Greek temples and statues) already a created art. Montage might be defined as that art of photography implying continuity because it represents a whole gradually, in selected parts, and according to the rhythm of presentation creates a mood for taking in by the eye a relatively complex object or scene at leisure, bit by bit.

I have not found one such but I can easily imagine a whole film of still photographs of Greek temples quite as formally satisfying as—probably more satisfying than—the Atget film I have mentioned. Such a film would be apt to be more dramatically abstract, quite as dramatic as it is lyric, and less nostalgic from the literary standpoint since it would have neither people nor places inhabited daily by people. Its object would be not to present us with the singleness of a noble ruin but to vary and internally multiply it by photographing it from different angles, with necessary repetition of architectural features, so that in the end we would have a composition like a painting, not an object like a building; besides, this composition would exist in time, like touring a great building inside and out, not to arrive at its total architectural concept, but to achieve a number of aesthetic perspectives that would hang together harmoniously.

Thinking purely in terms of still photography, one is filled with the idea that what injected a new spirit into both photography and painting was an impulse to *move toward* the subject of interest as if to see into it more deeply and precisely and variously, and thus to move the spectator's viewpoint inside a scene as if it were another environmental factor, not passively to remain outside it. That which I describe as an impulse is thus internally complicated—very much so if measured by the variety and extent of its parts, its development in several directions, all of which add up to a unique "rendering." By this path, film connects itself with a unified multiplicity, becomes not merely the notation of objects but embodies *ways of seeing them*. Thus it displaces interest from the mere integrity of an object—like the mummy of a king—to the agent of interest itself, to the eye which beholds it. Thus photography and its kinetic development was aesthetically aggressive and dynamic.

The subject of either photograph or painting in the nineteenth century tended to occupy a place equivalent to the subject of a stage play, divided firmly from the audience by a proscenium. What is known as "projection" both ways—from the actor and the action, in the case of a play, and from the audience in terms of understanding, identification and response—was thus totally a psychological matter, a mechanism that unified spectacle and spectator without what must be called mutual participation in any spatial/physical sense; the eye alone was the conductor, the welding agent. The architectural element of the theater's proscenium symbolized the firm convention of the barrier preventing what, in one modern term, is called environmental theater, which might be applied to Happenings in which an audience wandering through a given space (an informal "theater") don't necessarily participate but, according to physical capacity and contiguity, could participate if they wished.

A modern organization such as the Living Theatre instituted a kind of disorderly appeal from actors on stage to the audience to join them "orgiastically" in live-ins and love-ins, actions having no special dramatic structure, only a social structure. It has actors invading the audience to provoke emotional responses, pro or con, that would take physical or verbal form. At times the appeal itself, the provocation, was (à la Theater of Cruelty) a verbal or physical molestment. The procedure of a theater such as Richard Schechner's Performance Group somewhat altered the Living Theatre tactics by mingling the action of a well-known play (in 1969 it was Euripides' *Bacchae*) physically with the audience; at least, so far as the space in which the much revised Euripidean drama took place was untheaterlike enough to permit and encourage touching between actors and spectators as well as an exchange of words. The movement of the actors was literally around scaffoldings on which the spectators sat or simply among spectators squatting in groups on the floor; at times an actor would stop to whisper words into the ears of spectators.

Direct address of audience by actor is of course not new in the theater—it appears in the Elizabethan theater with the Prologue speaker and "asides" by actors only the audience (not those on stage) was supposed to hear—nor is mutual bodily participation quite new. As deriving from sacrificial rites in which the people of a district or tribe participated in choral manner, the ancient Theater of Dionysos at Athens (where the great dramatic competitions were held) preserved the old ritual form in the new drama largely by means of the chorus of elders or maidens, and by the orchestra of the amphitheater, where as it were audience space and actor space overlapped each other. The contemporary equivalent of this is the theater-in-the-round. Today, as a very modern descendant of the mutual-participation theater motif, there is the very late "amateurism" of stage performance; for example, the psychodrama, the improvised theater of psychiatric patients, a feature of which is immediate criticism by an audience of other psychodramatists, who have been watching and expect to take their own turns on stage. The latest form, as I write, is the Encounter Group, which would seem no more than a revival of the debating society concerned now with private/social rather than public/social issues, and very informal.

An important point in the development of mutual-participation theater was, of course, the plays of Luigi Pirandello, where the action on stage was rendered ambiguous by being self-conscious theater, seeming to improvise experimentally as it went along and drawing its cast, at times, from supposed members of the audience. It was as if Shakespeare's famous ironic *mot*, "All the world's a stage . . ." converted a dramatic spectacle into a moral problem. Pirandello's theater was inspired by the metaphysical consideration that, life itself being fraught with a struggle between illusion and reality, the theater should reflect this struggle as part of the creative process in the dramatist. The tragic pattern of fate and the comic pattern of morals was turned by Pirandello into a dramatic controversy among all values, the dramatic issue being in permanent suspense; thus his plays are conceived as searches after the identity between an actor and his action. This is precisely the search of the modern psychodrama, with the difference that the latter may not get as far as any positive dramatic action, anything to excite the emotions, anything to irrevocably *commit* the actor.

As a therapeutic ritual, the psychodrama in a way wishes to avoid action—through fear that it may be the "wrong" action. Hence all the talk, hence the absence of governing motive or a governing plot. At least, neither Sophocles' Oedipus nor the protagonists of Pirandello are prevented from violent and decisive action, however unhappy or "wrong" its outcome be. As for Hamlet, the corrosive irony is that violence comes on top of violence to no helpful purpose, as a series of dramatic blunders. Both Shaw and Ibsen are certainly "argumentative" dramatists, deeply concerned with social ethics. Yet they too allow the purely emotive act, even the purely irrational act. These days, the psychodramatists and the encounter groups, all doors open and window shades up, tend as dramatic spectacles to confine themselves to arguments, so that what we have on television and in halls are theaters whose utmost violence is a nasty personal insult, which, so far as identity goes, merely proclaims that men are rediscovering and reasserting hostility to each other. Naturally, there is an antidote, and this is the animal caress, meaning (through touch and/or words) "I love you." But the human effect in this theater of benignly stacked decks is sometimes incredibly phony. By this standard, the theater has broken down traditional drama to the domestic ritual of quarreling and making-up. Shades up or down, we are all at home, of course, there.

I doubt that Pirandello's drift, thus degraded, helps us much in our present search, so let us reorient the theme. It would appear that a photograph, whether still or moving, must remain an intact spectacle *by the absolute limits of its medium*. It is pre-accomplished, as it were, not accomplished during the same time (as in a play) that a spectator witnesses it, and what we see (moving or still) is a "reproduction." Furthermore, photograph and film have the window status of the painted picture that preceded them, and which at first they necessarily imitated. But I have already noted that at the very moment the film mechanism was advancing from primitive gadgets such as the gyroscope, painting was also destroying its static window-illusion by seeming to interfere with normal optical apprehension of objects and scenes, whatever the latter were.

The Impressionists made firm contours fuzzy and fuzzy contours into atmospheric blends, ending with the aggregation of small contrasting color dots of the Pointillistes: a rain of prismatic atoms. In painting nature, the stroking of a Claude Monet, as in the water lilies series, anticipated the ultimate stroke-abstraction of the Non-Objectivists and Abstract-Expressionists. The object was being dissolved. Then the Fauves came along to displace both natural color and delicacy of drawing by a gross, fiercely oversimplified color and form, as if to evoke clumsiness. The message was that life itself is not architecture or even groups of people seen distinctly and objectively, but a set of relationships that are essentially mobile, unstably changeful. Appearing almost simultaneously in easel painting and the theater, the expressionistic style made even a nonviolent subject seem violent by the nature of its drawing and the rough wildness of its brush strokes (look at a landscape by Oskar Kokoschka, an interior with people by Edvard Munch or a portrait by Chaim Soutine). It was notable that Fauvism had merely formal preoccupations (they did not treat "human situations" whereas the Expressionists regarded formal disorder as a psychological symptom of deranged or worked-up emotions).

The very step from mural to easel painting was, of course, a step toward intimacy of feeling, therefore a step toward the subject (the artist and spectator alike) by subjectivizing the object. Now what, exactly, is *the object?* Is it some sort of representation or is it living (or dead) reality itself? With this question we approach the very heart of the film. We are at grips with the theory, even if we cannot see exactly what it is. But we do know, I think, this much: reality is a set of mutating relationships more than it is a still, permanently measured and stable quantity. The shift that came into pictorial representation about the time that still photography had begun to think of changing itself into cinema was the moral/psychological shift from art as a mythic form of idealization to art as a higher variety of artifact. Myths, particularly religious myths, had once had stability; now they were subject to internal alteration. Before cinema, space itself, any given space, had never been considered an "object." Only its representation, if still, was an object. The virtue of the artifact was tentative and experimental; moreover, it did not precisely remain outside reality as an important and independent representation of it, but remained inside it, could easily be moved and, in groups, be moved *among*.

There had been a peripety, and before the reversal (which required time) both romantic and metaphysical values, regardless of religious motif, had reacted against science and reason and had returned to human aspiration and human excess. This explains romanticism in literature, which so easily accommodated social fervor, and new politics, and Pre-Raphaelitism in painting, whose vein of fantasy (despite often flat-footed anecdotalism) easily turned into radical politics and social rebellion. Remember that Byron, Shelley, Swinburne and William Morris were all fervent anti-establishment thinkers.

This was about the time when the influence of Jean-Jacques Rousseau and Napoleon Bonaparte was dually felt and the whole phenomenon of "romantic" reaction against reason and academic conservatism—so consistent with scientific postulates—had turned back to the instinctual search and emotional consciousness of the Earthly Paradise; actually, the Earthly Paradise was the dialectical child of religion and science felt in empiric terms of the social conscience. Now what is the Earthly Paradise but the world itself as an Ideal Object?—therefore the self-sufficient virtue in all idyllic or "romantic" painting of nature. It was removed from all physical participation except through the illusions of compulsive fanatics; in essence it was a metaphysical quantity only *resembling* nature itself.

In the light of these considerations, one discerns a deeper pattern in the veering of Eisenstein from mere social-revolutionary proletarianism—a philosophy supposed to convert even the Russian peasant to Marxism—to harmony with the animal instincts, to the idea of the hero not as a model of social and political progress, but as the protagonist of a dynamic myth in which he might just as easily be a pagan scapegoat as the successful leader of a modern people. But to have a politically acceptable myth—no matter what the art medium involved—one would have to depose the old tragic destiny and the old pagan vulnerability of the hero. The hero would be neither a haplessly superstitious peasant nor a demonically possessed Tsar like Ivan the Terrible. The trouble with Marxist psychology is that it developed by dialectic realization into thinking the world itself (in its special aspect of social organization) a metaphysical quantity. Passional socialism under the Communist-Marxist aegis posited this "ideal object" of a new society as virtually or inherently real, which is to say, psychologically, a *fait accompli*—a real object. Socialism is that state in which the tribe, through absolute unification, becomes an object to itself. It is Paradise Found. This means that there is no division in consciousness, no space between subject and object, thus no art because life has become not *a* work of art, but *the only* work of art.

According to the Marxist calendar, then, there are no tragedies or ironic defeats in the search for the Earthly Paradise because, essentially, the search is only a formality. The Soviet peoples exist in a "state of Marxism," therefore in perfection; it is just that certain individuals living there cannot "appreciate" this fact. Hence there are only "unfortunate accidents," miscalculations by those who are punishable for them, and "incidents" due solely to poor human vulnerability, still untransformed (since they represent unstable details) by Communist socialism. And why, then, the artifact rather than the myth? In the Soviet Union, we can evoke a logical answer: Because now the myth, being one myth, is a wholly subjectivized object, so that objects themselves, real objects, can only be major or minor details. Such a replacement, however, seems as plausible in a non-Marxist as in a Marxist society! Consider that the Art Nouveau movement, insofar as it broke out of literary "aesthetic decadence" patterns, turned to artifacts, to a life still represented by elements as useful as they were ornamental, to objets-d'art, to decoration and architectural environment. The wandering serpentine line in a jewel or a staircase was a way of destroying four-square conformity, the stuffy "upright," in both artistic and social/political sensibility. It implied a new freedom and spontaneity of movement on all levels of human activity. Now absolute movement and absolute stillness are equivalents; just so with absolute change and absolute permanence. But this is a motif of metaphysics; the arts, including cinema, do not represent absolutes, they only flirt with them.

Consider that Pre-Raphaelitism had its popular (albeit sentimental and moralistic) icons no less than its Wagnerian myths, and that the icons had their political side, especially as typified by Ford Madox Brown's famous painting *Work* (1852–65). If one expunged certain morbid accents from that epic work and "corrected" its mannerist formalism, it would do for a proletarian mural in the Soviet Union today or yesterday. Until Edward Burne-Jones's switch to mythology and mannerism, Pre-Raphaelite painting was notably photographic/realistic in style of representation: a phase of its contemporary anecdotalism that verged, at times, on trivia. At its middling level, it was a more serious form of fictional illustration, altogether in the Victorian mode. Yet exactly in this sentimental conception of "human situations" Pre-Raphaelitism turned away from the rigidly formal landscapes and portraits of the academy to actual humanity and its daily concerns as well as its moral myths. If physical labor could be dignified by myth, so could the casual moment of private moral illumination: see William Holman Hunt's *The Awakening Conscience*, which might, in fact, illustrate an incident from an early movie romance.

It shows a handsome young woman who has just been singing at the piano with an equally handsome young man, whose laughing expression indicates their songs have been gay. But suddenly—it is the "moment" of the painting—she has arisen with rigidly clasped fingers to stare, as if tragically, at some unseen vision even while their lighthearted pleasure still survives on the face of her surprised companion. Already we are with the alert photographer, snatching from the current of life its fleeting instant weighted with importance . . . The spectator, in a sense, is being invited into the movie house that is yet to materialize. *The Awakening Conscience* is dated 1852–54. Poe was then dead but Charles Baudelaire had still to begin *Les Fleurs du Mal* and modern painting had still to sprout its first buds of Impressionism.

Modern art was about to pose a dual new inquiry into time and space, both as objective factors and the modal perceptions of a subject, *as a psychology*. The film, nicknamed the movies, technically appeared within a few decades as one unsuspected but titanic agent of this large inquiry through token of the photograph: the haughtily dismissed and reverentially acclaimed photograph. Yet exactly in the fact that the photograph reminded everybody of reality as everyday life, it reminded people of the process of art—that art means selected, transformed, accented and specialized reality, a process that continues as life continues: a process that has no absolute climax, only relative climaxes. The paradox was that the photograph, like a painting, remained literally still, fixed; no matter how much movement it connoted, that movement was technically arrested. Film, or cinema, was the inspiration, itself necessarily technical, to animate this arrestment, to unfreeze it, and, as it were, liberate it into the movement of "life."

But this was not *just* the movement of life. It was also the movement of the life of art, which is to say, the movement of a dialectic, embedded permanently, I think, between art as a subject and life as an object, or art as an object and life as a subject, between which only mind can properly intermediate. Amid a great deal of confusion and pretension, amid much well-intended bad manners, this is what the mobility and environmental theaters, the psychodramatic and encounter groups, have been trying to do: to reassert the great and essential balance of an organic process, a joining and exaltation of opposites. The true access to this idea, and its embodiment too, is film; essentially and pre-eminently, film. At last, it seems possible to conclude that film has a psychology of its own. Time and space, however refined and complex, however "difficult" their intermingling, are thus merely the extended conditions of a supreme art to be called cinema.

"Supreme"? "Psychology"? Does the reader then imagine I am saying that film simply conveys more than other arts? It seems to me, not that it conveys more, necessarily, but that it is equipped to convey the most in terms of converting the experience of two things, *world* and *mind*, as respectively subject and object (or vice versa), with a maximum degree of the illusion of total reality in terms of audio-visual spectacle. This is so because film is situated at the source of the whole human apparatus of apprehension: it can affect and utilize the major senses, sight and hearing, into the most satisfying kinaesthetic spectacle of them all. This I would call a technically reinforced and aesthetically educated *psychology*: a psychology equipped with the most perfect instrument of self-expression yet invented: the sound-rigged film camera.

3

FILM AS SELF-CONSCIOUS SUBJECTIVITY

It would be a happy thing to glance at the historic accumulation of cinema over the world and find films which somehow were especially relevant to my approach here, films which are concrete illustrations that the focus of which I speak—the theory—is self-aware in terms of certain unique filmic events. Fortunately, I think, just the films we want are available. There may be others but at least there are two films ideal for our purpose; one involving the still photograph, the other, painting (which is "still" by definition): Antonioni's *Blow-Up* and the *Fellini Satyricon*. A scene exists in Federico Fellini's film where the Roman poet Eumolpus meets one of the young heroes, Encolpius, in an art gallery so that the latter, handsome and beautifully built, seems like a statue come to life. They form a boon companionship while the bawdy story—based on exploiting all varieties of sex and orgiastic situations—proceeds.

The original author, Petronius Arbiter, apparently depicted every phase of sexual "vice" and excess known to the people of that time and place. While nominally a satire, and even believed by some to have been written as an exemplary treatise for the Emperor Nero, Petronius' work in effect is a celebration of sexual lust, not as a social vice, but as a pure joy. As a social phenomenon, "vice" is only lucid and valid if specifically related to civil order and state prosperity. Even then it may function as an Establishment delusion, something on the statute books rather than a human reality in people's hearts and minds. Art, on the other hand, is free to tell us that sex, considered in terms of sensual pleasure and its animal climaxes, may exist quite independently of accepted public (for example, political) moral decisions.

Petronius' testimony is authentic and sufficient to itself but it has innumerable like companions that are quite as convincing and authoritative; for example, *The Decameron*, recently made into a film by Pier Paolo Pasolini. The more or less implied "moral censure" found at times in such works is very worldly, and beyond that, merely formal; that is to say, ambiguously salty. Observe that the Marquis de Sade, had he so wished, could have pretended that his most horrific scenes of lust and mayhem were intended, after all, to be morally exemplary, to warn humanity away from such models rather than to encourage it to imitate them. A true example of the strategy of fictional vice, presented with complete impudence as an "object lesson," is Choderos de Laclos' superb *Les Liaisons Dangereuses*, cleverly, if a bit cavalierly, made into a modern movie by Roger Vadim.

While the two young heroes of the *Fellini Satyricon*, Ascyltus and Encolpius, are plainly bisexual, their main romantic drive is toward their own sex, and concentrates on their rivalry for the boy Giton. To have faithfully imitated the *Satyricon* on film (the manuscript coming down to us has been filled in with later additions) would have meant that Fellini probably could not have gotten his film onto the commercial market. In any case, it seems that he wished to use Petronius' fiction as a theme for variations on his own, allegedly autobiographic, recollections. The fact is that Fellini's moral licence toward sexual custom (there is no faking in his film about the homosexual facts of the matter) points up, as much as does Eisenstein's *Ivan*, the purely technical as well as the theoretical aspects of cinema that I wish to emphasize now. In the last and widest, most efficient sense, artistic method is designed to *accommodate any subject matter whatever* and need not bow to limitations put on it by political edict or social prejudice, for the sake of this or that propaganda purpose. This is, moreover, why the politics of Pound's *Cantos*, even if historically useful and arguably correct, are ultimately irrelevant to the poetry in *The Cantos*. All that is *politically* required in the practice of genuine poetry, free poetry, is contingent permissiveness: noninterference from (virtually) noninterested authority; no harassment or dictation from any direction whatsoever.

This does not mean (as certain facile ideologies would have it mean) that artistic creation is "theoretically" unrelated to real life. Quite the contrary: it is abundantly, necessarily and self-evidently related to real life. Art and life are brothers and mutual critics. Yet a poem or a novel that happens to look like propaganda has disastrously fallen into the idiom of politicians who make speeches; that is, who (allegedly) wish to remedy what is at fault, what is bad. Politics wants a recipe, a program, for desirable change. Art cannot be such a program, simply because art represents what is true, basically, ineradicably true; art's authenticity and integrity, then, depend as much upon what is morally bad as upon what is morally good, which themselves are, of course, variables. Good and bad may change in social substance. Art, in social substance, never changes; its manners may change: not its destiny, its purpose.

Hence art and life are mutual critics, not on the basis of *what is desirable* but on the basis of *what is true*. This is one of the great points because life is always turning up new styles in the arts that contradict and tend to replace old styles, which, however, hang onto life by their inherently permanent qualities, so that we have an enduring category of art that is termed classic. The term classic rightly means simply "surviving truth." Classicism (or any more exactly named surviving "ism") is simply art that won't die with its individual creator's span of human life but stubbornly persists in the face of the strongest "replacement" arts and artists. So it happens that Fellini could take a classic work such as Petronius' *Satyricon* and revive it as both a symbolic autobiography and a period fantasy. Italy's Renaissance and Confucius' China provided just such period fantasies for Pound in *The Cantos* (which in a looser but material sense is also autobiographic) while the life of Ivan the Terrible, taken from the history of Russia's rulers, provided a period fantasy and an autobiographic form for the uses of Eisenstein.

That history is concerned with replacement orders, new orders, is self-manifest. But history by definition includes the history of the arts as well as of national governments, national and international religions and the fortunes of the planetary race. The arts may consciously reflect such transformation and struggle for survival or replacement in the social and political orders, but likewise they reflect—or "embody" would be a better word—the same transformation and struggle within their own domains. Eisenstein managed Ivan's personality so that it would include a ritual-like dance orgy—the all-male party which precedes the midnight mass in the church at the end of the two-part film. What we know as profane dance—historically both court ballet and folk dance—derived, of course, from sacred dance, which in distant pagan times was a vital part of ritual and also the art of theater deriving from ritual. The party and the dance in *Ivan the Terrible*, as pagan survivals, are at variance with the Christian ritual about to take place in the church; that is, nominally at variance.

The fact is: art not only synthesizes itself, it also synthesizes religion—and having arrived at this stage of my account, it is inevitably suggested that religion likewise does this. In any religion that is officially and widely practiced, there must be an original, perhaps persistent, issue between old elements and new elements, elements salvaged from the past and some introduced by the present. Even a fixed universal religion, as we should know well from observing our own latter twentieth century, is not perfectly static; it continually changes its rules, both formally by proclamation and by tacit, informal consent. It contracts with conservatism and expands into liberalism. Today, homosexuality is a declared feature of ultra-liberalism among Protestant churches. A perfectly lucid symbol of this mutability exists in physical form in Rome itself, where the Church of San Clemente is composed of three levels. The modern church is at street level, the medieval church at the level directly beneath, and the second underground level is pagan: a sacred place once devoted to the cult of Mithras, which sacrificed bulls and ordained a bath of bull's blood for its initiates. The antique symbol of the ravaged Acropolis at Athens suggests the rigors of such changes: itself a system of pagan overlay, it was reused successively by Christians and Turks as a sacred place—and at last, profanely, as a storehouse for gunpowder.

These historic mutations reinforce the eloquence of Fellini's final device at the end of his *Satyricon*. It is in line with the modern fashion of writing fictional accounts of artists and their works—something which, in *8½*, Fellini himself had explicitly ventured to do in terms of making a film within a film. In a sense, the device in the *Fellini Satyricon* is a more objectively phrased self-compliment than that in *8½*. Ascyltus having been killed, his mutual adventures with Encolpius (apparently Fellini's sign for himself) are at an end, so that Encolpius faces a new term of life. What is past is in itself dead, and this point, rather conventionally, is portrayed by the young man's departure in a ship: he faces a totally new life adventure. Yet, plainly, Fellini knows that nothing is ever totally new, or indeed humanity would cease to be humanity and require another self-definition. Yes, there is, to be sure, a conscious rejection by Encolpius of his past and this is relevant to the closing device.

In the last incident but one, however, Fellini seems deliberately to point to the slavish greed of power psychology in maintaining the social establishment (by which he may also mean, one hazards, the film establishment). A group of a dead man's old friends, notably mature rather than youthful, gather about his laid-out corpse to feed on its flesh. This is no Roman custom but the result of a whimsical clause in the dead man's will that leaves a portion of his wealth to anyone who will partake of that gruesome meal. Another human vice in the *Satyricon*?—the terrible animal baseness of greed?— the last ironic excess of body lust? Logically, one can hardly avoid this conclusion. But it is not simple, nor is it all . . . The stoic solemnity with which bits of the corpse are munched, as Encolpius prepares to sail with his companions, is not a cannibalistic orgy but a grimly depressing affair with physical nausea in the offing. Fellini now turns to art for the true meaning of his dénouement. It becomes a conventional way to end the film (not Petronius' way but Fellini's) and yet it carries its own peculiar weight.

The farewell shot of Encolpius, still young and attractive, restored to virility (rather than, as in Petronius' narrative,* left with the dead weight of his impotent member in his hand), fades into the image of him painted on a decaying wall as if he were a surviving fresco. As the camera backs away to show us the entire fragment, other characters are seen beside him. It is a way of conceiving cinema as a mode of mythical magic, as when Aphrodite listened to the sighs and prayers of Pygmalion and brought to life the statue of Galatea, only here inverting the magic of that legendary act. Fellini found his characters and the inspiration of his considerably altered story in a classic novel and gave them living forms on the screen. The last shot functions as a peripety in this process. However the film finally be rated, its revival of a human past is quick with the poetic imagination. Thus, once more in history, Fellini reasserts the right and might of artists to conceive a certain enduring humanity out of time and place, living buried in a book, to be discovered and prospected by another art. Many have attempted to revive the past in the genre known as the historical novel, but when unaided by the magic that only the imagination can command, the historical novel remains a more or less amusing, more or less respectable, type of archaeological reconstruction.

---

* The Petronius manuscripts as translated by Paul J. Gillette. Hathaway House.

Unfortunately for the *Fellini Satyricon*, the film artist settled for a mediocre painter to execute the fresco version of his cast; for example, the painted images suffer much by the most obvious comparison to be made: that with the beautiful fresco room in the Villa of the Mysteries at Pompeii. But the theoretic point for film is accurately registered: film is neither an expanding assembly of technical devices of its own nor a simple reflection of another art; neither is it a vast historic accumulation like an antique shop nor a wily synthesis that, while borrowing from traditional norms, seeks to be as strictly modern, as new, as possible. One even imagines that Fellini has added, as a contemporary filmmaker, a gentle satirical touch all his own.

Commercial film sedulously tries to be everything that film essentially is *not*. Throughout its history, in the midst of proliferating documentation in the form of words and pictures, and stifled by its own immense archives, the cinema has been forced to struggle for survival as a true, independent identity. This is why most films are *anthologies*, rather than *syntheses*, of other arts —of the stage's dialogue, the novel's narrative, the dance's visual patterns and, beyond art, mere historical data. The *Fellini Satyricon* itself, like the work on which it is based, is rather unsatisfactory, too episodic, in narrative structure. Still, with his final shot, Fellini may be supplying an aptly ironic comment on the fashionable gimmick of ending a contemporary film with a "freeze"— that is, a sudden arrestment of the depicted movement, leaving it suspended like a still photograph blurred with motion.

This same device was used as a facile climax for François Truffaut's *The Four Hundred Blows* (1958) and imitated by numerous films thereafter. It can, according to the sort of film it ends, be conceived as portraying an abruptness of climax with a subtle dramatic force behind it; or it can indicate merely that climaxes as such are often, humanly considered, relative and arbitrary things. The effect is aided, in the case of *The Four Hundred Blows*, by the fact that the frozen frame we are left with portrays an act of self-liberation before it is completed: the boy hero, alone, is running away from a reform school to make his own life. The Truffaut film caught the public fancy in being a premonition of the world youth rebellion: a throwing off of Establishment shackles, and so on (and so on). Actually, in general effect, the device tends to support the theory of film as a continuous "flow of life," the endless reel that has an "open end." In this view, the ending of every story would be a mechanical interruption of what, in objective fact, is a continuous action.

And yet, despite their being parallel, Fellini's last shot has just the opposite implication from Truffaut's. The images of art are always, in a way, laid to rest as dead men are; but the former tend to survive rather than, like human corpses, disintegrate. With his camera, Fellini has restored for us the pathos of distance after refreshing us by the pathos of proximity with what, as an original form of life, technically belongs to the past. Actually, the contact he makes is not just with Petronius' novel—that would mean, perhaps, only archaeological reconstruction—but with the basic stream of life which respectively Petronius portrayed in the Emperor Nero's time and Fellini portrays in the latter twentieth century. If Fellini makes free with the *Satyricon* manuscripts— and he makes *very* free with them—he is only doing what various forgers conscientiously did throughout the centuries to make up for the fragmented state in which the original came down to posterity. Yes: film, like any other art, must invent stories of its own while also recognizing that beneath the flow of time and the way it constantly transforms surfaces lies a stable identity of human experience stretching toward the past and the future alike. Everything concrete, every building or picture preserved by the past, every scrap in a museum and every national treasure (in Japan, human beings are declared such), every sculptured remnant, are reckonable by art simply because the living present is totally responsible to that whose survival it has both willed and tolerated. Art specifically concerns itself with the survivals that have been *willed*.

It is piquant to think that photography has meant also a vast, unpublicized dossier of casual snapshots, the family album, etc., and that this was going on during the creation of serious works of public interest, especially celebrity portraits, then journalistic photography and finally the movies, with their own divided and disputed destiny. Today we find home movies coexisting not merely with commercial films and art films, but lately with an "underground" movement that partakes of the broad art revolution that arose with Impressionism, Fauvism, Expressionism, Cubism and (anticlimactically) Dada and Surrealism. We find thus a dialectic split amid amateurism itself.

Partly an aesthetic revolution, this movement was a manifestation of film camp. Budding in the late fifties, the stylishly amateurish and static, quasi-realistic type of Underground film paradoxically drew a measure of its authenticity from the momentum acquired by the film medium as ipso facto a report of objective truth. Nowadays, the most decidedly hip films—part of the great wave of psychedelism based on drug culture—are often only direct reports of a life style, a new bohemianism, photographed with as much sedulous simplicity as would be some ritual of a savage tribe. It is merely that the setting is not the jungle but the corners of lofts in the East Village, New York City. An insidious megalomania filters into the family album and the home movie.

Of course, what is usually termed cinéma vérité did not, at first, dream of subjective specialization, of the connoisseur (or art) approach to filmic documentation. If it did seek exotica, the purpose was informational (like the long list of feature films about aboriginals) so that one honorable label of newsreelism has become the Information Film. It is a medium for showing us cities, industries, slums, moon lifts, disaster areas. Certain famous documentaries, such as two of the pioneer Robert Flaherty's films, *Moana* (about the South Seas) and *Nanook of the North* (about the Eskimos), were among the Information Film's exotica. Film buffs devoted to the documentary style argue at length about the high place due documentarism or cinéma vérité, in distinction to the humbleness of the newsreel, today altogether supplanted by the television newscast. Such arguing merely italicizes the old, old claim of film—not simply antiquated but ignobly limited—that it "reports the truth," this being the whole nature and function of photography, both still and moving.

Documentarism is a subpsychology of film whose influence is not to be underrated. It has bred its scholars (like Jay Leyda) and its full-blown theorists (like Siegfried Kracauer), but it is extremely rare, however cultivated or competent such investigators be, to find any leaven of irony in their reasoning about the truthtelling ideal, any adequate stocktaking of just what the immense potentiality of film really is. The true extent and variety of its theoretic domain actually goes far beyond cinéma vérité. In substance, the *exclusivist* argument for cinéma vérité, no matter what its precise complexion or incidental rationale, denotes another form of professional exploitation opened up by the discovery of photography. The aggressiveness of this professionalism, regardless of its (sometimes deceptive) liberal outlook, is totally antitheoretical. Show me a fanatical documentarist and I will show you someone who, however involuntarily, speaks in bad faith when he speaks of a film pretending to be a work of art, when the subject of film poetry, or any high-level analogy with another art, is at issue. The documentarist does not have to be a competing professional, he may just as well be a competing amateur. An amateur or "disinterested" scholar is apt to be just as competitive, these days, as a professional, even if the amateur field be only his own suburban neighborhood.

Speaking realistically, documentarism is quite as much a myth, in both favorable and unfavorable senses, as any other myth, and quite as much to be scrutinized for true value as, correspondingly, the most irresponsible fiction film. It is precisely the "good myth" of documentarism —for example, "the camera always tells the truth"—that my other revelatory film, *Blow-Up*, indicts and most ingeniously explodes while providing a virtual sermon on the truthtelling theory of film. With beautiful irony, one is reminded by *Blow-Up* that a major type of film in the archives is the detective story, as transposed from the novel to the film melodrama. The growing industrial status of this type of film insured that it go far beyond the standard suggested by the detective story's originator, Edgar Allan Poe. Poe made a subtle blend of blood and horror with impartial logical deduction in the solving of a murder mystery, but even in the brief form his fiction took, he created the detective-hero whose progeny rapidly produced a world tribe, stemming mainly from (to give its progenitor a name) Sherlock Holmes. Of course, Wilkie Collins had written the first full-length detective stories in the 1860s, but in those the theme and atmosphere were foremost. The detective's personality was isolated by Poe as the fanatically cerebral faculty of solving a puzzle.

What happened was that, when the film camera was invented, the idea was intuitively and forcefully grasped that this magic mechanism was a figure of speech for the searching eye and the responding mind of the detective himself. Casually, now, we come upon an existential situation that is of profound usefulness, really critical usefulness, in defining film as a psychology. It is so easy to distinguish among the forms of art, their resemblances and contrasts, their technical interrelations. Still, it is much more refined, it is downright difficult, to seize upon an art's unique psychology. Poe's version of horror was not at all trivial in introducing the element of scientific inquiry, the great game of putting two and two together and getting the wanted sum (not necessarily four). This is the detective's game, yes, but prophetically it was also, and the demonstration was not far away, the game played by the detective of the soul: the analyst, the psychiatrist.

The game of the detective is to uncover a hidden pattern, a whole objective pattern hidden both deliberately and contingently—because criminals seek to hide, to build around themselves both anonymity and false appearances. Most of the "anonymity" is ready-made by the complicated nature of space, the great number of things, opaque things, with which it is filled, no less than its sheer extent. All that a criminal builds around himself to hide his guilt collaborates automatically with the great universal blank covering nearly all things, including acts in past time that may leave little or no tangible evidence of themselves (except, as to murder, the corpse itself). These are acts which usually, if private acts, only a few people know or indeed care about, few remember or wish to remember unless they be filed thoughtfully away in a photograph album or a private letter or the unconscious mind.

There is a mythical body of public acts, of course, by which I mean acts of public importance—such as a President's assassination and the acts leading to his election, acts by legal bodies, labor strikes, contract negotiations, etc.; acts affecting whole nations and many communities, all composed of individuals. Facing this enormous mass (the social organism with its complicated network of tentacles) are, besides the good old journalism of print, the still camera and the movie camera, and unto the latter, with special vividness and honor, has fallen the eminent myth of public omniscience . . . that endless-dossier aspect of human existence and all its eyes, whose only job is to ratify the truth by photographing it. Thus has come about the proud reputation of the communication media, television being at this moment ahead of the rest, with the film documentary to instrument it and back it up.

How dramatic, then, is an act such as a *murder*, seeking to avoid public appearances, to erase itself! That, at least, is the official story. To this perpetual drama, in a time of intensive democracy, has been added that of political secrecy, the ponderings of a government with itself and the concealed motives of its public maneuvers, a secrecy whose legitimacy has been questioned in the United States by the unauthorized publication in the press of the Pentagon papers and the Anderson tapes: technically "stolen property." The highest court has ratified the legitimacy of exposing such secret files, reserving (in theory) its opinion on the publication of government secrets that might jeopardize a nation's welfare: the welfare of the people themselves and the welfare of projects undertaken by the government in their behalf. Naturally, the theory of what may or may not really jeopardize the proper success of a nation's operations on the international level is itself very vague and, to employ a sterling phrase, remains to be seen.

At the same time, there is that curious situation generally known as the invasion of privacy. This might be only a simple invasion by the police of suspicious or illegal premises, private homes, clubs, bars, gambling casinos, thieves' dens. But it is also those voluminous files, kept in this country by the F.B.I. and other branches of government, made of the private, semiprivate and public lives of citizens tabbed as dangerous or suspicious or maybe just "prominent." Wiretapping, other listening devices and the scrutiny of far-flung records from the bulk of such dossiers, while photography itself enters as a most important element of their sum of information. Right here, we are not at all far from the theme of the detective story, film psychology as such, and that diabolically relevant film, Antonioni's *Blow-Up*. Not that *Blow-Up* is altogether without significant precedent. The film camera's awareness of its inevitable role as truth-teller, indeed as insistent and aggressive truth-teller, was perfectly demonstrated in a film of 1946 called *The Lady in the Lake*. The nature of its main device is highly strategic and immensely important here.

Somebody, sooner or later, was bound to think of this highly charged device. For virtually the length of this crime-detection film, the detective is played by the camera eye as substantive for a man's body and, of course, his eyes. The camera's movements, that is, indicate the open-eyed passage of the detective's body through space wherever he pursues his clues. The psychological nature of the camera's vision, in this case, is emphasized by the fact that recurrently, though only in glimpses, we see parts of the detective's person when his face happens to be caught in a mirror or he extends an arm or leg in front of him. The value of the extra tension provided is obvious: the spectator technically is identified with the detective, and so *we* feel—comfortably or uncomfortably as the case may be—his peculiar responsibility to solve the crime. The artifice of the thing, however, must be equally present for spectators. *Our* minds could not be exactly *his* mind, so that whatever we see (assuming we note, optically only what, and as much as, he notes) our thought processes still must differ, perhaps vitally, from his. Because seeing, it should never be forgotten, is an optical process that cannot be dissociated from a psychological process.

The objective truth of what is seen by everyone operates only so far as the most primitive identification of objects goes. If a countryside scene is present to several people, each sees the "same" insofar as his retina registers at mathematical limits what is there: trees, hills, a river, a field of flowers, a fence, mountains in the distance, a path or a road near one's feet. Therefore, with *The Lady in the Lake*, we are reminded that within the changing field of vision, no matter what it be, the sum of objects is within the context of a particular psychology, and this psychology mainly concerns a murder that is a mystery insofar as its perpetrator is at first unknown, "invisible"—at least, as the perpetrator. The point is to find him, arrest him, etc. Everything seen by the detective is charged with this one known, but invisible fact; everything is connected with a corpse, its human identity and history, specifically with that "lady in the lake," why and how she got there.

Presumably the detective, as an expert in his profession, is highly trained visually, experienced in identifying significant sights, significant words, and more than that, all-importantly, the way those sights and sounds add up to a "solution," yield the desired pattern to which all the clues have contributed their special parts. In many a detective story, the wanted murderer is bodily present from the beginning; it is simply that his identity as the murderer is unknown. However, the crucial importance of a crime's true logic—its authentic and convincing plot—may be demonstrated when someone falsely, for whatever reason, confesses to a murder. Theoretically, tentatively, we have before us the answer to the puzzle, the mystery, but the mere words of confession, "I am the murderer" or "I killed him," may tell us a lot or virtually nothing. For if the confession is false, so may be the motive if calculated to mislead; even if the confessing person had a death-wish toward the victim, it was not sufficient to make him the actual murderer. The actual murderer, thus, had not only his own motive but the hardihood and means, perhaps the extra ingenuity, to commit the crime. A false confession is but another obstacle in a detective's path. So the famous guessing game of a mystery story resolves itself into the presence of one hidden but unbreakably true pattern, which the detective is supposed to seize and lay bare.

Here abides the very great moral force of the detective-story form, whether as novel or film. Its ideal of truth is the right answer in a guessing game, the right—that is, the conclusive—answer to a given puzzle. The ending of the mystery story, the *solution*, awaited by the reader so avidly—the reader who has ready his nervous thrill, the snap of his release from psychological suspense—is really the most false assurance of truth, correctly defined truth, that art could possibly furnish. Pause to consider that Sophocles' *Oedipus Rex* is so great a play, not because it is an unusual detective story and correctly identifies the criminal (thus satisfying what is romantically known to this day as justice) but rather because it is the outward structure and inner sensation of a tragic human guilt.

In all of time, very few detective stories have been told from the viewpoint of the criminal, and for the simplest of good reasons. His identity as known from the outset would transgress the rules of the established guessing game. Reader and spectator must have the precious thrill of continued suspense, the keen lust of the hunter and the all-too-dubious moral/emotional triumph of finally seeing justice done an evildoer. Besides, is it not true that this last "triumph" has less, perhaps much less, importance than one's identification with the detective's triumph, which is virtually inevitable? At least, in the detective's triumph, one takes a more conscious pleasure, while seeing a bad guy "get his," and possibly masochistically identifying with him, is one's more or less *subconscious* pleasure. Again I say, *Oedipus Rex* is so great a work because it demonstrates that, on a profound level, the realization of guilt is a far truer token of justice than its punishment. *Hamlet*, in a different way, is great for the same reason.

Here, however, our principal concern remains a specialization: the way the film, as a set of given works, criticizes its own psychology by particular examples. The whole film strip and its revolving images are simply an embodiment of the way the mind works in the widest sense of psychology—or perhaps I should say the most naked, the most literal sense of psychology. If it be also the widest, that is because a good part of the myth of filmic omniscience is true: nothing in prose or painting can match, for immediacy of presence, the optical image derived from actual or mechanical eyesight. The word and even the hieroglyph are already a conventional, accepted *translation* of eyesight. Put together, words make the art of prose while also creating an image of the world; put together kinetically, photographic images make the art of film while also creating an image of the world. But the former is an art and an idiom *by one remove*; the latter is the closest we can come to the world's naked presence through a medium, till perchance a machine be invented to record the image-by-image processes of the brain. Since film is a medium, it is a psychology, and *not* a psychology of physical reality if by "of" is meant that the medium and the objective facts are interchangeable. No! *Everything* comes to us through the mind: the brain's ceaseless nervous responses. Thus any medium showing these responses is basically an interpretation. To avoid being a formless conglomerate, a wild anthology of consciousness or its mere dictionary, the film must be a psychology of *art*. It has, I think, the potentiality of being the most exact psychology of art . . . one might even say the most critical . . .

Blow-Up seems to assert exactly this truth, this potential, this correct theory of film. Every cameraman, in short, is a detective. Every cameraman is responsible for the ultimate meanings of the imagery he records. In the photograph, basic human meanings merge with the most particular and tenuous aesthetic aims, those subjective responses of which the photographer tries to make his instrument the accurate medium. The whole myth that the camera "does not lie" is betrayed by its own simplism, which fatally limits its meanings. Surely, a photograph of an assassination, successful or attempted, is more conclusive legal proof than the word of the most honestly reputed witness, who may have some obscure reason to be lying or some odd compulsion to believe something he doesn't, on thorough reflection, quite believe. But a photograph is mechanical, as truthful as the electric apparatus conveying words by telephone; so that, once optical identities be established, an assassin or would-be assassin can be convicted on the evidence of a single still photograph.

We should stop to ask if this sort of legal evidence is really foolproof. It is not. Consider, for example, the film footage accidentally taken of John F. Kennedy's assassination. Even if, in a hypothetic photograph, an identifiable man be seen firing at his victim, he may have missed, and another's bullet may really have done the work. Therefore, proof would have to rest upon something quite real and quite unphotographic—that is, an analysis of the bullet in the victim's body as compared with the barrel of the suspected murder weapon. If the bullet extracted from the victim did not come from the murder weapon supposedly in hand, the search for the true killer must begin again and the photograph is shown to have deceived by appearances. The purpose of reason, like the purpose of art, is to look behind those appearances that are opaque surfaces (for those surfaces may be most misleading), to look beyond the technically visible areas (for there the true clue may hide itself).

The cachet of art, its whole subtlety and clarity as opposed to life's crudity and deceptiveness, is that *its* surfaces, no matter how technically opaque, are purely transparent—at least they become so, rhythmically and progressively, as the act of art (among the time arts) proceeds; so that, at the conclusion, all the surfaces are true: *they cannot tell a lie.* Here lives the whole quarrel between "art" and "truth" as objectively dramatized by modern novels and plays—Gide's novels, let us say, Pirandello's plays; and, among films, Fellini's 8½ and the present film, *Blow-Up.* True, elder modernism tended to be more explicit; these latter-day films of Antonioni and Fellini tend to be freely fantastic, slip into symbolism and perhaps covert autobiography. We should note that in André Gide's *Lafcadio's Adventures* and *The Counterfeiters*, novels composed of variations on aesthetic and moral ambiguity, a novelist within a novel, Baraglioul, is himself a surrogate (logically) for Gide, who still remains "another" in that he is the novelist outside the novelist.

The element of surrogacy is the only nontransparency in works of art where the truth remains technically ambiguous. But why so? Because our premise is that truth is something confined to literal and monolithic terms and is untranslatable. This happens not to be correct. An artist becomes the *auteur* of life. Just as the world itself, in the eyes of mystic philosophy with an ancient tradition, is illusion (technically a lie, an appearance, a thing mortal and otherwise vaguely vulnerable), so is art, and the surrogate for mystic philosophy in art is symbolism. If the symbolism be accurate and persuasive, however, the art is as true as anything can be. It is what the fresco painting of Encolpius and his companions is in the *Fellini Satyricon* and what the crucial photograph taken by the unnamed hero-photographer of *Blow-Up* is. It is basically what I meant when, above, I referred to film as the supreme exemplar of the dialectic—dramatically or comically inflected—between the work of art, the image standing for the truth, and an image (say one "taken from life") which seems, in whole or part, to coexist with the art image and yet contradict it. Truth may *seem* to be plural, and thus confusing, till it be redefined as a single lucid system of relationships created from mental operations.

Thus, even if a photograph be instrumental in identifying and convicting a murderer, and thus "tells the truth," it is still no better (though a small wonder) than that hypothetic film camera of Élie Faure, that can reach back or forward in time and register, let us say, a performance of *Oedipus Rex* in the Theater of Dionysos about 429 B.C. It would show us the sort of triumph to be found in millions of detective stories, on record today, in factual as well as fictional form. Yet the truth which that magic camera would tell, in its own right as a medium, would be only statistical; it would have photographed a play and be itself a work of art (or, for that matter, a work of ethics) only by proxy, like those films that competently document whole ballets.*

The truer truth would be in the art that was mirrored, not in the mirror. Film art "plays with" ready-made art in the way the mind plays with an idea, an intuition, an emotion; the way a film adaptation plays with an original work, whether God's or man's. What matters is the outcome: the way the story turns out. The young hero of *Blow-Up* is the Passionate Photographer in his fledgling form, the devotee dazed by the magic camera, without divining, however, just what the true nature of his great toy is: the depth and power of its magic. Critics who disdain *Blow-Up* as a piece of showy trivia, an elaborate film stunt with no substance, know nothing of film poetry, intuit little or nothing of the true theory of film. Well, maybe I split, here, one of the bountiful hairs of truth! I daresay *Blow-Up* could easily have been more exactly poetic had it not insisted on being so exactly theoretic. The point is it's true: true from front to back, all-around transparent.

The nameless young photographer is a symbol of chic, very mod chic. He does fashion-model work. And he's very sexy. But not so very adult about either sex or his arty craft. Like many a camera professional, he has an

---

* Best example: London's Royal Ballet production of three works with Margot Fonteyn: *The Firebird, Swan Lake, Undine.*

odd attachment to the carriage of his craft, the camera itself, almost as if—or quite as if?—it were a sort of acquired organ: another hand, even another penis. This is nothing that *Blow-Up* "says" in literal terms or conscious symbols; it is what the young man's personality and actions manage, together, to convey—to establish, as it were, as an early-on clue. The point is very prettily, niftily made when, indoors, in that febrile, heady, overfluid manner of certain professionals of the top rank, he takes a rapid series of shots with an experienced model who obviously knows what is expected of her—to be right, she must be a little "wild," a little quirky, a little insolent, a little droll, altogether hip, effulgently overassured, and very, very quick. The photographs, you see, will look like that, and maybe only a single one, among the dozens taken, will be used. All this is a parody, but not so exaggerated a parody as not to be poignantly recognizable.

That the young photographer is rather jaded with the game of sex as well as the game of his craft—the "coolness" of both being a deceptive surface—is shown when he yields to the importunities of two girl aspirants in the modeling profession. The scene ends in a mêlée of wrecked décor and orgiastic sex. That the whole thing is only a passing irritant becomes quite clear in the dénouement: the girls fade, the photographer wanders. He speeds off to visit an antique shop and is lured by the pleasant, empty greenery of a park across the way. As customarily, the fetish-camera is slung from one shoulder. What does he want now? Nothing he knows of. He is on the prowl for a "subject" even when idling, perhaps just when idling. He wants a subject to drop from the sky. And one does.

He is now the yearning amateur of the open, not the effete, trig professional of his studio; he is the amateur experimentalist whom Jean Cocteau advised to take his camera out into the world, without preconception, and begin shooting. There would lie the "art of the cinema." As if anyone could exist and act entirely without preconception, or at least preconditioning! Be sure: both Cocteau and Antonioni knew their ironies as well as their positive precepts. And they were not talking of the assignments given professional "field photographers": the wide open "go out and bring in some pictures" thing. The most accidental of human experiences, to be of value whether artistic or moral, must be geared to a certain preparatory key, must profit from that unconscious vigilance known as intuition, that sleeping intentness known as inspiration.

In the park, it may be the particular manner of a tallish, pretty woman who is with a male escort that first arrests and stirs the photographer to action; it may be the way she seems to be steering him farther and farther into the park's more isolated recesses; or the palpable nervousness of both of them. They seem to desire to be hidden— is it for the love act? This is something that in itself might quicken our young photographer. But why, he asks himself, the love act in what, however deserted, is after all a public park? The couple seem well-to-do, are far from being tramps. As he snaps them several times, he seems to have been detected by the woman, perhaps by both. So they become his "quarry." He's sure that he can, if persistent and ingenious, surprise them at least in an embrace. And he does. And he catches the woman catching him at it. In fact, she leaves her lover and pursues the now retreating photographer to claim his strip of still shots.

He declines, he parleys, he is struck by the young woman's good looks and by her obvious anxiety that he not retain his pictures. He suggests a rendezvous where they can work things out, and reluctantly she accepts, returning to her lover as the photographer leaves the park. The rendezvous is, of course, in his studio and there the deal, rather speedily figured out, is for her to go to bed with him in exchange for the unprinted camera roll. They go to bed and he hands her the camera roll as if it were not the dummy it is. He has retained the pictures he took, and when she has hurriedly left, he starts developing the negatives. Now comes the crucial question and the whole film's ultimate significance: Why is he so obsessed with these pictures? What does he hope to learn from them? Has some suspicion of the truth he is to learn already entered his head? And if so, just when did the suspicion have birth, at what point in the episode?

Cannily, Antonioni does not, to the end of the film, reveal the technical answers to these technical questions. They do not really matter. It is enough that his camera (the one taking Antonioni's film) shows the physical externals: the photographer's professional reflex in the park, the sex motif, his demonic will to find out "something," to penetrate to a secret between two lovers. Perhaps it is more than the desire to snatch a few moments of necking in an isolated spot; perhaps some sort of exhibitionism is involved, perhaps something more significant than that . . . The point is that the only way he can find out, now, is to reveal something the camera's eye could have registered which *his* eyes failed to register. Besides, the camera's eye can see a little farther than he can—but not far enough. Moreover, a photograph, though technically (as a "still") only a glimpse, can be studied at leisure, can survive indefinitely the instant it originally occupied. He catches, in the blow-ups he proceeds to print, not just a deep embrace between the lovers but the woman's anxious face turned in his direction with a certain alarm on its features . . .

Is it this which he himself caught, which excited him, made him suspicious, aware of something extraordinary going on? Evidently, from his absorbed and hurried action in making more and more, bigger and bigger blow-ups, he hopes to find that "something." He does. It is the dimly spotted, but clear enough, figure of a man in the tall foliage to one side, a man who seems to be aiming a revolver . . . At this point, the whole detective-story mirage unfolds itself in a glimpse and a gasp. We detect the pattern simultaneously with the aroused photographer. The woman has not really been in love, or smitten, with the man she allows to kiss and embrace her: she has (such is the melodramatic suggestion) deliberately lured him there to be killed. She seems the villain if only because she became so alarmed at the idea that the action was being photographed. She might have had another reason to be alarmed. As it is . . . One good look at the fatal blow-up and the photographer is on his way back to the park.

It is nighttime now. There, at the spot where he remembers to have seen the couple embracing, is the man's corpse: he has indeed been shot; his innocently inquiring camera has exposed a murder. It is now, when away from his studio, that he realizes he has made a grave strategic error: he has left the revelatory blow-up pinned with others on his studio wall. Since evidently the woman is the accomplice of a crime, she and/or her confederate, having been balked by the trickery of only seeming to yield her the negatives, will be coming back to steal them as soon as he absents himself. Such is the criminal logic—and so it turns out. When he returns, his walls are bare and all the negatives of the film roll are also gone. As of now, all evidence of the crime is erased. There are no clues . . . except, he suddenly bethinks himself, the corpse! But his and our worst suspicions are realized.

Returning again to the scene of the crime, he finds the corpse gone.

It is all too good, and too bad, to be true. The detective-eye camera, with encouragement, has performed wonderfully well: it is he, the human being behind the lens, who has been both clever and clumsy—fatally, absurdly clumsy. Somehow, with obscure intuition, he has uncovered a crime and then, through ineptitude, through childish excitement and nonthinking, he has let the evidence evaporate after verifying its existence. Has he, unconsciously, fallen so hard for the guilty woman that he has concealed from himself his own involuntary complicity? Certainly the film does not enlighten us on this point of the photographer's motivation. Yet one answer, a pivotal one, seems to become apparent regarding the facts we do know, and it seems to become apparent to him and to us too; that is, if we have become as involved as the disturbed photographer has.

The whole thing has sprung up too suddenly, gone by too fast, to give the discoverer the time to grasp its implications all at once. As mere spectators, we the audience are necessarily passive; we can only await developments on the luminous screen set off from the dark of the film house. But he, the technical seeker, the detective's surrogate, the inquiring photographer, even the questing libido, *he* has been caught, despite his quickening, his bright flow of intuition, *unawares*. True, he has not been looking for a murder. No. But neither has he been looking for a "plot," a work of art. Consciously he has been in search only of some interesting shots, some picturesque subject, some casual attitude of decorative value or a bit (that classic search!) of "human interest." Then, all at once, like successive thunderclaps, he has been introduced to the passions of crime and other, only hinted, doubtless deeper passions. The poor, clever, dumb, young being, the man with the camera as inquisitive as a child, has stumbled upon all art and all existence, as if he had stubbed his toe on a rock in the pathway.

The young photographer has shown the eye of a budding film-maker—or a budding novelist, a budding detective—in short, a budding artist. But at the moment of experiencing that peculiar impulse to go behind simple appearances, behind the strange public face of existence to its inner, familiar privacy; from its disjointedly visible and suggestive fragments, really parts of a hidden whole, to an organic and visible plot of the mind, body and emotions; at *this very moment*, the young man has suddenly, violently discovered himself a helpless neophyte, a mere beginner for all his casual cockiness, his air of taking women by the forelock of their photogenic looks. Nor is this sheer speculation. The doleful, puzzled, frustrated young man goes to a painter friend to tell him the story, perhaps get some practical advice or friendly consolation. The painter takes a bland, superior attitude and, pointing to a detail in one of his own paintings, says, "That's the clue."

The photographer is not consoled, appears hardly to understand. Yet all the painter can possibly mean is that any detail or special area of a work is a part that fits; a part that, just like a piece of a jigsaw puzzle, is necessary to fill out and complete the whole. *All* details in a work of art are significant, for they are selected to harmonize, to accent and develop, to interweave and contribute to a superior and pregnant unity which is *the work*. First, the whole, the unity, must somehow be known in advance; there must be a *theoretic* conception to be filled out in concrete terms. The trouble here is that the elusive whole belongs entirely to the objective world, the way a crime to be solved by the police does. The photographer has not meant, consciously, to create anything in the way of work but a "photograph." Anyway, *he* has no moral obligation whatever—at least not now when that photograph has disappeared.

Yet this hero's theoretic situation should detain us. Psychiatrist, police detective and artist alike seek that hidden wholeness, that organic personality of the work into which each part must fit, but which at first remains mostly invisible to the one creating it or discovering it. An art expert can tell from a couple of square inches of an El Greco, a van Gogh or a Tchelitchew, who the artist is, not necessarily because he recognizes just the picture from which the fragmented square is taken, but because he recognizes the painter's style of strokes, the very anatomy of his brushwork, the curve of his drawing. In fact, perhaps some such blazing intuition struck the young man with insight into the manners of the couple glimpsed in the park—there was something "special," a bit unnatural or overtense, about the woman's conduct. Knowing women so well, he could tell that much, perhaps, at first glance.

But the external driving force, for the time being, was enough; all he wished was to grab those few instants in his camera, so he could carry home some fresh work, something to print up and judge, discard or save; maybe use. First, he is only a still photographer, and thus unprepared for a drama in cinematic terms. His various shots, we can reflect, are actually "frozen" bits of a continuous action: the passage of the couple deeper into the park, deeper into the relationship that will make them abruptly intertwine in seeming love. The crucial blow-up is really an intensive close-up which the photographer has progressed toward by accident and then pursued with piqued interest. It is not at all, on the surface, an important detail of the embracing couple, but a vague background factor, part of an ordinary photograph's filler.

Thinking in terms of the title of Henri Cartier-Bresson's book of photographs, *The Decisive Moment*, Antonioni's young photographer has aimed at one "decisive" moment and hit (he finally learns) quite another. This hidden, but very much present, moment implies not a still shot but a moving shot, a series of images; it points to the plot of a mystery story and thus implies, in terms of his craft, cinema. *Blow-Up* is a dramatic object-lesson for the *auteur* film-maker in terms of a weighted search; the search, not for one beautiful effect, one rare gesture or "bit" of human interest—these, like murder mysteries themselves, come by the thousands, these represent even the best commercial photographer's daily assignments—no, the search demanded here is one for a really weighted human action, a drama in visibility, a work of film art.

Do I exaggerate? I shall not egotistically add, "Well, then, I exaggerate." For I don't, in the least. Perhaps *Antonioni* does. But I don't think he does; nor should anyone else think so, I imagine, provided the conclusion of *Blow-Up* be put in correct focus. Our photographer is at a decidedly loose end. He can hardly start searching the city for the young woman: she would logically have decamped pronto or gone into strict hiding. Yet we know that something important has happened to him, something more than just having a mystery story snatched like a book from under his eyes. Antonioni has made sure that the curious magnitude of what has happened, and its inner nature, won't be lost on us, even if it be lost on the photographer. At this point, the photographer begins representing the proto-artist who has somehow missed the boat: the gifted craftsman who has lacked the efficient impulse to be an artist—one might even add, relevantly, a film artist. In his urban peregrinations, the photographer has encountered a group of people on a bender or trip of some kind, a group which now, when another day has dawned, he meets again.

Evidently, they have been carousing and pursuing their own idea of a Happening by staying up all night in their clownish costumes and riding from house to house, spot to spot. The photographer has wandered back to the park, near a tennis court, when again the roisterers appear. They pile out of the parked auto and two of them, a man and a woman, take the tennis court and start a game in pure pantomime, with neither balls nor racquets. Seemingly they know well the real game they are mimicking. The photographer is much too deep in a brown study to more than glance at them as if they were absurd exhibitionists. The tennis pair are indulging in their pantomimic charade as if practicing the art of Marcel Marceau. Perhaps we, the audience, still don't get the point of *Blow-Up*; perhaps the young man with the camera slung on him doesn't either. But Antonioni is going to proffer it to all of us with a positive—if symbolic—gesture.

It would seem that the playing pair on the court, made up as conventional clowns, have noticed the lone photographer and perhaps been piqued by his lack of interest in them; or else, seeing a prospective spectator, have had the aesthetic impulse to expand the realistic scope of their pretended game by involving him. Anyway, they pretend a ball has been batted out of the court onto the greensward where the photographer is about to lose all interest in them. The mimes remain mute, and in another moment, the young man's turning away might have made their ploy too late. But he catches sight of their articulate gestures that he return the ball, which they indicate has rolled near his feet. After a moment's hesitation, he lazily obliges, they thank him with gestures, and for a few seconds more we see his gaze resting on them. Then he himself, standing there, disappears and all we have is the empty greensward.

The little dénouement is a symbolic figure for just what has happened to the photographer. I suggest it is, in effect, a moral parable. The whole film has been remarkably laconic and these last moments are as deliberately silent as those in which the photographer followed the couple in the park and snapped their pictures; as deliberately silent as his discovery of the crime in the blow-up, and his discovery of the corpse in the park. All important thought processes are rendered in terms of silent cinema in *Blow-Up*—all but that didactic sentence of the painter's: "That's the clue." The invisible ball of the tennis game is equivalent to the bullet which shot the man in the park. First we see the corpse; then we don't. First we see, at the fadeout, the living photographer; then we don't. It is a play on one of the cinema's oldest tricks: optical prestidigitation. But here the comic reference, like the clowns' costumes, is deliberately weighted, and partly with Antonioni's sovereign irony. The photographer too has "played the clown" and done so without the art of these knowing clowns. *He* knows nothing of the function of the invisible; *they* know all.

Part of every important design of the real world is always covered at any one moment, from any one angle, for reasons well known, reasons I have already mentioned. But they *exist*—may exist, should exist—in the *consciousness of the mind*. They exist in the *imagination*, whether corresponding to objective fact or subjective fancy, or both. They are equally important as fact or imagination. It is the artist who first makes them opaque, and then perfectly transparent, in a complete act of the imagination. Whatever is technically visible or invisible in a story—again the analogy is with a jigsaw puzzle—the story is visible *as a whole* to the artist; to anyone, in fact, who *thinks the world* . . . Yet, as for *Blow-Up*, the sad fact is that its story is about a hero who is a non-artist, a man who has to have the lesson of art flung in his face to gain even a glimmer of its majesty, its meaning. Fortunately, the real hero is his creator, Antonioni, who invented the parable in which he is the comic-pathetic lead. The film, by the way, only uses the original short story as a simple springboard; its events and meanings are *totally* different from the short story's.

Blow-Up is a work of film's self-criticism. Antonioni is the critical work's high intelligence, his hero its low. Let us consider the general grounds on which film can have a criticism of its own—one not belonging to film reviewers, who only dabble in values and ideas. One of the main functions of creative work is self-criticism, criticism of the work and of the author; that is, creative work is other-criticism primarily through the sense in which the author, as a private individual, inevitably joins, inexorably becomes involved with, the whole human stream and its widely distributed problems. No author, however devastatingly or adamantly "critical," stands outside his material (for example, the social body itself) as omnipotent judge. Whatever he creates, whatever he criticizes, he also, in the same acts, creates and criticizes himself by the visible evidence of his canons, his standards of beauty, his knowledge of the world, the extent of his grasp of ethical behavior.

Blow-Up is so theoretic (just right for my purpose) because its hero represents a failure to understand the object lesson of the film in which he appears. This was to make *Blow-Up* more than ever a didactic film. But if, most probably, the lesson is lost on our young photographer, it is not necessarily lost on us, or on his fellows, who may be more ambitious, more intelligent and sensitive than he. Only illusively, at the film's end, does the young photographer stand alone; only illusively does he disappear into thin air. He is still here, an opaque, enduring and alive body. And he is many. He is many a bogged-down critic, alas! many a bogged-down filmmaker.

4

THE BREAKTHROUGH
From Film to Filmed Mind

One of the universal problems of creative work—one might say the chief one—is "getting the first line." Usually a writer, a film-maker, even a painter, has thought long about a certain floating idea that has arisen from his general devotion to his art, from going around perpetually thinking in its terms; this, in fact, is why I say that the truly distinctive thing about film, psychologically speaking, is that it always begins by being a film reel exposed to the daylight or the "special lighting" of the mind. So, when it comes to exposing a physical film reel to the actual lights of the studio or the daylight of the world, the worker is simply attempting to reproduce in final, objective and elaborated form a process whose fetal stage has already reached a point of womb maturity in his mind. Thus the opening shot of a film, the opening sentence of a novel (or for that matter an essay or a chapter in this very book), is a sort of birth pang suddenly brought to a head, a breakthrough *from* what is still subjective and invisible to the naked eye *to* what is objective and visible to the naked eye.

Naturally, a whole speculative or theoretical process has preceded this moment of emergence, so that at the time it takes place, there exists behind it, both physically, in figurative space, as well as temporally, by the clock, a greater or lesser trash pile of discarded material: things seen, thoughts formulated, narratives traversed, metaphors constructed, general ideas floated in the brain's air. All of these, technically, have vanished; or, more properly speaking, have been absorbed in essence and their "matter" has been excreted. What is left in the mind has built up new forms, fresh configurations that are held in suspense, struggling to issue forth, but held in bondage, and perhaps themselves destroyable . . . but leaving, eventually, a more viable vestige, something that holds the secret élan of the breakthrough, which may be at the instant of emergence, release, realization.

And the breakthrough usually *does* come; the work *is* created. So far as the technical baggage of the film goes —all the craft books about films, how they are made or how to make them—what seems most important to the present issue is that all such lines of thought are concerned with post-mortem material, insofar as they compose the generic anatomy of a particular film or of the generic thing known as film-making. One cannot think a set of rules, a repertory of camera manipulations, is anything but a shell, and a shell without pre-determined shape or extent. Some books about film-making are virtually "grammars" (as we know from the title of one), others, leaning to the larger, more speculative side, are virtually "rhetorics" and deal with the higher aesthetics. Appended to some books—take Robert Gessner's *The Moving Image*—is a glossary of terms informing us, in short dictionary style, what the repertory of moving-picture devices consists of and what the names of various physical elements of the film camera are: its auxiliary machines such as the boom, the dolly and the zoom's extended lens: all "visual effects" that may have discarded their old mechanisms for new ones. Such books, which often are very learned, are much like anatomy lectures over human corpses that explain how a living man, in general, "works," how this or that of his organs functions, how the constellation of the body's vital energies—the blood stream, the muscle and nerve systems, the brain itself—operate in concert to make possible all the physical and mental movement of which a living man is capable. However, with unbeating heart and the total blank of unconsciousness, only man's diagram is left.

Such books, if well written and well informed, can be endlessly fascinating to film-makers themselves, especially the learners, and to film-buff critics, who can treat whole films as if they were great machines constructed by a canny compilation of devices. Any film can be made to seem, as a result, a veritable garden of technical flowers. But all that, however beguiling and legitimate, is not in the least *what I have in mind here*. I would like to ignore "the film" as a sort of computerized fantasy of camera effects and concentrate instead on its organic nature, viewing all such material means and classified effects as irrelevant, insofar as they are but mechanical details whether they pertain to "creating a film" or to a "created film." Like the craft analysts of film, a medical man can explain how a child is born by describing the inseminative origin of the fetus and its start (the script), the way it is nourished and grows (the production), and the structural mechanism by which it is projected into the world (the camera and the projector). But all this, I wish to point out, is automatic in that, as an analogy with birth, it is a process that nature takes care of without consulting man or relying on anything but man's passive consent that these instinctual things (with his help and precautions) eventuate. Technique is sufficient to the motives thereof, but technique is never a substitute for motivation.

A baby is made, not invented; it is a will in the nature of things. And the baby grows, moreover, into a man or a woman just as automatically, achieves maturity by the same will of nature, in which man, more or less voluntarily, participates. An art, on the other hand, is wholly the invention of man, who utilizes the peculiar faculties of his brain to create it. The material implements he uses in the case of film-making—the camera and its paraphernalia, lights, actors, props, natural and artificial backgrounds—are but incarnations of thoughts he has had, thoughts he has willfully developed. If at times his thoughts behave "automatically," it is only because he has set them in a certain bed of unconscious germination. Their final mold, their emergence into consciousness and an external form is entirely the result of his willed movement: a movement, it is to be hoped, matured by long training and experience.

Hence the object produced as the final result—the film—is essentially but a reflection of a huge concatenation of an individual man's willed thoughts. *What* these thoughts are, and above all why and how they are thus concatenated, is the world theory of film which I am trying to define. This theory, therefore, quite transcends the function of the film camera as a passive recording agent of what takes place independently of it, what *would take place* without its assistance or any intervention between us and the world. A few sentences ago, I made a distinction between a film work's emergence, the physical and projectable thing a finished film is, and the "emergence into consciousness."

It seems to me that, while in effect temporally simultaneous, these two emergences are not really identical, equivalent. For the moment of pure creation is that mechanism of psychic consciousness when thought is directly translated into action; this takes place, yes, the film artist shoots a scene, the painter does an hour's work on a canvas. The finished product is still to come; it is a mere stage in the evolution, a part of the whole, reworkable in itself and readjustable to the whole. All right: creation is a sum of accretions when the direct translation of thought into external form by an act of will happens to win an instantaneous, basically automatic breakthrough. This is a peculiar moment of time when the result, the external thing, the palpable (here visible) form, is all the creative worker has to show for the complicated process that has preceded this particular result. Now he is, at last, totally committed to all his "intentions," the meanings he has nourished and selected and arranged in his head, perhaps, experimentally, given certain tentative forms. Can it be denied that *what* he has committed himself to is only the outward or objective mirror of an inward or subjective process?

It is too easy, really, to concede this and not go further with speculation and analysis. There is a sense in which all works of art—a symphony, a painting, a film, a ballet, a poem—are truly, when finished (and performed), "objects." But nothing is ever, totally and finally, an object per se—an "absolute" object. In order to exist—even in order to pre-exist—an object needs a spectator: from among spectators, creators must come. Metaphysicians try to pretend that ideas exist outside them or in some impalpable world of which one can have only intuitions and glimpses. For example, the philosopher Carl Jung believes in eternal objects, the Archetypes, as having existence prior and external to man, and independent of him. Jung does not claim that these are composed of matter, but they are, necessarily, forms; hence they are "metaphysical objects." We can imagine a parallel, quasi-metaphysical situation in which the created world of man, our planetary civilization, the very face of the earth, post-1971, is bereft of human beings (all animals, indeed, except cockroaches) by the fatal use of the atomic bomb. A movie, *On the Beach,* based on a novel of the same title, was made about the prelude to this event: the world of human consciousness is awaiting its extinction, but the "things" it has created are expected to remain for an indefinite period. One point brought out by the film was quite accurate although, on the whole, it was a sad and sadly sentimental movie. Film photography of a world untenanted by man (the streets of a modern city and a great army base) brought to men themselves, the spectators of this fantasy, an awareness of their own self-created world nominally, technically and finally divorced from their participation. Man had made this world no longer "his," insofar as he was foreseeing the time when mankind would have no hope of survival, become virtually extinct. The fact that *On the Beach* is revived on television makes one think of those thousands of television audiences, aloft and safe, in that science-fiction fantasy . . .

These particular optical portions of *On the Beach,* man-untenanted, were an objectified act of imagination by men who, in order to witness such a vision, had still to be alive, a circumstance that contradicted the very premise of a man-untenanted world. As a matter of fact, the explanation was not intended to be supernatural, as if some robot camera had continued to unwind film and photograph the world without man's help; no, the reason that we, here and now, could view here a seemingly man-untenanted world is that a few men who have been left alive in a submarine—suitably appareled in gear that, like that of astronauts, can resist an earthly condition deadly for man—are supposed to be investigating what they think is some sign of life left on the planet after zero hour. Basically, these men are showing the same instinct that inspired mankind, in the aforesaid science-fiction story, to view our planet's destruction via television.

Yet not the science-fiction aspect—as a factual possibility—is important here, but the psychological aspect: the importance to the imagination and *to film* as the imagination's vehicle. In *On the Beach,* a campy sort of irony was attached to the loyal human search for some sign of life following the atomic devastation. Inevitably, the first idea suggested to those searchers was that if, at that moment of hopelessness, there were conditions somewhere that promised the survival of human life, those conditions might provide a cornerstone for the continuance of the race. Man's scientific faculty would, of course, discover what the conditions were and somehow promote them. But our story here is "tragic"— the searchers are balked when they find that the wireless signals they could not make out were the freakish result of an accident when life had experienced its final interruption at the army base to which the "signals" have attracted them. A Coca-Cola bottle has fallen over only to become anchored to the string of a window shade, so that the motion of the breeze coming through the window is knocking the bottle against the signaling instrument and causing the indecipherable "message."

We need not assess the pathos or the artistic ingenuity of this story device, or indeed the ethics of the case, beyond presuming that man would be loath to depart the planet he has historically occupied, taken charge of, and developed so phenomenally. Actually, however, the film's climax is structural to its narrative: it spells the deadend of all hope. Yet let us look at it again *outside* its given context. Is the constellation of (1) the Coca-Cola bottle, (2) the communication instrument, and (3) the avid interest aroused by its message sent to a far point, not one of extreme suggestiveness? Like other communication instruments, the wireless is a sign of man's pride in scientific achievement, in what is commonly referred to as "unifying" the planet. Television at once comes to mind as the greatest human achievement of this type, insofar as a complete image of reality be concerned, for it compasses as well the human voice and all sound; its purpose is to encyclopedize the world, the act of *living everywhere at once*.

An especially arresting detail of the given context is the Coca-Cola bottle's presence and its freakishly mechanical, totally accidental function. Despite the solemnity of the occasion and the good faith of the makers of *On the Beach*, it might occur to a spectator of the movie that the image of the Coca-Cola bottle constitutes what is known as a "plug"—it has an unavoidable commercial resonance and might be mythologically interpreted, with excruciating irony, as (assuming the searchers had been a newscast team) the "last TV commercial," the honor falling to Coca-Cola as a product of worldwide fame. I hold the common belief that there is no great frontier which this particular beverage has failed to pass. Still, what I indicate is not a piece of irony, campy or otherwise. I point to an image of the typical time/space of film in the culture of television, and to the apparition of the Coca-Cola bottle as dramatically capturing this image.

Let us simplify matters by referring to limited notations of space with special functions as, in this instance, boxes: generic or abstract boxes. The television studio, where programs are broadcast, is a sort of box, and so is the receiving set to be found in private homes and public places, which themselves are buildings, or partitioned boxes. A box, whatever shape, is simply a convenient container. On the other hand, it is precisely the intention of communication systems to transcend all the barriers provided by boxed-in spatial limitations and to do it (such is the madness of nearly everyone's desire for news of the world) in the shortest possible time. Even were there no physical barriers in space, space itself, as distance, naturally provides an empty barrier to communication by way of the eyes and all other human organs designed to receive signals. Of course, we read of prodigies of sense perception, but these, when too prodigal, are rationally attributed to ESP (extrasensory perception). This has nothing to do with the fact that the very shape of our planet, related to the rigid straightness of the plane of television transmission, provides an obstacle that must be overriden by supplying relay stations.

Live broadcasting, as it is called, has a distinct TV spectator value, such value that it is a regular practice of TV newscasting to print across the image of the film we are seeing "Live from such-and-such-a-place" or to have a voice report at broadcast's end that portions of the program have been pre-recorded. This means that a team of reporter and cameraman (two at a minimum) went out in the field, photographed an event and brought it back to be mixed and edited in the studio; hence we see it projected on a screen whose sight and sound seem simultaneously available to us. Otherwise a television camera would be on the spot relaying events to us by way of a central broadcasting station. The crucial element is dual: there is a decreased interval between us and the event even in "instantaneousness," and unless, as rarely happens, the broadcast be suddenly cut off the air, there has been no evident "editorial" medium. So whatever we see or hear, theoretically, is life in the raw.

The television film's *durée*, therefore, has a special character. What philosophy calls duration (Bergson's *durée*) has a definite time/space status, and in the case of television this special duration is the key to a special mass psychology, meaning, in the present focus of interest, one aspect or domain of the psychology of film, one sort of filmic time/space *durée* as opposed to another sort. The situation of this *durée* as instanced by *On the Beach* is fictional, melodramatic and extreme. But one importantly suggestive thing that this film does is to place dramatic emphasis on the element of communication in a supreme human crisis. Yet it is perfectly logical and is deeply embedded in human history as the chief primordial drama: signals connecting one human being with another used to be loud cries from the human throat, gesture when the signaler was visible, the beating of drums, and ascending smoke. At one time, the welfare and occasionally the very life of men depended on such signals, which united the tribe through a physically barriered space, including distance, and aided it against all conditions posing peril: human and animal enemies as well as natural accidents.

Such signals formed a language system. Being meshed with the whole life of the tribe, their importance eventually assumed a symbolic status that developed magical rites: dance and music forms of imitation that projected success in the hunt and the needed fall of rain, human and natural fertility, and the all-benignant rising of the sun. The *magic* signal thus not only governed tribal survival and welfare but through the power of example also organized the tribe's activities, became gestures toward improvement, remaining not mere measures of defense, ordinary interhuman battle strategies, but presuming to control and instruct the mysterious forces of nature, the weather itself: influencing human and animal spirits no less than human and animal embodiments.

The exultation of victory dances and mating dances, the orgy of the act of sacrifice, both real and symbolic, produced a communal state of psychic expectation that today we call wish-fulfillment. This, in mental terms, is visionary and hallucinative and has a material effect on the emotions and the nervous system. The primitive ecstasy of "seeing things" is well known and historically recorded but it has a dual nature of good and evil. The skill of prophetic vision, peculiar to shamans (magicians or medicine men), would extend by psychic suggestion to the whole tribe; the shamans were simply its myth- ological movers and nerve centers in an unofficial capac- ity. Supposedly, the priests of established religion, along with the kings, had such affairs in hand and governed them; indeed, priests were at times the political op- ponents of the shamans.

What was destined to triumph in the psychological sense, regardless of internal events and struggles, was the seeming *given unity* of the tribe, to which, with rigid logic, perfected systems of internal communication were essential. Today, it is technically the complaint of whole nations and of individual political thinkers that the woes of the world are due to internally determined lack of "un- derstanding" between one great human group and an- other, whether racial, religious or political. Owing to the complexity of modern civilization, such obfuscating interests and motives are subtly confused and go far be- yond that old primordial oneness of the tribe that used to govern interhuman relations. Therefore certain given and tacit contrarieties of interest, rather than the ab- sence of an analytical and true understanding of these contrarieties, are the modern causes of conflict between nations. Analysts of world economy, indeed, trace these sometimes deceptive disagreements to an irreducible and prime economic base. That assumption does little to bring about the harmony of international solutions; it does explain the formidable superstructures of international hypocrisy.

Not surprising, then, that we find a poet-thinker such as Ezra Pound recommending a return to the last historically operative survival of that ancient, seemingly foolproof, oneness: the feudal family in the modernized form of the fascist state. Pound, the poet, sought to particularize while he poetized and mythified. But his basic human sentiment is the same as that of the historic personage who proclaimed the supreme political value to be "my country, right or wrong." Who is to say that, despite all religious and humane considerations (whose reality, being deeply historical, can hardly be denied), modern nations do not behave according to that simplistic rule of thumb, so reassuring, tribally subjective, and perhaps not so *very* anachronistic: "my country, right or wrong"?

Let none accuse me of being at all politically motivated. Modern politics is simply an end product of what I am describing, and if some of these observations sound politically "cynical," that is only because, to me, many social values with high currency and journalistic credit seem greatly inflated. I am getting at a relatively hidden yet historically ratified idea necessary to the present purpose. There is a latterday world movement I would roughly term existential. In effect, it means wiping out the legends of history, their many lessons and sometimes terrible logic, as merely cumbersome to living inheritors: too much a haunting, heavyish load of conscience for slaphappy, hurrying, paranoid humanity . . .

And *there* is the key word, the key human fact: paranoia. Spatial paranoia, which in truth makes the boundaries of state, of acknowledged nations, so preternaturally sacred, is really older than the hills in that it reverberates with the old, old struggle for life among planetary denizens, a struggle whose "terrible logic" seems before us in material and visible consequences. Well, is it so present, is it so material? The mania for communication, giving us the various "magic" arms of the media, the whole machinery of news reporting and the myth of its boon for the most obscure citizen, is based upon a phobia: the deep urge of a tribe, a people, a modern state, to unite itself mentally by *technical consciousness* of the world, though not necessarily *real understanding* of the world. The myth of forming a bulwark against the rest of the world is but itself a great signal: the magic sign (providing a motif for the lives of the historic heroes of consolidation: Stalin, Churchill, de Gaulle, Hitler, Napoleon, Ivan the Terrible, Genghis Khan, Alexander the Great) that a people must unite within so as to form an invulnerable front and a fearsome striking force that will daunt one's enemies without (and incidentally those lingering within). Conquest is a part of this transtribal unification because it reduces the spoilage potential from outside by increasing the centripetal pressure of an augmented government and augmented quantification.

Base fear was coadjutant with happy expectation in the first prehistoric, and many a later, human mind. What was desire fulfilled, even to overflowing, was morally tempered by fear—by premonitions of death, certainty of the risk of death, and death itself; fear of starvation, an enemy's stone, spear or arrow, flood, landslide, a lightning bolt, even snow and ice. Where to hide, to establish headquarters, to have refuge and safety? The primitives started to invent walls, boxing enclosures, they found caves, hollowed out rooms in cliffs, put up barriers: they also organized the tribal base from which the band of hunters went out to slay animals and human enemies. Space, considered generally and conceptually, was more or less an *elastic box*. *Lebensraum*—to emphasize it by using a language other than English—is perhaps the most primitive mental feeling to deserve the name of concept. Living space was the home, the burial ground and the hunting ground, the grazing and then the planting ground. In daily experience, space was an expandable, contractable box existing partly as abstract but also as a concrete "magic" entity.

This box was extended, made roomier, by the weapons of the hunter, by his strength and bravery. It was aided psychologically by magic, seemed safer and roomier through a moral physique, a new dignity and picturesqueness of the person himself; a sheer power flashing from his eyes and his show of strength through style and dance gesture as well as through performance. The dance circle of the encampment and the instinctive compactness, both of the animal herd and the roving horde, were the benign forms of malign risk, were a dual and utter commitment to the struggle for life. When I went to Madison Square Garden, New York City, to behold something I especially wanted to see—the matador El Cordobés perform a corrida in Spain—I was taking advantage of a modern miracle of spatial communication and also partaking of the extra thrill—as a generation has tried to persuade us all—created by witnessing a distant event of importance simultaneously with its actual occurrence.

In the huge building, the seats occupied by a friend and myself were excellent: directly opposite, on a perfect seeing level, one of the four boxlike giant screens where the images were to appear. In fact, this was part of my thrill because it brought to my elbow as a physical manifestation something I knew by report. Right next to me was the rather large box—only just too small to contain a huddled human adult—whose mechanism was sensitized to airborne forces sent far in the upper air from the source to a circling manmade satellite, and bouncing off it, coming down again to New York so that I could witness El Cordobés' performance (and those of two other matadors) virtually as it was happening.

Surely such a thrill is without novelty. By 1972 it might even be called banal, yet it continues to touch a universal chord in humanity. For instance, suppose the graceful, magic hero, El Cordobés, was humiliatingly gored, or killed. Witnesses, however much shocked and saddened, could cherish a certain satisfaction: "I was there when it happened." In fact, most of the witnesses with me in Madison Square Garden saw what happened better than those Spanish citizens who necessarily sat rather far from the performers in the ring, the bull and the matador. We in New York saw it not "scenically," as on a removed stage, all at once, but in close-ups mixed with distance shots; that is, at vital moments, in clear detail. Undoubtedly, if El Cordobés had been killed by one of his two bulls, we would have known better than the audience around the bullring just how the fatality took place: the precise design of its intimate calamity. Consider the shooting of Lee Harvey Oswald, viewed by millions of Americans in the privacy of their living rooms.

For myself and my friend, it was an artistic event even more than a sporting event, and the time/space thrill of simultaneity (the product of a communication medium) was minimal to us. For me, it was simply a movie: the art was the dance, the drama a surviving ritual, alive with human magic. Film aesthetics in the form of its exponents and practitioners must face the fact that "simultaneity" is a distinct film value only in terms of newscasting via TV film, thus not an aesthetic factor but a popular sentiment. In the case of this Spanish corrida, time acquires so much of an added value because, in terms of measured planetary extent, the intervening distance is so great. True, a historical force, or rather reinforcement, is also present because of the perspective I have been evoking: that of the very primitive psyche of man that to some degree all of us inherit. Even so, there remains a distinction. In total terms, the artistic element not only of the event, but of the art of vision known as film, is minimal to the mass audience, while the sporting element for this audience is very great; part of the sporting element here, one may say, was the audience's own vestigial superstition—a mass hangover—that a thrilling event was taking place via a medium that "magically" united the world and annihilated the inconvenience of geographically obstructive space.

Manuel Benítez (El Cordobés) is a young, handsome figure of a man with a vital, smilingly magnetic personality that is eminently projectable; in short, he is a real "actor" with the skilled grace of a dancer and almost an excess of verve. Needless to say, he is much appreciated by a nation of hero-worshipping aficionados. As a matador, Benítez is daring and inventive in an inspired manner, though his style, from the classic viewpoint, is unorthodox and corrupted by antic features. To be sure, he seems to prolong the preliminary stages of the fight with serene indifference, with deliberate risks that evoke gasps, applause and disapproval; he kneels during his passes perhaps once or twice too often—not standing to kneel again but swiftly shifting his knees as in a dance figure—when logically his victim, the charging bull, is already much tired, drained of energy and properly befuddled, so that Benítez is suspected of showing off. Nevertheless, one of the most theatrical feats in bullfighting is to "play with" a seemingly dazed, already defeated bull, who may have just enough energy left for that unexpected last, close charge when a horn will manage to connect with his enemy's body. By courtesy of the camera (which could also have been watched at the locale of the fight) we witness a superb exhibition of dance skill, of grace and dramatic timing. The fact that the medium is so real, in vivid color and larger than life (that is, larger than it would be on the actual scene or a home television set), is incidental to the aesthetics of dance, which seems more than ever pyrotechnic in a situation where the dancer exposes himself to death.

Fortunately, I have witnessed other versions of the bullfight, one of them during a documentary about Benítez, showing some well-edited bullfight sequences—none specific and complete, but the more cinematically effective for that very reason. The point is that, aside from all realism about a specific event or type of event, the exhibition of bullfighting becomes more cinematically effective the more "artificially," that is unrealistically, manipulated it be with special effects: close-ups that mask off the complete figures of bull and matador, repetition of action, superposition and slow motion, so that we get a continuous effect like Action Painting without losing our awareness of the subject's identity. Another film about the bullfight, exclusively motivated by aesthetics, was made by the French film-maker Denys Colomb de Daunant. This is able to show us how film is doubly subjectivizing: both by rendering, through kinetics, the rhythmic features of a dance (the bull's and his sacrificer's) so that the matador's inwardness of physical effort is grasped, and by letting us, through this same means, enter with the matador into this same inner state *optically objectified*. Both performer and witness of this art are thus supremely subjectified, respectively and in unified concert. The formalism of the medium is precisely what brings them together in this unique relation, which otherwise would not exist. Such is our very real illusion . . .

As I say, we cannot as yet have a photograph of the inner processes of a matador during the fight or of our own, the spectator's, inner processes, no matter which part of an anatomy be concentrated on. Besides, there is yet no codified system for understanding what we might see in this unknown way. In a brief documentary film, the interior of the body has been filmed by way of the throat and pretty far down, but the result, however extraordinary as a scientific exploit, is only of "scenic" interest. Imagine being down there! Rather ghoulish, of course. Still, if there were, say, a film reel exposed to El Cordobés' brain *as connected with his eyes,* would not what we see be something as strange and mesmerically rhythmic as what we see by an actual film camera and its resources? Yes, but like that personified camera, the detective in *The Lady in the Lake,* almost nothing would be seen of Benítez himself; anyway, it would be another sort of cinéma vérité, perhaps to become as ordinary as the kind we know. Besides, the subjectivity of film I mean (its theory) is the privilege of a witness able to see the *maximum* quantity of an event.

As with this TV corrida, or any other subject filmed, there *are* lighted surfaces, we *see* lighted surfaces. As agents of consciousness, we recognize the nature of what is happening by a codified, completely apprehensible system of material (here natural) signs. By such a system of gestures and tones of voice, an actor conveys by his person the inner processes of the character he is portraying. In the instance of de Daunant's conventional-ized, poetically concentrated film, we see a purified agonic dance, of which the physical agent of the camera, variously governed, is the transparent medium; indeed, the sole medium. We can gather something similar from watching a mere eyewitness version of the Cordobés bullfight by courtesy of the TV camera—a courtesy, and our privilege, by all means, and yet not the same thing as the artistically designed, dynamically purified dance invented in de Daunant's camera.

Surely, in the documentary or cinéma vérité dimen-sion of film, the world is seen as optically objective, as external to the witness, whatever value or meaning the witness may impute to it. During the late 1940s, an Italian man of letters, Nicola Chiaromonte, attacked the communicative potential of the movies as negative be-cause a camera photographed only the surfaces of life, failing to endow them with meaning.* Of course, his attack was limited to the *ready-made* surfaces of life, and a mere vérité filming of them, with neither plastic editing (which might give a beautiful decorative effect as in de Daunant's *Forbidden Bullfight*) nor special pur-pose, such as one portraying a human situation, as in the art of mime. Again and again, whether in serious boast or serious disdain, we run into a critical hostility toward film that accuses it of being a technological show-piece, an "inquiry" whose only asset is the accumulation of sheer optical evidence—as if, in fact, its highest func-tion were "legal evidence," establishing acts and iden-tities that otherwise would be unknown or disputable, or doing even less: showing us anonymous evidence and unmotivated, perhaps "unreadable," action.

---

* "A Note on the Movies," by Nicola Chiaromonte, *Instead*, 4, 1948.

The present book assumes (as I assumed in the forties when I opposed Chiaromonte's argument) that such could be but half the truth of film and, actually, its lesser half. Yet this camera business of truth-telling, of providing a visual/auditory archive (assisted perhaps by telescopic and microscopic lenses), is of very great importance in the eyes of the public as a function of both entertainment and information, each (however) of a transient character. Few of those who sit before television sets to watch baseball games, favorite comedians or soap-opera serials, few whose favorite entertainment is a Broadway musical or who consider that watching the "Six O'Clock News" is a daily rite they would sorely miss—few of these, certainly, realize the fact, but the time/space technically involved with their lust to be thus "entertained" is really that of the external world, that of time-passing: the time of the clock that vanishes away, and so must constantly, "in toto," be renewed.

Strictly speaking, being a TV addict (one who takes his sports and laugh acts and crime melodramas *at home*) means accepting the medium of art and truth, the TV camera, as a pastime and nothing more: something like the stomach's requiring replenishment. This is the opposite of taking "external" truth as either art or history, both of which are concerned with aspects of permanence in time, aspects of intellectual (or subjective rather than geographic or objective) space. For most watchers, the filmic vision, whether seen in a theater or conveyed at home by television, is simply a substitute for "being on the spot." Why are information articles about directors and the problems they have with certain films, about the behind-the-scenes conditions of this or that film, about the actors, their private personalities and domestic relations, all so popular with the more "literate" movie-goers and TV watchers? That is because, to some degree, these articles technically involve the spectator with what has been "really" going on *behind* the fiction, *behind* the formal presentation; this helps him to subjectivize, however trivially, what otherwise would remain an aesthetic or merely "external" object: the film as a contrived surface, a calculated appearance, whose "reality" finally will—alas, alas!—elude him.

Here is the baleful result of the myth that reality can be attained *only by the penetration of opaque surfaces.* If such surfaces are not voluntarily and systematically removed by the consent of those involved with them, they can be circumvented by eavesdropping, spying, hearsay, or other figurative ways of unlocking closed doors. On the other hand, the true process of subjectivization through art (filmic or other) is automatic identification between the *subjectivity of the watcher* and the *subjectivity of the creator,* of which the created work is the apprehensible token, the lucid competent medium. What the spectator should seek to grasp through film as an art is not external time and external space (a thing which in any case is an illusion) but the internal time/space of the creator. For a work of film should be precisely, in theory, the *photographic reproduction of what has happened in the creator's brain,* not anything that has happened *outside it.* Whatever has happened outside this brain, without its instigation, is automatically transformed by the process of assimilating, or *mediumizing,* it.

In the interests of the present theory, we must grapple with the fact that a created work, in distinction to the given realities with which it deals (its transformed material), is an aggressive, not a passive, quantity; hence, the spectator's mind must, in a figurative sense, set its dial at the corresponding point of the receptive mechanism which is *himself*: the mechanism of his own personal sensibility and intelligence. Neither the TV set in front of him nor the film projector behind him is the receptive mechanism of what he sees on the screen: the receptive mechanism is, actually, the sentient capacity of his own brain. Nevertheless, there is a *mass* brain, a *social* brain, a *public* brain which, every day in every way, militates against this basic truth of the receptivity of optical/aural works by the qualified individual.

It seems to me that the only explanation for the existence of this mass or public brain is what I have already indicated here as primitive *spatial paranoia*. The dangers of our overpopulated, highly competitive and dubiously peaceful world are multiplied far beyond those of prehistoric times when the tribal group was being developed. Now we have the private individual in his looming collective, subjective (though mentally unresourceful) aloneness, who continually must be reassured of the safety of external space as it spreads beyond sight, and proportionately (he supposes) beyond comprehension, for the very reason that *it is technically unseen*. It is this individual whose anxiety neurosis, shared with an indefinite mass of others, is responsible for what may be called modern communication mania: the pushing avidity to conceive actual space as always available to the eyes and ears through word, image and (ideally) sound, properly staked out (that is, geographically distinct) and preferably (by all means!) well policed.

Here is exactly what I mean by the concept of space as a measurable, secure box (the world) corresponding to time as a measurable, closed circle (the clock). The conquest of that box, the world's space, is equivalent mythically to the conquest of fear. If, in human affairs, men are afraid of being late for an appointment, they are far, far more afraid of being less than the space occupied by the human affairs around them. Does this seem absurd? It is, relatively, absurd. If men find it desirable to transport their bodies from one point of planetary space to another by the quickest possible means (the jet airplane), it is even more desirable that their minds be transported in the quickest possible time (via television) through world space—through planetary space and beyond . . . for always, always, by the very definition of box-limited space, there is an unknown and insecure space-beyond, which must be, however illusively or sloppily, brought within and secured.

This psychic state accounts for what I shall call the pseudo-filmic myth of our nation's Space Program. This myth, I believe, is even more important than the ostensible aim of science to investigate the nature of the universe, or than the function of flights to the moon and back as simply a great sporting event. Why so? Because "space flight" is a symbol reassuring the mass brain, in its dominant paranoia, that the dangers of space can be put under control, theoretically, by various surveying apparatuses. Take the myth of the seismograph whose registry of some devastating earthquake, perhaps very distant, is somehow a reassuring fetish. Yet the seismograph is simply an obedient servant of disaster. In no way can it prevent it or (as yet, anyway) lead to its prevention. The most it can do is to indicate, by registering "warning" tremors, that human life over the untrustworthy region make itself scarce there. Yet scientific calculations (for instance, those regarding the restless state of the great "fault" beneath the city of San Francisco) have proved so untrustworthy themselves that citizens, as usual, place higher value on myths than on sheerly speculative facts.

Of course, there are more serviceable fetishes than seismographs. Private-circuit television is commonly installed in office and apartment buildings and even in homes, for protection against illegal intruders and (inevitably) for spying on employees and persons purporting to have incidental business on the premises. There is that constant "space-within" which is rather indefinite and likewise needs "boxing" and "securing." Filmgoers, older and younger ones, are sure to recall the prophetic scene inserted by Chaplin in his film *Modern Times*, when, via private-circuit television, Charlie's boss is able to catch him loitering in the men's room, where he thinks he is unseen and "safe" because he is physically alone. True, the worker, in his breaks from work (official and unofficial), prefers to be unsupervised, but such moments are when men wish not to be seen, not when they wish to see or be seen. The wish not to be seen is contractive, the wish to see, and be seen, expansive; each is fraught as much with fear as with confidence and satisfaction.

An impartial observer is now in a position to note this pivotal thought: the concept of space as a vast quantity, both theoretically and practically supervised with the help of mechanical seeing-eyes, is, politically considered, the precise *optical* concept of the fascist state. In political practice, of course, the fascist state cannot rely on television or any other mechanical eye to regulate and protect itself internally: human agents, functioning in the framework of various police bureaus, must accomplish this with the aid of various mechanical spying devices. A film titled *The Seventh Cross*, about Germany during the Second World War, portrayed just such a paranoiac conception of supervised space by making, in the eyes of a political fugitive, every German citizen a potential informer, the unnumbered individual seeing-eyes of a closed national circuit. This situation is quite consistent with one aspect of my theory: the potential TV watcher, the private citizen (specifically, in *The Seventh Cross*, a political enemy) becomes the *watched* rather than the *watcher*. It is a special, abnormal condition: a condition of internal strife when an anonymous individual is frequently to be victimized. As a peacetime condition, the occupation of space-watching, with its built-in paranoiac impulse, may work, at its own leisure and pleasure, the opposite way—toward confidence, amusement and delusive freedom.

If a watcher, conceivably, does not realize that in this sense the lovely miracle of television may be equivalent to the awful disaster of the police state, he is just being innocently happy. Fiddling with his TV dial, he is in fact enjoying the false moral guarantee of social unity that once was the hallucinative myth of the primal tribe: the tribe's surviving self-hypnosis now manifest in modern individuals. And still there is the lurking, ineradicable paranoia, an irony which the great public mass of film and TV watchers is most disinclined (and thus unequipped) to perceive. For what is the TV watcher, in particular, always witnessing *after* he abandons his ball game and his favorite comedian? He is witnessing the underside of that safety myth which is the logical boon of all-seeing space surveillance. He is seeing, and with thrilled interest as a rule, exactly the practical breakdown of his own illusive myth, the safety myth of the mass brain: he proceeds to absorb visually all sorts of disasters: the ravages of nature; floods, fires, cyclones and earthquakes, which specifically wreck communication systems, attack the public safety, destroy human lives; all the ravages of crime and the desolation of poverty areas; strikes and riots: perpetual threats to everyone's comfort and the proper conduct of life. These may occupy the more serious domain of his daily attention. Can it not then be said that such "thrills" are on a par with the thrill experienced when a member of one's "own" baseball team hits a home run or when one laughs himself sick at the gags of his beloved comedian or eats up the vision of a beautiful actress speaking of her "private life" on a talk show?

From the spectator viewpoint, entertainment may be thought of as the traditional escapist form, where the watcher not only escapes from his own problems, from inner "reality" to outer "fantasy" and "fact," but also, logically, identifies himself with some fugitive human being and wishes to escape that being's possible fate as victim. The humble private citizen's life often lacks (again this is the tradition) what is called "excitement" and "material rewards"; therefore he must find in the entertainment media a romantic surrogate for himself, defeated or triumphant. I speak only of the commonest form of escape mechanism in terms of entertainment media, whether in themselves artistic or inartistic. The fact is that, viewing the matter as a spectator norm, every watcher sustains in some degree, in this or that emotional or intellectual phase, a great micro-macrocosmic tension. The space-within exists—and must exist however consciously it be avoided—equally, co-extensively, with the space-outside. The science-fiction type of film, therefore, was bound to get around to viewing the interior of the body as an artificially constructed inner space corresponding with the real body's inner space, which in turn would be a trope for actual space: the "out there" space shared with all other men.

Here we are reminded that, just as there is an ecological myth of the external environment, there is an ecological myth of the internal environment, for example, the health of each individual's own interior body. If there were not this inevitable communication between inner and outer, in the medical as much as in any other sense, there would be no such thing as an "ecological" problem. The ploy of the science-fiction film *Fantastic*

Voyage deals with a magic form of physical diminution that corresponds to the publicly trivial, virtually unnoticed status of the humble, undistinguished private citizen. The fiction plot is that a group of normal human beings, a heroic medical team, are reduced to organic minutiae while retaining their original forms and then are injected into the veins of a great scientist in order to remove a blood clot that threatens his life. Just as scientists will do anything to prove a point, the movies will do anything to make a hit at the box office. The body interior becomes, of course, a gruesome labyrinth like an unknown mammoth cave, with disaster always lying in ambush for the valiant and resourceful explorers, who, after their laborious victory, have to find a way out and almost, of course, fail to find it. At long last, all of them, including Raquel Welch, the woman of the group, manage to escape through one or perhaps both of the scientist's obliging retinas . . . to be restored to normal life size: the grand reward of all popular fiction heroes. Or did one medico perish? Well . . .

Obviously, this film is a refurbished version of a very, very old story and becomes interesting through ingenious situations and the finesse of its camera tricks; moreover, it arrests us in this context because it is a microcosmic metaphor of claustrophobia, interchangeable with agoraphobia as the twin nervous sensations of what I call spatial paranoia—which itself is so much older than the adventure pattern of this science-fiction piece. It is spatial paranoia that created the original illusion of social unity necessary to the individual's psychic being from time immemorial to now, no matter what the size or complication of the world in which he imagines himself.

The point is that, with the modern multiplicity of things, and above all the varied media which communicate consciousness of these things, the elasticity of the world-box becomes extraordinarily, unpredictably variable, and thereby the more "exciting." It is natural, too, that the individual living in this world should seek some central bureau, as it were, where he can always find a reassuringly comprehensive purview of things. This bureau is the aggregate of the world's television studios while the magic box transmitting the complicated physicality he desires to keep under his eye is, of course, his own television set, with its seductively mobile dial. Each television camera, along with its vocal assistant, the reporter, exists as if at the end of one of the numerous tentacles extended in all directions by the octopi that are the nerve centers of the main TV networks. This is what typically defines the space of our man-inhabited world, both earth and air, and on past the stratosphere to other planets, such as the moon, to which humanity has already extended its conquest—a conquest that is going on, and on, and on even as I write.

part ii

CREATIVE REACTION

5

FILM FORM AS THE PARANOIA OF TIME AND SPACE

The theory of film I am proposing is that something exists besides this specious totalitarianism of all space, pseudo-monolithic, geographically staked out and optically supervised for maximum security plus the overplus of "entertainment." To the myth of the mass brain, unconsciously inherited from paranoid antiquity and nourished by paranoid modernity, I oppose the true psychology of film, by which of course I mean its art, not its technology; I propose a film of its own, its very own time/space. This is decidedly not the time/space of science, which keeps re-exploring the explored and trying to give the box of space a proper shape as well as authenticated contents, an occupancy that must, simply because it is real, external and mutable, be constantly assayed, disciplined and ascertainable. This is all very well as applied to canned goods sold by the millions of units but it has nothing to contribute to the structure of *intellectual* space and its durations. Everywhere the extent of the big-space box or world-container is assumed or given; else, as with the disputed frontiers of a nation, experts calculate how far it can be expanded, how far contracted.

At this point, there must be no quibbling. The space of the film I mean is infinite, its time is absolute, if we take the conditions of infinity and eternity as inner mental concepts, not concepts to be judged by actual time and space measurements. The infinite and the absolute are concepts difficult to grasp, either in the abstract or as evident in practice, perhaps just because they are qualities, not quantities. A quantity can be measured— even, as advanced mathematics has shown, the most difficult and paradoxical quantities—but a quality cannot be measured; a quality must be intuited as real, as present, through some mode of perception, some subjective judge, which can be designated only relatively, such as the rhetorical "I" in the formula: "I see." Surely, there must be an *event*, but also there must be the witness, and the witness can attest to the event without having any purely scientific or foolproof way to ratify that event as he sees it, reports it, knows it. Only the faith in signs, only the associations of like things, such as actual images, figures of speech or a common system of symbolic gestures, physical resemblance of look and behavior, the conventional meanings attached to language itself—only these things can assign the exact "quality" of an event or object in distinction to its "quantity," its scientific description or inventory.

Well, I assert these truths. They remain to be believed. And people believe different things on a vast gamut of judgment-norms, classifications, types, eccentricities. To "believe," we have to cope with blurred signals that actually are hopelessly confused owing to fleeting impressions, inadequate attention, a poor system

of mental reference (including poor memory), inertia
and carelessness of mind, prejudice of emotion, unconscious distraction, both accidental and self-promoted,
bad faith, deliberate deception from outside . . . Science
was invented to supplement and correct all this "human"
flaccidity, vagueness and confusion: science extending
from the memo pad to a theory of the origin and destiny
of the universe. We know how—it has been mentioned
here more than once—science itself rushes, via film, to
the aid of humanity in its paranoid quandary: its passion
to be both reassured and entertained. The genre is
science fiction, and the medium of film is pre-eminently
equipped to display its miracles, which are so wonderful
that it might seem witnesses would be inspired to leave
altogether this poor, entrapped, so-limited human condition and seek, as real possibilities (without waiting
for a cosmic accident to threaten the Earth), the logically
incredible avenues of existence as seen in science-fiction
films.

There are two works—one about time, one about space
—which utilize future existence as an experimental postulate of human reality. True, we are already entered upon
a Space Age in a more concretely promising sense than
we have entered the Time Age proposed as inherently
true (for example, possible) by the picturization of
H. G. Wells's *The Time Machine*. I shan't argue here
just how good is the form in which this story has been
transferred from the printed page to cinema. Potentially
at least, its events are more vivid as true optical imagery,
and the film script is reasonably well imagined. As I have
maintained in the past, we can often draw from filmic
endeavor, even commercial filmic endeavor, casual and
passing effects that are more artistically impressive in
themselves, out of context, than in the context of the
films in which they appear. Surely this phenomenon is

more than ever true of such films as *The Time Machine*, *Stairway to Heaven*, *Fantastic Voyage* (see above), and *2001: A Space Odyssey* (see below).

As it happens, while H. G. Wells possessed an intuitive imagination, he was a third-rate author, with the result that his fantasies are wide open to the worst habits of commercial films, even while the film medium naturally "takes" to them. Only when a spectator's gaze becomes aware of being forced to shift so as to take in a picture's totality, is the essentially static nature of his own viewpoint put in question—the curving Cinerama screen used for the proper exhibition of *2001: A Space Odyssey* makes the spectator's head turn in a literal sense unless he gets far enough away from it to take it all in with a steady frontal gaze. Naturally, psychological attention always qualifies what any individual watcher of a film or TV screen actually sees well enough to note and recall. The modern idea of cineplastics as not *a* film, not a work to be seen objectively, but an artificial environment that encloses the spectator—and which he can see only with a full turn of his body, led by his gaze, as though he were in the real world—is quite another matter, particularly when, as now, the said "environment" is changing from moment to moment. Elaborate discothèques sometimes try to provide this sort of thing as an aid to appreciating rock music while dancing to it; the spectator-dancer is immersed in a total world of changing color patterns and insistent rhythms. The movement, of course, is cyclic, like a repeated film sequence that regularly returns to its own beginning. This is a typical complement to the habit of drug-taking, however mild, because such a condition automatically disposes of the rational mental order which, separating subject and object, makes subjectivization—as when faced by a work of visual art—into an aesthetic ritual.

The Time Machine, as a primarily visual work, utilizes the still spectator-viewpoint as a myth of immortality, for example, that which endures as the world around it (or, technically, in front of it) changes to the extent of decades and even centuries. The decorative sleigh, all gold and red plush and meant to be horse-drawn, is the miniature model from which a young inventor and antiquarian, in the year 1899, constructs a supernatural machine with gearshifts capable of transporting its occupant into time future or time past. The same idea, interestingly enough, appeared in a film by Chris Marker, *The Jetty,* which supposedly takes place in future time when the atom bomb has decimated most of mankind and left the remnant sterile. By then, there is no belief in another life, so the only recourse to "immortality" is mental, a matter of traditional dreaming, as it were, hence the logical procedure is injection of a drug by which the subject, facing his own and his race's extinction, can relive the past or a wholly hypothetic future. The protagonist achieves, in short, the sensation of immortality, even while suffering physical pain and at last meeting, in fantasy, his own death.

In *The Time Machine,* too, an arrested immortality is conferred on its inventor while the real world changes in its old-fashioned, ploddingly chronological way. This leads to situations most wonderful, perilous, pathetic and embarrassing for the inventor, whose immortality, on the other hand, is based not on the well-known human illusion but on the supernatural faculty of his invention. Like Dorian Gray, he himself stays young as whole generations grow old and perish. The story is spoiled by the comic-strip crudity of showing the intellectual masters of the future Earth an underground caste that is degraded physically to being cavemen-monsters. On the other hand, the former fair-haired flower of the race has become a set of zombiesque slaves, periodically sacrificed by their hideous overlords, and living above ground in a primitive natural paradise which their strange masters disdain. In this respect, the film must be dismissed with a faint grin if not a downright grimace. These sequences hardly qualify it as middle camp. Howsoever, the lamentable state of human affairs which I describe has been caused by a now historic world war. The intervention of the inventor-hero, who decides to rescue the lovely zombies from their degradation, is simply stereotyped adventure fable. Not in this dimension do we find the charm or the significance of *The Time Machine*.

Rather, as Marshall McLuhan might say, it is the medium here which is at least the *superior* message; or still better, the message is the medium's self-consciousness of its magic power, its pseudosupernatural-ism—which, after all, is the exact point of the supposedly drug-induced hallucination portrayed by *The Jetty*. The key sequence in *The Jetty* is achieved by a swift kinesis of frozen images that, projected in smooth sequence, synopsize both time and space. The effect is similar to images in a dream or images remembered from a dream. *The Time Machine* is oriented to a more elaborate and explicit concept of time/space; its central device, the machine, bears much the same relation to the (then primitive) automobile as Élie Faure's supernaturally endowed film camera bore the actual film camera of his period, yet the supernatural faculty of both is oriented to time leaps, not space leaps. Read as a parable of television and the movies, the elegant red and gold sleigh-machine is but a theater seat or a lounge chair before a TV set. This is quite clear from the way material things change in time as if the decades made exactly such an edited movie as the drug-injected dreamer of *The Jetty* makes of his recalled past (or intuited future). The episode in *The Time Machine* works as a transition to a point in the future when the First World War is devastating London. The entranced occupant of the machine is moved to halt its operation and step out to question a uniformed man he believes he recognizes as a friend, whom he suddenly notices climbing the steps to a shop across the street. Because now it is some fifteen years later, the man turns out to be his friend's grown-up son. What the interim has shown, not in jerks but in smooth fadeouts and fadeins like meltings, is the swift change of clothes on mannikins in the shop across the street. Such a device would be quite natural, not supernatural, if it had been designed (apart from its context) to exhibit the way clothes fashions altered during a decade and a half.

At one point, when the inventor is away from his machine, his house is abandoned and the machine moved to a spot in the yard. Our hero, returning from his adventure, does not find it in its old place and must trace the marks of its passage on the floor and the ground outside. Since the machine has the magic faculty of transporting itself through time, it is found out of place at first in the *future* environment and finally recovered there; then, by shifting gears, the inventor can return it *in time* to his old home. In terms of physical space, it has been moved only a few yards, but because time duly transforms the aspects of place, even the machine's immediate environment has changed somewhat. The special pathos is that of the dramatic inequity of stable things in an unstable environment and unstable things in a stable environment. Space has been poetically freighted with time in an unusual way. The sleigh that is the Time Machine is, in general, a symbol of constancy; that is, it represents a good, a desirable, stability. It is a willed arrestment of "time in its flight." Yet, magically, it can also precipitate that same flight at the whim of its driver, who is able, if he likes, to observe centuries flash past on his speedometer.

Something that even a brilliant thinker such as McLuhan may overlook, in his heady glances at technological glamour, is that the will of the spectator (one might even call it a perceptual law) is, even like the will to immortality, that he remain stable while the world of time and space is made to turn this way or that at his pleasure . . . I say "at his pleasure" because the gearshift of the Time Machine, as we may notice, is another form of the dial on a TV set. By being able to visit this or that movie, one having a contemporary or historical theme, or to turn the dial to this or that TV program, the spectator acquires a sense of power over time and space, which he can make move here or there, back and forth, seemingly (such is his illusion and his neurosis) at his own will. Just how neurotic this same magic faculty can be, and on what emotional depths it can draw, is nowhere shown better than in Ingmar Bergman's remarkable film *Persona*.

But first let us examine a primary distinction most important to our case here: that between stasis and stability. Both essentially imply a fixity, but particularly so stability, which has priority in the moral sphere, where it is benign in meaning fixity of purpose, something always "upright," not liable to fall apart, and so on. Such moving things as automobile tires or planets are stable because they are fixed in orbit yet they are not static. Stability is always desirable even while, to expand its position in the ethical realm, it is open to criticism for representing the ultraconservative—that is, for taking on the undesirable qualities of stasis, which philosophers in the nineteenth century opposed to the dynamics by which society (in the Hegelian sense) would not stay put but change toward the plane of perfection. Stasis likewise implies a purely mathematical or scientific fixity, such as that which seems immovable either physically or according to the abstract laws of logic. Curiously, with high suggestiveness, the film *Persona* associates the common device of the frozen frame in moving-picture projection with the moral ambiguities of stasis and movement, stability and instability.

Sometimes, paradoxically, purely moral forms seem static (this might mean a dynamic criticism of society as atrophied) while a chemical substance, is subjected to other elements, proves stable or unstable, maintains its identity or changes into something else, losing its original potency. A film or a prose narrative that drags, that does not develop true and interesting new situations, is said to be "static." It lacks the natural pleasure and charm of growth that is associated with movement. For shock value, and as an esoteric sort of conceit, Bergman has placed at the very opening of *Persona*, before the first narrative scene and even the titles, a short and provocative sequence that seems a foray into surrealism. In the quick change of shots, rather static images of pain or sleeping (perhaps dead) persons, a skeleton dance from an archaic movie, a bit of animated cartoon and some serenely anonymous shots of rustic scenery, one gets something of the impression I described above of filmic animation produced by running a succession of still images on a strip through the regular movie projector (*The Jetty*).

Maybe Bergman's selection of shots and their sequence (like arranged clips swept up from the cutting room floor) have a symbolic significance requiring more study to understand. But at least it is clear that the sequence, ending with the image of a boy lying inert on what seems an operating table (he is covered to the chest by a white sheet), awakening to a bell, turning on his stomach and reading a book, surely relates to various events in the narrative that follows. Pain, death, anesthesia, inanimate nature, the antic skeleton-man, along with the sudden freeze of a little cartoon woman doing setting-up exercises, have obviously been parodies of elements in the grave human situation that eventuates as Bergman's main story. When I had seen *Persona* twice, it still had not struck me that what I identified as mockery of certain facile film devices (some now enjoying a fashionable revival) included reverse motion.

Usually reverse motion is easy to apprehend in film, if only because people are seen moving backward rather than forward or because the preceding action is repeated but in reverse. Yet there are times when the clue by which watchers detect reverse motion, if unexpected, seems most elusive and fortified against analytical detection. At the same time, one senses something "unnatural" in the movement; the explanation may be that, for some arbitrary reason, it has simply been run backward. Without seeing the film again, or reading anything about this opening sequence, the notion suddenly came to me that Bergman, in the final bit when the supine boy awakes, turns on his stomach and starts reading a book, had practiced a trick on us. When the little action was originally shot, I believe now that it *started* with the boy on his stomach, reading, and subsequently, when the bell sounds, he abandons the book, turns over and goes to sleep. Indeed, both this trick and the nature of its action relate more or less weightedly to subsequent actions in the following dramatic plot.

Surely, in the light cast by the whole of *Persona*, we can say that Bergman started his work by making an ironic comment on the film medium as a mechanical toy, which not only may arrest the presentation of physical movement (the frozen frame) but also reverse it in time and space. He clearly shows that this technique for arresting and reversing human motion may be perfectly frivolous (a stunt worthy of archaic movies, which made jokes or simple wonders of such things) and yet that it also points, as a technical faculty, to most important psychic and emotive stoppages ("fixations" and "withdrawals") in human behavior. For precisely such a case happens to be the theme of his story.

A noted dramatic actress forgets well-learned lines in the midst of a performance (the play is an *Electra*). She goes dry, as the saying is, and suddenly, after moments of anguish and a hysterical giggle, realizes that this stage or studio accident is actually freighted with dreadful significance for her: it is the first material symbol of a withdrawal from normal life that duly takes place. She will live, she will eat, she will smile and even read, but she will not issue from personal seclusion and she will not utter words to anyone. Her resolution not to speak remains stable except for a single instance of instability: when her nurse eventually induces her to pronounce exactly two words, "No, nothing." First, she enters a hospital, then, advised to go to the country with the nurse, seems to live contented, even mildly happy, in this withdrawal from her professional life, her husband, her little son and all society, till a neurosis bred within *the nurse* gradually, with threats of violence, breaks up the situation. Here the picture ends with an odd formal inconclusiveness. The nurse, not her patient, seems to have had a catharsis. And no one seems "hurt." But the feeling conveyed is one of absolute suspense.

Persona is so highly charged as to present a very formidable problem to interpreters, who may wish to give it a unified pattern. But at least certain of its quantities —if not one inevitable dimension of meaning—are identifiable. Both seriously and playfully, Bergman is utilizing the dramatic concept of peripety: the withdrawn actress's young nurse temporarily becomes a psychiatric patient so that technically the actress becomes her psychiatrist, thus reversing their original situations. Through a still screen image of a face, one half the actress's and the other her nurse's, Bergman visually, at one point, conveys the notion of split personality, a state well known as leading to psychopathic results of different kinds. The nurse seems to have a problem devolving on sexual guilt and her attitude toward her patient suggests it may well be a hidden lesbian impulse. But that neither a sexual nor a psychiatric reading of *Persona* is efficient or inevitable was startlingly proved when Swedish theologians announced their own interpretation of the actress's withdrawal: she represents God whose silence traditionally provides such grave dilemmas for saints and others who apply to him for a word of forgiveness or advice—in short, for personal recognition. *Persona* is rich enough in quality to sustain such an interpretation, although in that case, it seems to me, the mold of Bergman's plot, its personnel, and above all the strange moodiness of his filmic devices, should embarrass rather than reassure a theological reading.

True, it *fits*. There's the rub. And the rub is the more interesting thereby. However, it seems to me that *Persona* is more persuasive, indeed richer, for the present purpose than for any theological purpose. Expanded to this other wide context—to the purview of my theory— the film contains a number of relevant, tendentious, very large factors. Too, too easily, I think, we can do without theology in gauging the major portent of *Persona*. The most tricky-looking device in the work can, in fact, be related to the theory of film as I see it: as a psychology, a consciousness, an aesthetics of its own; and as, in the present discussion, a time/space of its own. The film medium's greatly suggestive manipulability is forcefully stated by the surreal sequence mentioned above as opening the movie. Film time can go backward and forward at will, a spatial path be retraversed, action go "in circles." Just as neatly, a psychic state that is stable and even dynamic can be disguised by "silence" and "stasis" through the act of withdrawal. Yet this same reversal of personality (the actress's) can function as psychologically positive, can purge, and indeed re-create, another personality (the nurse's).

Persona shows vividly that by no means do all personal withdrawals begin or end in catatonia or in that complete physical paralysis (a sexual instance is in Pasolini's film *Teorema*) resulting from deep psychic shock. This means, in more normal, generalized terms that what we know as "rest" can be easily misinterpreted by the thoughtless and light-minded as irrational stasis, perverse arrestment or pathological inertia. The need for privacy and a certain physical withdrawal is true of all genuine artists: it is the condition of their creative work. Artists and saints are themselves adepts of silence. Something that may well be overlooked in the context of *Persona* is that the actress's withdrawal situation is "abnormal" and "pathological" not by her own subscription, but by that of others; by the hospital's head psychiatrist, the actress's bewildered husband, the nurse commissioned to help her "come back"; by, in a word, not herself, but the society around her. God, surely, has no monopoly on portentously weighted silence.

An artist, in truth, is by profession (Bergman's opening sequence enigmatically states this) one who manipulates silences, rests, pauses, absences, as all literally part of the dynamic process of creation: a dialectic of its own. Therefore silence—that which by poetic authority "speaks volumes"—can be an attribute of a stable, rather than an unstable, condition. The more "silently" machines work, for instance, the better; indeed, their intrusive clatter is often a sign that they are not in order, are deteriorating. "Noise" typically appears in the form of meaningless dissonance: a breakup of some established rhythm. Silence may be but one of the ensigns of rhythm which itself is an indispensable trait of all art media.

A formal difficulty appears in art precisely when its subject—namely, the object of its attention—is some drastic breakup of rhythm, of the expected, of the usual course of human behavior. Modern taste and its ironic complexion tend, just as in this Bergman film, to juggle with such situations, to take an experimental view toward them, seeking deliberate risk as if tragically motivated, turning suddenly—as if to a safety base in a game—toward comic irony, toward an elegant sense of play, making everything tantalizingly inconclusive and ambiguous. Although I think Bergman has gone too far here in such experimentalism, I also think he has ingeniously stated a theory of film that entirely coincides with mine. This theory depends on the willful sovereignty of the actress Elizabeth Vogler's inward subjectivity, which covers itself with an outward mask of silence.

There is no indication that her withdrawal state is "deadness," actual staticity, a deterioration. Her incommunicativeness is simply a social condition that she elects to impose on those around her. The charm of its power has been revealed to her when, utterly distressed at first by forgetting her lines, she quickly hails the event with an exuberant giggle. Hers is the happiness of a *triumphant recognition*. Like God, like the artist, she can will her privacy, make it hermetic, be invulnerably subjective.

Naturally, it is a shock because she has not realized, before, this potential of intellectual creation: this withdrawal "to think." I once knew an unhappy individual, mature in age but not "old," frustrated in her moribund marriage relations, for she herself was still vital, a woman who felt a real desire to change her life but never mustered the strength to make the first gesture, much less the strength to go through with it. She was overwhelmed by a fatality of inertia even while conscious of intense unhappiness. She, by all odds, was *static*. Often she would say: "If only I could go somewhere in the country, be by myself—and think—then I could decide . . . Then I might make the break [from her husband]."

That magical event the woman could not bring about: old human ties (she had grown children), old romantic sentiments, lingering memories of happiness, held her back, shackled her; froze her, literally, in her frame. But the same magical event effectually befalls Elizabeth Vogler, the actress, as if by accident. The great point is that Elizabeth recognizes the sign *and obeys it*. It means cutting off past human relations that still abide, severing herself radically from all society. And yet she welcomes it—welcomes it, indeed, as if it were a nun's vow of silence. When eventually she goes to the country and lives a secluded rustic life with her young nurse, she grows tranquil like a nun, even cheerful like a nun; it is the nurse Alma's aggressive neurosis that surfaces, torments Elizabeth and spoils the tenor of their life together. Maybe, all this while, Elizabeth has been a suppressed lesbian; maybe she does not fall in love with Alma, but Alma with her. All the same, Elizabeth may slowly have been realizing her own identity as a lesbian . . . a realization that only the stage accident and her withdrawal have brought about.

If one liked, one could think of *Persona* as a refined

sexual fantasy, in which an auteur-voyeur chooses a difficult lesbian situation to juggle with, thinking of it as a mock psychiatric problem, even a mock formal problem, but weaving tensions in which two women, subconsciously attracted to each other, resist the attraction for complicated private reasons and end up frustrated, in hopeless antagonism. It could represent a sadistic impulse on the part of the auteur-voyeur, even a didactic gesture. The film could even be high professional camp, showing Bergman's rivals how clever and resourceful he can be, how daringly obscure and baffling. . . . We do not know; that is, we cannot be perfectly sure from the evidence as presented by the film.

What we do know, I think, is that Elizabeth Vogler is asserting the power of the human creator and that Bergman, because he *is* a film-maker, has variously but directly conveyed this by uniquely filmic devices. Yes, they are devices with a will-o'-the-wisp instability, but their function, in this fuller light, is revealed as ironic: it is just this always threatening, contingent, environmental instability from which the creator must protect his own watchful, willed subjectivity. Without that armored subjectivity, he could not create. This, then, is how what I call the very strong *filmicality* of Bergman's film came about: he felt, like his heroine, great pressures against an inner essence that constitutes a theory; in his case, it is being an authentic film-maker, in Elizabeth Vogler's case, being an authentic human being. Whatever art be involved, whatever its subject or scope or peculiar significance as an individual work, for it to be first-rate, to rank at all, it must be, respectively, *painterly* in painting, *prosish* in prose, *filmic* in film-making: it must achieve its triumph in terms of its own medium.

Nothing could be a worse error at this point than to assume of an art that "the medium is the message" in the sense that a film is an aggregate of interlocking filmic devices; that a true film, as it were, is any sort of mediumistic stunt. The fact is that Bergman's heroine is indelibly a *filmic heroine*. Everything she must resist to maintain the preciousness of her inward integrity attacks her in terms of an *instability* which happens to be *one of the wrong theories of film*. I mean, for instance, the formula offered by Professor Susanne Langer that film is basically a dream mode, a medium that reproduces as a psychic mechanism the hazy, illogical, technically irresponsible, unsatisfyingly fluid, anticlimactically forwarded shape of dreams. For Professor Langer, a professional philosopher, the film makes an ideal dream-form because dreams characteristically have no beginning or end, no arranged or preconceived shape; viewpoints and scenes change arbitrarily; entrances and exits are unconscious and unprepared for; human identities are vague and chameleon. Time as a disciplined logic, a chronometric system, is ignored by dreams, while in its place appears an arbitrarily prolonged, inverted or ellipsized, immeasurable and usually jumpy duration. In other words, dreams (and films as the functional interpreter of dreams) display a psychically spontaneous, purely subjective world that is the direct opposite of the objective world with its coherent, orderly, measurable and verifiably "real" systems of behavior. All the empiric evidence of film archives to the contrary, film means, to Professor Langer and her associates, the inevitable medium for man's irresponsible psyche, its finally uncontrolled and tacitly incoherent behavior.

This thinker might be considered to have borrowed a cue from Surrealism to formulate her film theory. However, her academic coolness and detachment, her purely topical and actually curt interest in the matter (her published essay on the subject is very short) belies any conclusion to that effect. Surrealism *willfully* exploits irrationality; it wishes to be an instrument of passion and wholly responsible for "dream acts," whether keeping them within imaginary borders or inserting them among the facts of daily life. Still, I wrote above that the strange little montage sequence introducing *Persona* was "surreal." I have not mentioned that it ends with the little awakened or going-to-sleep boy finding a moment to caress the huge phantasmal image of a female head, an action which, repeated at the close, gives the film a cyclic aura despite its abrupt suspension of plot.

Who is the boy? Is he Elizabeth's son? The plot brings out that she has both a son and a husband—and that the boy is not quite well or normal. Suppose we suppose that one of the son's compulsive habits, before bedtime, is to dial-twist the TV set at home? He might get something like that bizarre sequence run off to lead into the film's main action. Yet he loves his mother (the caressing of her imaged face would show that) and obediently, at a signal, goes to bed and quietly starts reading. It might be, however, that his compulsive behavior, his desire to wring amusement from TV antics (rather than to go to bed) is merely the "toy model" of his mother's desire to entertain an imaginary, desired, but also truncated, unachievable life. It might be a lesbian life, it might not. The point is that it is not her present "real" life; it is a *theoretical* life whose essence is subjectively present and finally powerful enough to make her (through forgetting her lines in the play) yield to the sway of the truer fiction inside; the fiction that is part of her and *only her* psychic life; a fiction that does not belong to a play—the imaginative work of another—or to the real, unprofessional orders of her life as mother and wife.

All Elizabeth has to do, to reverse the established relation of reality/unreality, truth/fiction, order/disorder, is

drastically to repudiate her "objective life"—her withdrawal expresses this—and start privately entertaining
her "subjective life." She imposes directly on herself,
that is, and indirectly on the world, the practical continuity of an armored subjectivity. As I said, the world's
reaction to this is to consider it pathological and at once
to set about destroying it: this rescue process is called
breaking down the barriers erected by the withdrawn
individual (what the young nurse personally sets out to
do), re-establishing the individual's contact with the
world, with its "love," and so on; in short, bringing her
or him back to "normal life." But the psychological fact
is that as soon as Elizabeth Vogler successfully withdraws, without going into catatonia or total paralysis,
then the apprehended world, proceeding normally in
orderly fashion, as it did before, takes on nevertheless
that arbitrary and annoying intrusiveness, that disturbing instability, which is canonically attributed to *dreams*,
and also (if we are to believe Professor Langer) to *films*.

All that we term normalcy, objectivity, reason, measured time and space, become, to this withdrawn actress,
simply the institutions of paranoia. As Freud observed
(and as I once noted in connection with an analysis
of Antonioni's films), the paranoid personality is established by the delusion that, as isolated and anonymous as the individual may be, the world is everywhere
involved with him and his doings; all space holds for
him danger, threat, seductive promise used as traps; there
are always lurking ambushes—lonely women with a talent for paranoia imagine a rapist in every shadow,
around every corner of a street. The obsessive habit of
the TV dial-twister—that master of television, that
"producer" (I quote McLuhan) of baseball TV replays
—becomes the antiparanoiac device of human beings sensitive to the fears of paranoia, longing for anything in

the world to "ecstasize" themselves so their latent fears can be allayed, dissipated. This not only *includes* entertainment, it is itself a form of entertainment: a power-fetish against boredom as well as fear. Yet, to someone exposed to it in another, while himself *indisposed*, it can easily look and sound like pandemonium in an insane asylum—different sets of sounds and images on TV (with commercials providing valiant help) dash in and out of consciousness with neither rhyme nor reason, or rhyme and reason so trivial that it's kindergarten all over again. Such a thing provides a perfect parody, a camp farce, of Professor Langer's concept of film as "dream mode." When commercials *are* obliquely or ironically connected with the programs they interrupt, the effect is dreamlike to the extent that it is "surreal." Actually Professor Langer's theory makes no allowance for specifically *surreal* instability.

Dial-twisting, truly, is a deliberately artificial form imposed on what already, in the total order of existence, is extremely complicated in terms of time and space and the multifarious, endlessly reaching actions accomplished therein. Any day's sum of one television station's programs is but a pale and tiny reflection of this immense complication. But the artificial small form of it, brought to life by a dial-twister's whim, is that same subjective psychic procedure, that same desired *durée* of the mass brain I described above. As applied to *Persona* this *durée* is no fantasy of mine (conceivably based on the opening montage sequence); it duly, in fact, becomes part of the film's action. And what it expresses, precisely, is the world of home television as *the apparition of a terrifying paranoia*.

Elizabeth is still in her hospital room, prior to her trip to stay at the seaside cottage, and happens to be alone except for the TV set, which is performing. Presumably she herself has turned it on for her private distraction, but in fact, according to what eventuates, she has probably forgotten about it (in the way one can forget about television when in home action), or she may simply be dissociating from it as perhaps she had to do at home where her little boy was, hypothetically, so avid a TV watcher. Previously, in her hospital room, she has been listening to the set (or perhaps the radio) when a drama is being performed. Suddenly, she requests the nurse to turn it off. So, in effect, we have a duplication of the moment when she forgot her lines on stage: a speech has been abruptly discontinued.

At present, she is pacing the floor, at some distance from the TV set, when with horror she becomes aware that the newscast has flashed on the image of one of the Buddhist priests who publicly immolated themselves in Vietnam. We, the audience in the film house, are shown what Elizabeth, with signs of agitation and fear, is watching on television. It seems to be an authentic movie that was taken on the spot by a news camera. We see the seated priest in flames, spectators on the scene, and other cameramen (beyond the priest) taking still shots of the dreadful sight. Why is Elizabeth so especially horrified? Why is the impact of this tragic scene so positive and dramatic in the context before us?

Because, as if through a slip of the imagination or an idle mechanical gesture, the actress has exposed herself to exactly the sort of world-intrusion that her act of solemn withdrawal has sought to protect her from. One of the world's most alarming aspects is now visible to her eyesight, achieving a duration which she knows is real, not fictitious, for a Buddhist priest has truly performed this act of self-sacrifice. We must be sure of understanding, here, just what is involved with the actress's withdrawal as a conscious assertion of absolute privacy, of armored subjectivity. Since hers is palpably not the act of a trained artist, who simply wishes privacy to create, there is a personal risk, a grave crisis, involved with it. She is experimenting with herself; her own involuntary act has surprised her true self.

The risk she runs is the possible extinction of consciousness as well as of personal identity, and the priest's act happens to symbolize this fatality through the actual extinction of his life. Totally withdrawn persons are regarded as moral suicides. Elizabeth is aware that, whatever life and inward personality she has to protect, she is traveling a very dangerous path; the inherent paranoia of it is precisely what is revealed to her when she catches sight of the priest immolating himself. Yet *she* knows and *we* know that this same tragic act, thus magically transported in all directions on the airwaves, is also the appetizing diversion, the obsessive habit, of millions of spectators who desire only to be acquainted with everything that's going on, no matter what; if the event is tragic, ugly, a disaster, freakishly horrible, depressing— well, all the better!

The world's objective order, obviously, has broken down. But all things "break down," don't they? Congratulate yourself, citizen, that a particular misfortune has befallen someone else, not you. Go on patiently constructing your visual/aural antidote against common paranoia, that spatial paranoia which I am convinced is the world's most popular theory of film. The odd mistake made mutually by Dr. Kracauer and Professor Langer is that a "theory of film" requires an intermediary computer, programmed one way or another, properly to establish itself. Vain fallacy of scholars! The world—that is, the people in it—has already established this theory—

beyond Professor Langer's dreams, beyond Dr. Kracauer's faith in physical reality . . . Still, it is an incorrect theory and, as I have already postulated, it means only the opposite sides of the same false coin.

6

THE TIME/SPACE
COMPUTER AS FILM HERO

Insofar as they are not mechanical transportation systems, work hours, meal hours, bathroom duties, sleep—the orders of the world—are mass theoretical delusions, superstructures of long-acquired social and private habits based invariably on the natural world; habits morally obeyed by human nature, biologically by nature. If all the natural orders of the world were exempt from irregularities, there would be no doctors, no medicine, no hospitals; no courtrooms, no jails and no police. Hence, our society is always in a state of greater or lesser attack from forces easy to identify, at least, by name. To counteract this uncomfortable and embarrassing situation, that monster, the computing machine, was invented to reinforce mass delusions as well as to facilitate the mechanical operations supporting them. Humanity is to be persuaded that programming as many functional aspects of existence as possible, and instantly getting the right answers or cues to everything requiring laborious calculation, have the conclusiveness of a mathematical equation: the supreme exactitude of a sum in simple addition.

I mean, such is the computer myth that has so high a place in modern society. It would be very wrong to consider the computer as a mere mechanical fact-finder, whose glorious function is to save time and eliminate error. The very theory that it is so useful and without error is a myth; mechanical breakdown is only one of its Achilles' heels. To people who have great faith in it, to these above all, the computer is, first, a myth; second, a servant. By and large, it is the incarnate robot-emanation of the mass brain. Thus, if romantic, fancy-bred and frivolous movies cheat us, if we are befuddled by headlines, compromised by facts, and moan (as we have moaned through the centuries) that things have seldom, if ever, been so bad, we can always turn (if not to one of the new lay religions or to the latest brand of remodeled Christianity) to—no, not to mere entertainment, but to the myth lying in the wonderful innards of those computers, whose automatism has the fascination of the Robot Queen pictured in the 1927 movie classic, *Metropolis,* or before that, the demonic charm of the mechanical chess-player that could beat any human being at a man-made game and that another wonder-movie duly enshrined. Remember a German movie called *The Golem?* Much later, it was remade with Harry Baur in the title part. There the myth of the conquering hero as tribal savior (here of medieval ghetto Jews) was illustrated by a mechanical man.

Popular film has had a hero's triumph in the way that the telephone, the steamboat and the airplane have prevailed—laughed at, pooh-poohed at first, even hated, any magical gimmick that can be universally serviceable to the race will go on relentlessly to victory, honors, and "end" as a lasting monument to human pride. As soon as the germ of spatial conquest, closed in man's heart and rooted there, abandoned the earth to go skyward, one could not expect it to return except as proof of its success, the way the astronauts return from their flights to the moon. The same sacredness has been reserved for science fiction, whose predictions of new triumphs (and a modicum of new horrors) have been phenomenally underwritten by reality and the nature that still seems to support reality—reality, of course, being mostly another man-made invention. Thus, one theory of film to be coped with at yet another turn is the Kracauerian beyond-which-not-reality. This means that, in alignment with the highest reaches of scientific exploration of the universe and man's inveterate megalomaniac delusions (second only to his paranoiac delusions), the conquest of space, modestly termed by Dr. Kracauer "physical reality," is not only unstoppable but virtually unlimited.

The most pretentious testimony to reach film screens of the space-conquest myth, to date, is 2001: *A Space Odyssey* (1968). Its story is a heartfelt collaboration between the director Stanley Kubrick and the science-fiction master Arthur C. Clarke. It is a resourcefully charged up (for example, fictionally much programmed) adult fairy tale with a darwinized human past—incidentally disproved, lately, by anthropology—and a superhumanoid future, which reassuringly, at the end, presumes to look "timelessly" human . . . For what could be more timelessly human than a human fetus with big doll-like eyes? Are the eyes rather *too* big? Well, *plus ça change, plus la même chose!* As all film buffs know, 2001 is an elaborated, classy, lavishly imagined reconstruction of previous science-fiction movies as archaeologically verified by having gone to the archives.

Don't forget that 1950 winner, *Destination Moon*, even though it showed astronauts as heroic guinea pigs palpably suffering, with wonderfully contorted features, gravitational pull in the interior of their space rocket. Yet there's nothing like (supposed) outer space to make a cliché look bright, shiny and fabulously new. In *2001*, self-outdoing science was celebrated by making future astronauts, now deserving the title of cosmonauts, look as comfortable as if they were walking around the lounge of a 747. There's only one kink: the cosmonauts are notably deadpan—possibly (only possibly!) because there are no smiling 1971 hostesses to react to: their far-flung mission is too serious for that. In 1968, stereotyped science fiction had already supplied film audiences with humanoid creatures attuned to the vicissitudes of robot romances of the future, including interplanetary melo-dramas; these had (and have on TV) the look-it-isn't-quite-human! theme along with the dynamic reflex the burden of that theme inspires in human beings on both sides of the screen. Home Underground movies, not sur-prisingly, parodied them with that induplicable good faith in camp which Home Underground movies always have; one grotesque result was a thing called *Sins of the Fleshapoids*.

You see how easy it is (and perhaps always will be) to make fun of *2001*. Though it earned millions, the film was pounced upon and withered by hostile criticism (sometimes as curt as the demand for ticket money back) from both the mass brain, representing the citizenry, and the caste brain, representing the critics and the élite. Some critics were honestly divided in their own minds; eventually, a certain percentage of them fell down and worshipped with the public. A curious conjunction of bravos came in the form of telegrams addressed to Kubrick by, respectively, two Italian film directors,

Franco Zeffirelli and Federico Fellini. The former can hardly be rated as a serious artist, the latter can. Hence their consensus (their telegrams have much the same emotional tone) is quite strikingly suggestive. What does it suggest? It suggests, as usual, the worst that may truthfully be said about the best aficionados.

In a way, 2001: *A Space Odyssey* could be classified as simply the balmiest of high-camp efforts to lift its own weight in gold to the greatest heights of illusion yet successfully scaled by film. But the sad thing about science fiction, exactly at its most ambitious as here, is that it has not developed a method in film or on the printed page to distinguish convincingly between *de*humanization and *super*humanization without landing back (thud and bump) with the grand old sentimental clichés that have always worked with juvenile adults and adult juveniles. I don't mean just all those apes as obvious testimony to the superhuman sublimity of man's achievement. No, no! To interpret, as does this film, Johann Strauss's *Blue Danube* waltz by setting it to the revolutions of a luxurious future spaceship is as grand and as old a cliché as any filmgoer or TV watcher could possibly respond to and like. And Kubrick is curiously right in his "prophetic" capacity.

That cliché will be logically, all else being equal, just as grand and old and serviceable in the year 2001 as it is now. As I watched the film's authentic cinerama screening, I was not immune, myself, to a certain charm. How terribly, terribly easy it is to become a child again, providing the feat be momentary enough! Despite the big reach of technical time in this film, precisely such *momentariness* is what Kubrick relied on to ensure the grandiose cliché he knew his film had to be to succeed at the box office. True, statistics seem to say that young or young-minded audiences really made the film a box-office smash, because the audience at the original invitation screening, composed largely of professionals and professional critics, was (it was noted with alarm) decidedly cool and unthrilled. Everything was explained later when it was estimated that the range of spectator age at this preview was from thirty-five to sixty, while the bulk of the mostly enthusiastic public that later saw it was allegedly under thirty-five.

Starting with apes is another way of taking us back in time—back to the original beasts we so lamentably, and comically, were, and to which—another departmental theme of science fiction says—we might some day backslide. In *Planet of the Apes,* a spaceship lost in time and space apparently stumbles on a new planet, where it seems (they can breathe its air without apparatus) that actual anthropoids form the political and cultural élite and are at least as intelligent as Hollywood's most gifted minds. However, they live in a style situated somewhere between caveman legend and the elegant simplicity of ancient Crete, though not with that island's elegant costuming. The human hero (no other than spellbinding Charlton Heston) soon digs the situation, however flabbergasted he is, and behaves as one might expect: in the tradition once set—it is still admired today—by the Tarzan-like Douglas Fairbanks, Senior. In other words, while incarcerated as an interesting curiosity by the apes, Heston escapes the clutches of his enemies. But an intellectual pay-off, in terms of an honorable socko finish, has been reserved for audience pleasure. Free and having won, during his Buck Rogers exploits, the love of a fair maiden, Heston is cantering along a seacoast of the bizarre planet (horses are also the slaves of this anthropoid civilization) while we prepare ourselves for the usual farewell fadeout. Then a most curious sight makes him pull on the reins and grow rigidly still as he shares the amazement of his fair companion: it is the remains of the Statue of Liberty, toppled from her noble uprightness and rotting away over waters where (as of here and now) she still presides . . .

2001 does not deal with devices so ingeniously primitive. After all, Miss Liberty, as familiarly she used to be called, belongs to the nineteenth century, now a "guilty" century because its strange ideals, despite the intelligence of twentieth-century computers, will apparently lead us all to the Planet of the Apes. Life, think Clarke and Kubrick, should be, even today, more sophisticated, up-to-date and optimistic than that. The symbol chosen to represent the metaphysical beyond, the incarnate ideal, the mystic lodestone and grandiose future of man (whatever setbacks he may experience throughout time) has the shape and proportions of a downscaled modern skyscraper without windows; it is also very like the three-dimensional oblong with which some abstract sculptors start as a basic form. It is black and emits, moreover, a strange sound that may (just *may*) be a message. McLuhanism seems not to have triumphed in those days to come, although, for all the "success" with which the language of the black monolith is decoded (for example, none) its geometric form and sound must remain for us as both the medium and the message.

But here—as elsewhere—the time for making jokes has ceased. If creative jokes must be rivaled by critical jokes in the present instance, it is because evidence has to be lined up in every argument. People are prone to forget so easily, attention is so quickly distracted: it's part of the contemporary paranoiac pattern. Hence I apologize if, to some, I now seem overscrupulous. The black monolith is a romantic symbol of the metaphysical pretensions of a great deal of science fiction. For all that it is ever made to mean in spiritual or intellectual terms, it might as well be an overgrown television set with invisible screen and concealed mechanisms. It may be, indeed, a radioactive storage battery posing as a mere monolith. While *2001* is superlative in its "special effects" —whose secrets of manufacture were duly exposed in a paperback compiled about the film—it has such plain reference to many of its science-fiction predecessors that it could be called a super-riot of clichés.

The aforesaid monolith suggests not just the sighing statue of Memnon in Egypt but the "musical" Coca-Cola bottle in *On the Beach*. As for the anthropoid contrast which forms the prelude to *2001*, it is a thing of shreds and patches, its solemnity strained and pedantic. The film's subjective version of the conquest of the solar system, through the astronaut Bowman's determination to break the clown-barrier in such antics, comes straight from the environments of discothèques and the more impetuous abstract color fantasies on film, while the presence of the formidable Space Pod in which he makes his fabulous journey (finally seen as a decorative object in the apartment he inhabits in his old age—on Jupiter, presumably, or we may be back on Earth with Charlton Heston) makes a neat parallel with *The Time Machine*. Even more: Though I had to be reminded of it, the pseudo-elegant period rooms of Bowman's apartment, where he lives like a rich but eccentric overlord who has chosen monkish seclusion, are supposed to be a sort of cage—that is, a prison—where the superior intelligences of the world he has penetrated are keeping him for observation (ah, yes! there was also Heston, kept in jail for observation in *Planet of the Apes!*). Bowman's place looks a lot like a megalomaniac version of a display suite in a department store which had elected to predict how "period effects" might look several centuries from now. So why not have them, pronto, in your own home? And the Space Pod becomes a grand token for the projected immortality of Pop Art.

You, who have also seen, know how little I am kidding. The truth is spectacularly flat and McLuhanish; flatter and more banal, by far, than the hypersensitive but innocent technologist McLuhan has meant any of the truth to be. The central plot tension derives from a master computer taken along on this sensational voyage. His name is Hal, and most unsurprisingly, if with a proud air of ingenuity, he turns out to be the villain of the piece. But, as more than one spectator observed, a villain whose necessary annihilation, if only because he has a quite human voice, stirred some hearts with paradoxical pity. Like traditional robots, he seems to get delusions of grandeur (namely: can't he outthink humans?) which puts him in line with the soulless tyrants of history who have crushed mankind underfoot. Meanwhile, one of the two deadpan cosmonauts has fallen victim to Hal and floats off, as good as dead, into space; his comrade, Bowman, survives and after vengefully destroying Hal, in spite of his pathetic pleas, decides to go all out for—for what? What did you think? Spatial conquest, of course! Originally, Clarke had proposed to Kubrick that the film's title be *How the Solar System Was Won.*

Yes! That wonderful box again. That box which so palpably and tantalizingly lives outside us, and which film documentarists, among others, have sworn to explore and explore and explore. You know: the Mysterious Universe. I don't deny that the said universe is full of wonders that can be caught by cameras in the hands of daring and imaginative cameramen who are ambitious scientists. But the result is still a notebook of moving images: it is not *film form.* Together, Kubrick and his ardent colleague, Clarke, make quite a pyrotechnic team, but Kubrick, forced at last to fall back on the imagination (as the film's superfictional postulate compelled him to do), could not come up with anything better than a screen-filling fetus with phenomenally goo-goo eyes. Inevitably it suggests (one feels that here is the sort of creator who both knows and doesn't know what he's doing) that Bowman—the man of the future who has left sex and family and humanity back in those moldy old centuries we now live in—is no more than a sportive megalomaniac, hell-bent all this while on getting back into the womb. By this self-evident analogy, all spatial conquest (and spatial paranoia as well) would be the Freudian superstructure of an all-too-human impulse bred by primitive agoraphobia.

I know, of course, that there are opponents of Freudian and other "metaphorical" interpretations of human behavior, and that these (very possibly Kubrick too) would protest any such interpretation as the last one. Why can't the fetus merely symbolize a rebeginning, a grand rebeginning for what, after all, is a grand exploit, and will be, by all present signs, even grander? One can only respond by being literal. That is something which it takes poets to know. Pseudo-metaphysicians and exalted discothèque-dazzlers won't do. The point, happily enough, issues from the medium's connection with the message. It would take someone extremely positivistic, evangelically manic, and (I would add) overconfident, to say that the meanings of 2001 are perfectly plain and need arouse no quarrels. They are not perfectly plain unless, again, we have "the medium" that "is the message": a proposition which, incidentally, automatically silences all that we know as criticism.

If the present book has any point or any raison-d'être, we must concede that 2001 is full of arguable attitudes and quantities, whether as fiction or philosophy or the "art" of prophecy. The truly literate, the only satisfyingly poetic, viewpoint to take is that messages do exist in art and that the art medium, in its specific devices, inevitably inflects the nature of its messages. Thus the human fetus as the farewell image of *2001* establishes beyond quibble that it is a metaphor for man as an occupant of space as a superwomb, not just the human womb of his mother's body. Yet superwomb means super-mother—and what is actually gained by this? For it is only an inflation, on an infinite scale, of what is already given. Basically, the notion is already something of a platitude. Its expression in *2001*, furthermore, is by no means joyously optimistic any more than it is lucidly tragic. The dying Bowman in his luminous, luxurious suite is about as lucidly human as a rat dying from some medical experiment conducted here and now. Is Bowman's the existential boredom, perchance, of a man who has "had everything"? Certainly, according to *2001*, it might just as well be the boredom of an animal species, the "last of its kind," dying in some contemporary zoo. The film could have ended, of course, with that image. But it didn't. It ended with the eerily immense fetus: an out-of-whack kewpie doll.

Every fetus, we can gently reflect, is literally a "sign" for the future child and the future adult, whatever his provable capacities. This particular fetus is not, at least not self-evidently, made from a mechanical womb. But even if it were, it would not necessarily mean the first stage of extrasensory perception in an ordinary human being. It might be just the result of a mechanical way of producing real human children without the aid of a real human womb. Would that eliminate claustrophobia? And what of agoraphobia? Hal's hypothetic female counterpart might have been designated to produce the cineramic fetus. Moreover, the children of such a machine would be, from all the looks of this product, like the children of today except that the social complex we know as the human family might be no more, and some educational system—perhaps the state itself—would be such a child's sole parent.

In that direction, of course, lies a science-fiction field such as that of Orwell's *1984*, which has a quite different legend of paranoiac space: the space where the fascist state has become a claustrophobiac machine, reducing the individual to the strictest condition of surveillance and imposing on him all reality beyond his immediate sensory domain as a conspiracy of "false effects." It is as if the world were a film studio: a very large film studio. Men are made to believe that society is engaged in a war that actually doesn't exist but which morally justifies the hardship of the sacrifices and restrictions that all must endure at this future time. Now you see what I mean by a previous statement. Space is supposed, by a theory of film that would compass *2001* and *1984*, to expand and contract in a supposed chronometric continuum (a "time box") where the main (the *only crucial*) problem is the terms of its *social* control. If we made a flow-of-life reel of a diverse set of science-fiction films, compacting *2001*, *1984*, *The Time Machine*, *On the Beach* and *Planet of the Apes*—and let's add *The Tenth Victim*—we would have an incoherent fantasy of man's paranoiac brooding over what's going to happen to him tomorrow, next year and in eternity. This theory, thus, is only a mechanical compilation of man's mentally stimulated fears and hopes: the most abject of them and the most romantic. Despite isolated moments of visual majesty, the prevalent style of such filmic efforts of the imagination is the way-out comic strip, where everything appallingly sinister and emotionally jolting that man fears and dreads, on one hand, and that he sadomasochistically enjoys and welcomes, perhaps loves, on the other, is seen in terms of strenuously hoked-up fairy tales about that well-known superhuman hero whose personality, self-evidently, is so unwilling to die. It is simply that, owing to the notable instability of filmic imagination, we have perpetually revived versions of heroes seeming too much like Tarzan, too much like Buck Rogers, too much like those heroes who escape by a hair from what would have been a fatal ordeal of brainwashing, turning them not into great adepts but great zombies. Bowman, modishly enough, has touches of all three types. Yet, so far as any romantic glamour he creates about the human personality goes, he rather leans toward the zombiesque.

From the most ancient times, I take leave to remark once more, man has had an irrepressible yen to plot the full nature as well as the full extent of his living space. From *The Divine Comedy*, and before that *The Aeneid*, to the cheapest comic strip of modern times, the basic armature of myth and fairy tale and hero legend has been the ritual ordeal, in which the individual—usually as the explicit hero—must save his life or earn some supreme reward by surviving a planned series of encounters with dangers material and elusive, puzzles and traps to test his physical bravery and mental resources. The old Greek tragedies clearly contain the "ordeal" pattern and so did the ceremonies initiating applicants to the old mystery religions. In terms of the initiation rite, around which the whole tradition of hermetic wisdom was built, various scholars have tried to reconstruct an archetypal test, necessarily including the vestiges of the primordial rite of human sacrifice, when a scapegoat's punishment cleansed the tribe of evil and guilt. No, indeed, we aren't quite done with Bowman! The most extensive and vivid scholarly reconstruction of such rites is probably Edouard Schuré's attempt, called "The Sacred Drama of Eleusis," with a version conceived for the stage, in his book *The Genesis of Tragedy*.

Religious sensibility having lost intensity since the sixteenth century, public religion has replaced the pagan hero and the adept's spiritual tradition with the priest cult and above all with mass salvation. Mass salvation is supposedly "for everyone" and is administered by a priesthood or else, in our modern opportunistic and individualistic times, by a peripatetic evangelist. Hence heroic individuals have tended in the last four centuries to be men of genius devoted to art or philosophy or science: so we have the great artists, the great Renaissance philosophers, the great inventors—and, because government too has been a sort of experimental art or science ever since Plato's *Republic* was written, also the great politicians. Surely, all these overshadow the great saints. The one big obstacle to the survival of this commodious tradition of individual genius has been the question of evil, its social and religious status, its rules of application, and of course its living office in the persons of its administrators. A conflict of ethical interests was the eventual upshot, so that state and individual, church and individual, church and dissenting sect, church and state were constantly at loggerheads even within the structure of the state itself, not to mention the racial and national quarrels that have led to international as well as civil wars.

If I recapitulate within this loose context, it is because of the theoretical nature of my argument: the issue is not only the situation of film's archetypal heroes, but also their identity. If there be a hero in front of the camera, and if the subject matter or message is his story (his ordeal, his victory or defeat), there is likewise a hero (or if you like an antihero) behind it, the film director who is the work's and essentially the hero's creator. We must reflect that, in view of all the screen biographies, romantic or factual in spirit, that have been done of artists, scientists, inventors and politicians, there has existed a double set of heroes or "antiheroes": the one conceived before the camera, the one conceiving behind it— the master of the camera's, and the master of his own, fate. It is on the responsibility of the latter, above all and first and last, that a theory of film must concentrate.

The author, the creator, the auteur-director, the dramatist, even the painter—each is directly responsible for the conduct of his heroes in that it is he who judges their, perhaps factually "prerecorded" behavior, and picturing it, explicates it; thus with all the films about kings and statesmen, inventors and artists, bar none. The great defect of filmic biographies about historic personages, the main obstacle in the path of their imaginative art, has been their lack of subjectivity *on both sides of the camera.* In other words, it is the continuing and deliberately fostered error of cultivating a supposed aesthetic of the objective (the checkable) facts, as if these facts had been supplied not by human impulses but by a carefully programmed computer, which for lack of a better name we may call "history."

In this sense, all the past is a time machine equipped with answers; as space, to the scientist and the documentarist, is only a partitioned box to be inventoried, so, coordinately, is time. As I said, there is no explanation of the black slab and its message, in 2001, beyond what might be found on the walls of a super-discothèque, no explanation of Bowman's inner destiny beyond what may be discovered about an anthropoid isolated for observation in a science laboratory. And if we have to rely on what Kubrick-Clarke are willing to report of the latter, our outlook is both misty and meager, and, I should add, altogether dim. All this points to the ethic of the computer which is based on determined human worship of the machine, and is the only true robot. Here is the fallacy of science that has always threatened to be likewise the fallacy of art and everything else.

The historic example of a creative genius such as Leonardo da Vinci may be most misleading. True, he inflected the art of painting toward science so as to discover truths as yet uncodified, truths of archaeology and common cause-and-effect in the physical world; as everyone knows, he was a proto-scientist. But this sum of extraordinary knowledge and experiments is only analogous, not identical, with the purely spiritual co-efficient of his painting. It is only that profound science of human divination which made him catch the great human nuance in the face of Mona Lisa; in other words, only by a transvaluation of value in the Nietzschean sense do we view *The Madonna of the Rocks, The Virgin and St. Anne, Mona Lisa,* and the surviving image of *The Last Supper.* As much as Leonardo was concerned with mechanisms, he regarded them ultimately (aside from their practical use) as mysteries. Just so, the mechanism of an ingenious murder-mystery novel involves something that, to acquire significance, needs to be "solved" by a moral philosopher or an artist after it has been "solved" by a detective. The conventional murder mystery *ends* where truly vital mysteries *begin*: with the identification of the murderer. Theoretically, the detective in a mystery story is simply the surrogate for a computer's answer to a question: give him the correct data and he is programmed to come up with the right answer. Yet it is not Oedipus' legal or "courtroom" identification that matters to *his* drama, but the identification behind that identification: the quality of the specific human plot *within,* and in a sense also *behind,* his topical acts of murder and incest.

In the same sense, it is not the clinical classification of Elizabeth Vogler's case as "total withdrawal" that matters in the Bergman film I have discussed, *Persona,* but Elizabeth's own purely subjective truth, her motives for withdrawal and what articulacies her cloak of inarticulacy conceals; at least, the profound and precious nature of their presence, if not their specification, is their value; for we are never told their specification. Elizabeth's case can be compared with that of Josephine in Kafka's masterful little prose fable, "Josephine, Singer of the Mouse Folk." Kafka's allegoric theme is the deliberate withdrawal of a great singer, widely acknowledged by a mouse élite, but, according to a sudden, arbitrary decision of her own, persuaded that her society does not sufficiently remunerate her *in terms of understanding.* Thus the author writes this striking sentence, putting it in the mouth of a narrator who is himself a mouse, a member of Josephine's society: "She hides herself and does not sing." It is a difficult fable whose subject is the artistic genius's alienation from the rest of society; it remains a mystery because Josephine's position is that while her art is much appreciated, it is not rightly understood; so it happens that she ceases to perform and "hides." The fact is, she is compelled to do a certain amount of uncongenial work aside from her singing and considers, independently, that her singing is quite adequate to justify her economic place in her society.

This is the way the narrator expatiates on the insoluble situation: "Josephine wants not only to be admired, but to be admired in exactly the way she decides. Admiration alone is of no importance to her. And when you sit in front of her, you realize that what she squeaks is not ordinary squeaking." What emerges from the narrator's judgment is a sort of conundrum: the mouse folk, including himself, *think* they understand Josephine's singing although she denies that they do. It is an impasse of immeasurable depth because it is the lone individual subject (here an artist) pitting himself against all objectivity, setting himself up, as it were, above all judgment by others and declaring his economic self-sufficiency *in theory*. It is the myth of art as the ultimate hermetic quantity, the impregnable élite, the ultimate subjective authoritarianism whose destiny is an obscure aloneness and that pesky economic "disqualification."

Now, if we consider this myth in the light of Elizabeth Vogler's insistent withdrawal, and the signs which she is provoked to give a society that questions her right to that withdrawal, the content of the myth—though technically, in *Persona*, it too involves an artist—is automatically reoriented to the individual's right to "live in" society without "being of it," that is, without participating in it or communicating with it. With *Persona*, the economic problem is not part of the ethical quarrel. From the standpoint of Christian religion, Elizabeth is guilty of the calendar sin of pride: that which certain saints had to cope with, both in their own personalities and in regard to church authority; hence, so far as theological interpretation goes, Elizabeth can just as well represent a rebellious saint as she can represent God. For that matter, even as Josephine, she might represent the artist in the Soviet Union, or any fascist state, whose cooperation with society, whose contribution to the state's welfare, is mandatory on the economic level. Today's totalitarian state, with so many doors closed to international commerce, theoretically cannot afford to let its artists be self-indulgently, petulantly silent. Each one is not only needed as a variety of worker, he is needed as a propagandist, so that his articulacy must follow general, politically viable lines; if he wishes to state his private case as an artist, and insists on stating it, he is condemned to silence, exile and perhaps worse; preliminarily he is put under surveillance, as was Sergei Eisenstein, or subjected to censorship and harassment, as were Boris Pasternak and others.

Another of Bergman's films, *The Silence*, treated the issue of social communication quite differently, making silence not the simple self-dictate of an individual, but a mysterious technical contingency, as of one broad communication system that is disconnected from another. The linguistic quantity operates here in terms of different nations but there are also other levels, just as in *Persona* there is the artistic level and the human level: the "humanity" that nominally means the world collective of higher gregarious animals. In a way, the human situation in *The Silence* is quite the opposite of that in *Persona* and through the single faculty of *will*. The vestigial family of three in *The Silence*, two adult sisters and the little son of one of them, are apparently displaced persons in the process of seeking refuge because of war or revolution, so that here the untoward complex of international accident is what creates the problem: an imposed, arbitrary "silence" isolating three persons in a momentary social vacuum. Yet it soon appears that this abrupt objective situation is but a symbolic reflection of that silence notoriously imposed by social and family hypocrisy: that secretive, a-morally tolerated division within a family group that leads to neurosis and tragic outcome and that is briefly, spasmodically broken only by the sexual communication that one of the women establishes with a pickup: a waiter in a cafe she visits alone. As in *Persona* the focus is on two isolated women, at least one of each pair being suspect as lesbian, except that it is at the *end* of *The Silence* that one of the pair (she is the plot's animator) withdraws in proud isolation. She is suffering from a nervous disease that means progressive suffocation—its cause may be the suppressed passion for her younger sister—so that at the climax, bidding her sister and her little nephew goodbye, the elder woman remains to die in the hotel where they have been forced to stop, while the two others resume their "free" life.

This rule flows from my theory of film: It takes a "subject" to know a "subject"—however much the known subject be vowed to silence—and let the "objects" fall where they may! What the artist learns (it is his sole and solitary science) is the outward signals of inward, or spiritual, activity; these he learns by heart and they form his technology: all else is his enlistment of devices to explicate, give proper and accurate form to, this adept learning of signals. Yes, the devices themselves inspire, just as a great pianist is first inspired by the sound of someone else playing the piano; so that, in order to give his inward feelings external expression, he first has to learn the operation of a given, difficult machine. Having committed this to memory by way of the heart, he is prepared to perform his prodigies, perhaps even compose them himself. Thus, too, the composer who would create symphonies must learn the behavior of each musical instrument and how they all combine in sounds and silences.

In respect to being an interpretive instrument, the film camera is exactly the same. Its prodigies are many; indeed, they may be thoroughly inventoried. Still, the greatest error of which a film-maker can be guilty is to assume that these peculiar technical advantages, this vocabulary of effects, are ever, rightly speaking, applied to manipulating what is called the real world. It is true: the documentarist's ambition to be expressive may use editing methods that are simply a special arrangement of reportorial footage in which the camera previously has been merely a passive agent, moving only in order (as in televised baseball games) to cover this or that detail of a whole action. There is, as I said above, a category of imaginative documentary (such as de Daunant's *Forbidden Bullfight*) yet the film process in such cases has been a deliberate subjectivizing of the objective world: a transmuting treatment of the given material. In *Forbidden Bullfight* too there is *simultaneity* (literally a rhythmic superimposing of time figures in a single moving group) but that film made the *work of art* rather than the *fact of communication* (as in the El Cordobés satellite broadcast) a "wonder" of simultaneity.

When a film-maker tackles the project of using an original literary work with unavoidable symbolic and allegoric qualities (as Orson Welles did when venturing to film Kafka's novel *The Trial*), he is actually putting himself on trial as a film artist. Welles himself is mythologically memorable in film history for a reason quite pertinent here. It was he who, as producer and director of a radio feature known as "The Mercury Theatre of the Air," pulled off a stunt that parodied the sensationalism of a communication medium so successfully that it could have been a deliberate hoax. Here is a perfect instance—indeed a sublimely apt instance—of the operation of the human race's spatial paranoia. Supposedly, a radio performance is interrupted by a station's news service to broadcast the "fact" that a force of planetary invaders—strange creatures like "Martians"—has just landed and threatens to take over the planet. Despite periodic interruptions explaining that this simulated reality was a routine performance of Welles's theater group, thousands and thousands of listeners were instantly panicked by it so that they did not stay by their set to learn the truth. Some fled from their homes without ado while police departments, radio stations and newspapers were deluged with frantic phone calls, and chaos reigned among switchboards. The event helped make Welles a more famous public figure and—I greatly fear—a worse film director.

In *The Trial*, the adventurous Welles fails by trying to translate the work's really hermetic subjectivity back into terms of real space, which the camera's version of actual three dimensions inevitably suggests, both paranoiacally and megalomaniacally. In that same supposed susceptibility of the camera to external space lay the danger to Welles's project. For Kafka's design is *entirely subjective*. The protagonist K.'s trial is not the imitation of a real trial and therefore not about even the real world: it is not a fancied-up courtroom melodrama, a restaged enactment of an actual trial. Nevertheless, Welles treats it as if it were. The book is the trial of the protagonist's own paranoiac fears of persecution, a kind of Grand Guignol of the horrors of facing punishment for unconscious guilt, for negative "psychological" crimes, the shames and terrors of the tempted imagination; or else it is the pure experience of the "innocent" hallucinating improbable complicity with the world's guilt. That too would be paranoia.

In choosing a picturesque, abandoned railroad station for the background of much of his film action and using it as a bizarre, complicated stage set, Welles furnished exactly the wrong spatial mîse-en-scène for Kafka's studied drama of hallucination. The film's artificially arranged spaces, corresponding to scenes of the story, are "stagy" because they don't exist in the correct envelope. *The Trial* has nothing to do with fantastic staging. One place where Welles really gives away the frivolity and foolishness of his methods is the house of the lawyer to whom the tense and frightened K. applies for aid after being arrested and temporarily released. In Kafka's novel, the lawyer's home is a mere hovel lit expressly by a single candle; thus it is an image of K.'s own gloom and the desperate poverty of his confidence. To give himself a big role and a big scene, Welles, playing the lawyer, makes the focal point of the domicile an immense "ducal" bed where he lolls like a drunken millionaire, forced apparently to economize. Moreover, instead of being lit by one candle, the place is lit visibly by several hundred artistically grouped candles so that the scene suggests a fantasy number in a musical revue rather than Kafka's story. Welles aimed at framing his film action in grandiose and bizarre space—as if it were the fruit of some mad architect's endeavors. But the "physical setting" of a film is truly a matter of dynamic, not static, space; it should be notably unstable here, making sudden transitions from point to point as in dream action.

What, then, are the qualities of dynamic space in dreams? Depth in dreams tends to be shallow, not at all precise in the way of planetary vistas, with their implicit vanishing points and perspective laws; while paths of action, which in the real world can have such various scenery or "settings," tend to be tunnel-like in dreams or ellipsized into odd geometric fragments. Above all, such space is not the equilibrated dynamics conveyed by firm uprights such as buildings. Space in dreams, while we may feel a thing like headlong propulsion inside it, has vague edges; shapeless, as if unseen, contours. No matter how bizarre human actions, motives, apparel may seem in visual media, if the implication of the medium portraying them be that they are taking place in the real world, then these things are eccentric, basically extraneous, not inevitable. The true dynamics of film action easily knit together the most fantastic elements with the most ordinary so long as space itself, its particular shape, is clearly defined *by the action alone*, not conventionally framed by the casual and contingent, essentially static, partitions of the real world.

Of the action in ritual ordeals, we may relevantly note that it has a rigidly imposed continuity; logically, there is no time to dawdle, to turn aside, to ponder at leisure—all problems must be instantly met. Yet K., in *The Trial*, perpetually ponders, wanders, "squanders" his time. This is Kafka's special paradox, this "stolen leisure," the secret of his equivocal dynamics of movement. The ceremonial aspects of bureaucracy, taking up an uncomfortable space on the clock, serves generally in Kafka's work as the antithetic elements of his film-type dynamics that are so close to dreaming. Kafka uses obstructive, time-consuming technicalities, the whole official etiquette of bureaucratic processes, as counterfoils to the paranoid, instinctive immediacies of dream confrontation. Space extends before the Kafkan protagonist, one might say, wish-fulfilmically. *The Castle*, as well as *The Trial*, testifies to this. It is as if the protagonist dreamed up the "bureaucratic" obstacles he encounters in time and space as desirable postponements, physical shields against an anticipated moment of guilt-awareness: the moment when he shall stand in the presence of half-yearned-for, half-repulsive self-consciousness. In the domain of neurotic tensions, the paradoxes and surprises of spatial continuity are always *compressions* of time and space— exactly the "linkage" and "collision" of classic film montage given extra force and acuteness.

In contrast, *2001: A Space Odyssey* is like a boring, metaphorically much overelaborated lecture featuring a supposed object-lesson. It is indeed about a subject that has dreamlike aspects as well as the ordeal pattern common to *The Trial* and *The Time Machine*, but its particular substance is vulgarly sweetened by sensual lures along the way: baits for an initiate who meets death only in mummery because he has accomplished a superduper stunt, a marvelous if ambiguous exploit on which Welles's Martian hoax is a quaint little variation. Movies in general are for those who have failed in ritual ordeals and thus been rejected; just so with death befalling real astronauts, as proved by the state funeral for the three returned Russians who were killed by a technical misfire of their space vehicle when almost back on Earth. The efficacy was the life of their action, not their lives as enactors, since fortune proved them voluntary scapegoats to be smothered in ornate "immortality" as soon as they were again on terra firma.

Kafka's protagonist, K., is a failed applicant in both *The Castle* and *The Trial*. So is Oedipus, not killed but exiled in disgrace at the tragic revelation of his guilt. However, reaching Colonus as an old man, Oedipus is celebrated as a hero and given the highest public honors; that is, the ordeal pattern is reinstated in Sophocles' trilogy through Oedipus' acquired eligibility: his exile has purified him and he is recognized as an honorable survivor. This is the crucial point of mortal ordeals: surviving them with grace and honor through innate wisdom. Oedipus is proven eligible for man's greatest destiny, welcome into the realm of the gods, because he has attained the ultimate wisdom through tragic human experience: the successful initiate sloughs his former personality, that is, to assume a new, more vital one. At the end of *Oedipus at Colonus*, the hero is not executed (as K. is finally executed in *The Trial*); he is endowed with life's supreme enlightenment. No! Oedipus is not, like Bowman, the star of a superficial, super-athletic, super-planetary feat. Oedipus' heroic status, in a word, is internal, not external; subjective, not objective. I am afraid that Bowman is just the newest, naïve version of the antique (and never very interesting) Everyman hero.

The general structure of dream action echoes the purely formal pattern of ritual ordeal: it is action condensed into special meaningfulness, to which no detail, however signally "enigmatic," is extraneous. Take the scene in *The Trial* where K. discovers the Whipper at work as if in some obscure, blank-doored covert (apt to be missed) in a large office building. This sort of dream montage in prose is literally the true dynamics of film as a strict continuity of mental images. Its only "place" is the mind itself. It is by no means, as in Welles's film, an accommodating stage space imitating in three dimensions K.'s strange "visions" and his participation in them. Obviously, the final scene of K.'s execution, ordered without due process of trial (as criminal execution of innocent persons have often been ordered), is a mentally formed ellipsis of space characteristic of dreaming. It is just like the action of K.'s execution itself, an anachronistically toned stabbing, as if the act were a mugging, not an execution (this is Kafka's fantasy), and his executioners a couple of bravos hired by a personal enemy. While irrational and arbitrary in the original context, this act is emotionally and mentally (though not spatially) real.

The "physical reality" of photography, with its automatic imitation of the space witnessed by everyday vision in everyday life, posed for Welles here, as it would have for anyone filming *The Trial*, a disadvantage to be overcome by filmic technique, not a ready-made trait to be exploited by the production of a theater spectacle. Yet a theater spectacle is all that poor Welles, blandly if somewhat haltingly, could make of Kafka's masterpiece. One might think it was a parable of life as lived in a totalitarian state but conceived as a macabre, unmusical comedy. Space in film, my theory says, is not the photographic reflection of external space (space external to all individual human beings) but rather the dynamic relation specifically created by the interaction, physical and mental, of things contained by space; time in film, coordinately, is not duration as occupied by the clock's measurement of physical objects in motion, but rather the duration of the time required for the produced images to represent a limited motion in those physical objects—literally, it is simply the running time of the film. And film space is not that "out there," it is literally the shape of the space in a given film.

7

HERO AND ROBOT
Film Theory versus Film Totalitarianism

In trying to set up a competent theory of film, it is sense-less to believe one has to point to this or that film and say, "That is a perfect realization of my theory." The world is full of well-liked films, flatteringly liked films, and also, of course, of well-liking critics and those de-votees we call buffs: the film addicts; wise men enough, a few of them, but also (more numerously) the pretend-wise. Every film critic, or for that matter every literary or art critic, was at one time in his life a buff, one who had fallen in love with a medium and had not even paused to consider that he required a "theory" about that medium; or, above all, about that favorite film or novel he has seen or read six or seven times. In this respect, those who become film theorists are just like those who become film-makers, since both are very close to the critic, or knowledgeably committed person, that man or woman who has turned to professional taste-making by formulating a facility for uttering opinions about the objects (movies) that have adduced his or her addiction. All the top-levelers are by way of being adepts: people who "know their stuff," who can be called experts. Surely, an expert can feel free to theorize . . . if he likes. . . .

Theorizing is as much an academic occupation as anything else that can be "taught." A facility for theory is quite close to a facility for languages. If one is a professional, a critic or a teacher of film, it is advantageous, if not de rigueur, to develop a language of theory; such a facility, in short, helps one put across one's more controversial opinions. If challenged by contrary opinions, by the sheer blank wall of obstinate likers who prefer their likes to yours, their dislikes to yours, the most obvious and convenient strategy—whether or not you're a professional—is to reply with a general rationale for your point of view, respond with a theory that backs up your opinion. This department—naturally it would be departmentalized in colleges—is called a course in Film Aesthetics or Film Appreciation as distinct from a course in Film Craft or just plain Film-making, in which last you begin—if you *are* a beginner—by handling a camera and being instructed on how it operates so as to produce satisfactory images.

Our technological age, not dependent on a thing like grandeur to be perfectly self-confident, is habituated to think of itself naturally and straightforwardly as "technically informed." Add to "technically informed," "technically informed in a cocky way": the overbearing one-upman, suave or plangent, is rife among us and very detectable. Anyone in a conversation over dinner or cocktails, at a party or a convention, who is embarrassed by some contradictious person unable to see a certain film the way he does, will smoothly—if he's a clever one-upman—slip into technical or professional shoptalk, thus implying that *his* opinions are not defensible only by that "I know what I like" cornerstone, but rather are the result of being better informed about certain relevant, perhaps basic, facts. For "facts" in this case, one can read "technique": that is, ways and means, or what the whole technical patois of the film studios is about. Of course, technical patois gets insidiously mixed with promotion jargon, but that aspect seldom gets noticed. It is as impolite to notice that professionals are being professional as to notice that cripples are handicapped. If some fractious person counters your maneuver with remarks about culture or the filmically misfired merits of an original novel, if he speaks, in short, of general values and the issue of significant content or message, you would be only conventional to meet him with a McLuhan-derived sneer and the charge, spoken or unspoken, that he's a boring intellectual, a mere crank or wildly pretentious and off the beam.

He may well be told, regardless of his credentials, that he doesn't dig the movies. I heard this very accusation, in so many words, leveled at one of our better known serious film critics, and nonchalantly as you please, by his own son. Maybe I exaggerate. Maybe I haven't gotten around much lately. Well, I do know that properly sober professors in the academies hold highly charged feelings about the movies, and to their positive advantage as an art form. Still, such enlightened types of instructor are bound to be, as yet, a minority. God knows, the world is full of pretentiousness, which is a human impulse not in the least particular about its modes. Yet the world is equally full of pedantic unpretentiousness. I imagine there are still professional holdouts who, with the shadow of an apologetic smile, may be expected to say, "You see, I hardly ever go to the movies." Or else: "*Gone With the Wind* seems to be the last movie I saw, and after all, the original novel was no masterpiece." Or: "Bergman? Oh, yes, I suppose he's a very good film-maker, very serious, but he's no more to me, I admit, than a name. At least, I *believe* I've never seen a film of his. I only go to the movies [wry smile] when my wife manages to drag me to one." I actually heard someone jubilantly say—he remains a stranger to me for I refrained from learning anything more about him—"*My Fair Lady* was the first film I saw since Garbo retired . . ."

The above passage may seem a long prelude to my confession that the theory I have been expounding is not intended for specialists of any type. A specialist would not know what to do with it. I fully realize that point. A specialist must have more specialty than a true theory holds. What a specialist requires is a program becomingly titivated with a theory, perhaps unblushingly disguised as a theory, but actually a "this is how it's done" golden rule. With a program having the rank of a golden rule, one has something to go on. With a *theory*, well—so much *depends*. Theories are useful sometimes; sometimes, not. It is even hard to tell if a theory be a true theory. Take Dr. Kracauer's theory. It was not really a theory; it was, almost nakedly, a set program. Professor Langer's indeed was a true—I mean a genuinely constructed—theory. And yet what can be done with it? Nothing whatever. By itself, it simply stands there; or rather, since its essence is instability, it *doesn't* stand there. And there you are: without a film leg to stand on.

Much aestheticizing about film, once the particular idiom is mastered, can be rewarding; it can make one brood. And (at least in the U.S.A.) brooding is a preparation for action. Yet even pretty good aestheticizing, I think, is more apt to make one brood over things accomplished, what they mean and how good they are, rather than over things *to be* accomplished. In the large sense, film aesthetics is an antitheoretical realm in that, while duly sustaining a larger, enlightened purview of the art of film, it offers a kind of guide for making better, more refined judgments, more "accurate" judgments that can't be driven into the corner of "Well, I know what I like—and I simply loved *Shoot the Piano Player!*" (Straight look of careless defiance accompanying such words.) Hence, the total labyrinth of the aesthetically well-structured response to films is too apt to behave like an "appreciation course" fully mastered. It shifts the accent, willy-nilly, to the way of criticism rather than to the way of creation. Have I run into a paradox? Isn't the way of creation the *technological* way? No. But I saw this paradox coming and I am prepared to get round it. There is the technological way and the aestheticizing way, and both may sustain a moderate technical wisdom, but neither is the correct way, the correct *theoretic* way. The really right and serviceable theoretic way is to provide for film a general mode of *inspiration*: a separate groove for the imagination. The degree of inspiration depends wholly in the degree of grasp obtained on the true, the essential, nature of a specific medium. This is bound to stimulate the imagination toward the special uses of that medium.

It is so easy for one to point to Jean Renoir's *Grand Illusion* and *The Rules of the Game,* to Marcel Carné's *Children of Paradise,* to Sergei Eisenstein's *Potemkin* and *Ivan the Terrible,* to Jean Cocteau's *The Storm Within, Beauty and the Beast* and *The Blood of a Poet,* to Vittorio de Sica's *Bicycle Thief,* to Federico Fellini's *Satyricon* and that director's *La Strada* and *Cabiria,* to Ingmar Bergman's *Wild Strawberries, The Silence* and *Persona,* to Akira Kurosawa's *Rashomon, Throne of Blood* and *I Live in Fear,* to Michelangelo Antonioni's high period, excepting the film he made in the United

States, to Satyajit Ray's *Apu* trilogy and Marcel Pagnol's *Fanny*, *Marius*, *César*, and so on; not forgetting distinguished Hungarian and Brazilian films to flower lately, or small great films such as Jean Genet's *Un Chant d'Amour*, Luis Buñuel's *L'Âge d'Or* and *Un Chien Andalou*, Sidney Peterson's *The Lead Shoes* and Maya Deren's lyric autobiography . . . and to say, "Let *these* inspire you!—let your theory, like your practice, grow out of those films."

Yet I wonder profoundly about the attributed inspiration of concrete examples: too many people like things for too many different reasons. So I have concluded that such a procedure would be wrong, because to analyze the above-named films by the severest standards would be to expose their defects as well as their incontrovertible virtues and outstanding distinction. All that such an assessment would accomplish would be a standard system of rating. And that would be a theory-injected aesthetics. What I propose is an aesthetics-injected theory. This will allow me, I think, to tackle some of the above-mentioned films as theoretic illustrations. Every created film, after all, is both a corpse and a living act—and part of the living act, though the part least likely to be seen and appreciated, is its theory; or rather, *the* theory in which, with other films, it spontaneously, probably unconsciously, participates.

After all, what is the "literary gift"? Words. Words, that is, in the advanced art of their use as language. Ezra Pound—whose mature literary gift I have already here, in a sense, condemned—is so exalted an artistic figure in our century partly because he consciously labored to show, in so many words, just what the art of language is, so that he was theoretically reviving that art even as he was illustrating it with his own creative product, climactically *The Cantos*. Great artists may, in this way, be great teachers. Pound likewise expounded a theory of how to read. Marcel Proust, for his part, emphasized theory by constructing a new sort of novel based—to be quite literal—on the psychology of words, or words as the vehicle of memory: "the past recaptured." His was a theory of the novel not as a series of notated physical acts and moral relations, given the shape of an action plot, but rather a series of memory mechanisms erecting an elaborate verbal plan: an illusive structure that was a single grand piece of architecture, not made of stone or other substance, but of air—that is, the brain's densely lucid air. Art, whatever its resemblance to our externalized life, to that life's spatial design and time elapse, is intense subjectivity given an objective hold on life by endowing it with a form separable from life, a form having its own time and space. Film is *one type* of such a form; films are various entities illustrating, participating, in this type.

More: Film is a type-form that, not accidentally, is close to the so-called psychological novel as well as to the quasi-aesthetic forms of the psychodrama and the "living theater" and to painting as an "environment." All the recent formless forms of art, minimal art, the demi-arts, are strategic substitutes for art, tours-de-force that represent the desperation of insistent but undersubjectivized artistic impulses. Underground films, as a popular bane rather than an avant-garde boon, share in this movement of boastful pseudo-subjectification—*art* (that is, objectively formalized subjectivity) *at any price*. Small, independent-minded film-makers, disdaining, at first, commercialism and sincerely admiring "film poetics," have felt the curious and positive pressures of our age as much as have the most commercial, the most professionally involved, film-makers. The density of this pressure, so far as art goes, is concentrated in the popular fetishism of imitating (a) external life and (b) common life. It is dedicated to reducing the margin between art and reality to a point where, however blurringly, they merge and seem to flow together. This rather "ups" the space concept of film by ignoring such things as "borders," hence spoiling all the distinguishing technical marks of a "story."

From the old-fashioned space-adventure serials, more than a quarter century old, to the huge technological vanities of 2001 (compact with studio tricks), the commercial film has hacked out a path to the stars whose most vivid implication is that some super jet plane, at a time not too distant, will carry thousands of ordinary Earth beings to the moon with as much éclat and safety as have ever been associated with those exceptionally favored humans, the astronautical experts. To the *moon*? I mean, of course, to still more distant "oases." The exact aesthetic status, and the perhaps disturbing sum total of moral implications, of this particular achievement by mankind is not to the point, in the worldly sense. What is to the worldly point is the transportation of material bodies to splendiferous distances and the "theory" that, in this way, a certain crucially important, indeed limitless, communication is being achieved. Communication! I ask:—with what? With the future? And what, pray, is the *future*?

The speculative ironies of this process, of which even the commercial film has become aware (vide *Planet of the Apes*), are just as little to the point in the great popular film world. That mass brain of which I spoke above—doubtless a bit contemptuously—has resigned itself to the idea, indeed one might say to the theory, of what current idiom terms "power failures." Something, sometime, somewhere, *has to give way*. It's in the nature of things. Why? Well, because mankind is not perfect; anyway, not

yet. Such a thought, such an abiding morality of tolerance, is a way of soothing the embarrassing and dis-
tressing manifestation of the human disease I have been
calling spatial paranoia, a disease active, I believe, from
the most distant Earthly times to the present moment.

When a society is organized against this broadly irksome, deep-rooted paranoia, it may mean a revolution—
oh, yes! But the upshot of that isolated if victorious
revolution, as in the Soviet Union and China, takes
the form of things we have dubbed the Iron Curtain,
economic isolation and so on, as seen from outside; and
as seen from inside, a form of the crudest, most old-
fashioned way of solving the quarrel between great or
small tribal enemies: simple, thorough extermination of
the hostile group and systematic forms of brainwashing
(when necessary) one's own group. Brainwashing may
pass for what kinder urges to improve and civilize the
superior animal, man, historically term education. In our
strictly contemporary world of factional societies and nations, it is a very special thing to conceive a disinterested
theory of any kind of higher work, a theory to remain
independent of political concern and the stiff bureaucratic supervision which, regardless of scale, that concern naturally invites.

It is not just a grotesque fiction that, in a politically
oriented mystery thriller, *The Ipcress File*, a man is im-
prisoned in a hermetic little box of a room and bound to
a chair so that artificially induced hallucinations are supposed to unhinge him and compel him, through a sort of
automatic terror, to divulge his secret. Of course, this is
a particular feature in a counter-espionage system of the
most advanced kind, yet it is actually a new version of
a very ancient activity: inducing the confession of guilt
through the most horrific physical torture. It may seem
odd and facile to cross-reference the situation of the

man trapped into a perilous psychedelic experience in *The Ipcress File* with Bowman of 2001 trapped in his Space Pod and enduring the psychedelic consequences of superspace conquest. If I do thus cross-reference the two situations, with their closely comparable patterns, it is to italicize that the paranoid nature of man's mental experience—today, in the future or long ago—relates logically to the totalitarian state as a social organ eliding spatial megalomania with spatial paranoia.

To return to Earth: Not only trapped professional spies and intelligence agents are under fire by such drastic devices as that in *The Ipcress File*. There are far more insidious, well-disguised methods of attack to be directed at someone who shows signs of personal dissidence, especially if they are aggressive signs, if their mode is habitual public expression. Beset by disturbances big and little, in nominally peaceful and nominally belligerent times, the arts have had to resort to what moral philosophers think of as strategies; that is, calculated ways of survival and prospering under more or less adverse conditions. The artist too is cornered, and sometimes treated, like a spy—how subtly, ambiguously, he *is* a sort of spy, I have been trying to indicate. But brutal and overt persecution is by no means the only tactic adopted toward him.

It is not news that, at this hour, the "radical arts"—which is to say, the arts concerned with social problems and with exalting minorities to public recognition and all sorts of status—are being patronized in great hunks by the cultural bureaus of the rich foundations that give away money. It does not take a very radical political viewpoint to define this situation as one in which threatening social elements are being bribed to keep the peace, to tolerate the reigning status quo, provided they are allowed various public forums, nominally of an educational or artistic character. Thus we have had, in the last decade, a formidable growth of black theater (now extending to black, that is *totally* black, movies) and black education; not to mention the steady moral propaganda for the tolerance of blacks tending to equalize them economically, if not also socially, with whites.

This is no place to go into the ironies and contradictions of such a white-establishment program in behalf of the black minority (which, after all, is so major). But the point does relate to my theory of film because such rehaulings of that ailing thing, the capitalist world establishment, make a group of compensative mechanisms for the ancient human disease I think so central to filmic phenomena: both temporal and spatial paranoia. We must remember that one of the inalienable provinces of mankind, tending to concentrate itself in small groups and individuals, yet a still identifiable "tribal" institution, is that of fantasizing; for example, using fantasy as an automatically empiric theory of "safety" both passively and aggressively. Magic, in brief, is simply a primitive theory of the universe with man at its center. Safety, then, for just what, just whom? Why, for (besides the individual) the tribe, the nation, the government, religion, and those fluid and several human-group interests we call trade and economic prosperity, as well as those we call the arts and culture.

Promptly, I must point to the whole abstract art movement as a strategy by artists—those dedicated preservers of the quality and power of subjectivity—to preserve the high standards of sensibility threatened by the photograph, which, even as it seemed to triumph in the field of portraiture, gave the craft of mirroring the world's objects in enduring form so very common a look: a look that made conventions static in the unimaginative sense; barren, lifeless, with no room (such was the initial reflex) for idealizing or romanticizing. Photography wished to make a conquest of the world of reality? Let it! What, in fact, animated the ensuing abstractness of painting style? Its basis was geometry. Yet long before the nineteenth century, geometric principles of structure for "building" human anatomy as well as spatial compositions were formulated by master painters. Hence (inspired by the strange obsessions of Vincent van Gogh and Paul Cézanne with inventing structures more than they copied surfaces or imitated appearances) first the Fauves and then the Cubists, desiring complete liberation from photographic-retinal art, simply excised all retinal copying from painting and regarded the geometrically based armature (man and nature as a set of hieroglyphs) as the *sole subject* of painting. Therefore the objects we know as Cubist paintings and Abstract-Expressionist paintings are merely simple transferences of subjective ideas into objective forms.

I do not contend that thus abstract art eliminates the human reference, the reference to objective life; in fact, I have always maintained the opposite. There is a constant *passage* back and forth from spectator to art work that makes impossible a total abstraction from the realities of human subject-matter; indeed, such total abstraction itself would be a triumphant form of robotism and that is virtually inconceivable; it is the *futile ambition* involved with robotism that we have to fear. In painting, even the most commonplace geometric humanoid figures are not precisely or necessarily robots. Even in this sphere of conscious subject-matter (*robot* represented as replacing *man*) there is a dynamic and continuous exchange that prevents any specific robot-identity, however technically stable, from being static. By manipulation (a certain kind of skip cutting), human movement recorded on film can be made to look jerky and mechanical, perhaps ridiculously or repellently so, perhaps amusingly, according to the subject and the way it and its context have been revised by the mechanization. Satiric and ironic reference is a psychological element, moreover, often used with the robot-idea and never to be ignored; the artist's intention, through plot and style, will determine all this: the artistic quality, the moral inflection, the relative scope of the idea.

To modern spectators, certain portrait photographs of very old vintage look ridiculously robot-like because the primitive camera necessitated a subject's holding very still; besides, the new invention placed more responsibility on the sitter himself than did the old invention of painting. Painting was a gradual, a patiently and easily revisable process; photography, on the contrary, meant everything was decided in the fraction of a minute. Photography, at first, tended to make the sitter too self-conscious. One should note, moreover, that seventy-five and a hundred years ago, the value of photography as an item of antiquarianism, old photographs as romantic charmers and delicious camps, simply did not exist. Photography was a recent scientific invention and therefore a great novelty. Very quickly, having become the movies, it began competing on every artistic level; with the stage and the novel, even with the circus, as well as with painting. Academic painting flattered itself that photography could be absorbed; after all, in classic painting, beginning with the Renaissance, there arose an ideal of realism based on anatomic accuracy. Only eventually, with the age of reason and the rapid growth of science, was the old ideal of "accuracy" exposed historically for being more idealistic than accurate, more romantic than realistic. It would take time, however, for a complete revolt against the sovereignty of the retina, and when it did come, it would rely only marginally on exotica, as a phase of Cubism relied on African art.

Pre-Raphaelite painting absorbed the technique of photographic (or let us say retinal) accuracy while utilizing the most romantic, even fabulous and exotic, content. Its political and social attitudes, once "radical" and "progressive," evaporated into the deadly earnestness of revolutionary Marxism. With Art Nouveau, which came along as the new century approached, a decorative style quite replaced anecdotal human themes—as romantically conventional as these were in nineteenth-century painting—and used a subjectivizing strategy by creating special backgrounds-for-living: actually, in the modern sense, *environments*; for instance, Whistler's Peacock Room; which is why, in some ways, the Pre-Raphaelites of the 1850s can be identified with the Hippies of the 1960s and 1970s. Both represent skip-time and skip-space revivals. In important respects, the Hippies are still anti-urban and their proliferation in big cities is not a sign of partiality for cityscapes and their polyglot cultural resonances, but rather a behavioral tactic taking advantage of the tolerance of the democratic metropolis, its easy way of absorbing the most diverse communities.

The thing we call "life style" today is but a set of conventional terms for society's renewed, as it were refired, effort to maintain certain subjectival traits, "tribal" traits because they resist the transmutation of the human into the world-robot, the type-slave of a world system. As of 1971, the totalitarian state is the only broad application of this concept of universal robotization: man as the completely objectivized slave of fascist bureaucracies (see Fritz Lang's film *Metropolis*). The current furor by minorities, major and minor, is—however we estimate it in particular cases—a *planetary* furor. Even today's contention between racial tribes, as scandalous and bloody as it may be, as anachronistic as it may seem, actually provides a block to the advance of world robotization. What the minorities themselves do not realize (since fanaticism is not only part of their life styles but a dynamic law of their being) is that a thing like documentary film, among techniques that can be utilized as propaganda, has only the most *indirect* bearing upon the status of free culture, and in fact can function, come into being, *only* in a liberal democracy. For this reason, the true theory of film must reject the documentarist viewpoint as minimally relevant to the direct creation of works of art, to the active formation of a high, independent culture. Élitist? This culture is élitist only through natural selection. If the masses joined up with it, they would not be the masses.

The disconcerting, rather sudden, switch in painting style as a connoisseur value from Abstract Expressionism to Pop Art becomes quite plausible, if no less lamentable, if we consider Pop Art as a strategy identical with the historic strategy of abstract art—that is, a continuous and aggressively revived *subjectivity* that is the fundamental rule, the very law, of artistic creation. That subjectivity took an abstractionist rather than some other form, as the new century took shape, was only a particular historic coincidence. Art will resort to anything to maintain its identity; in that respect, it is like a plant whose roots instinctively find whatever source of water is available. It is not that one can make a facile metaphor for art as a biological instinct; no, it is an organic function of its very own.

The art process is literally and corporeally the translation of a pure subject into a pure object. The subject originates in the artist's head, it ends in the world of all objects; that is, it really *begins* there. Art in itself as an organic object never pre-existed as given. It is an entirely new object and therefore it has to be created in toto; it is a reflection, it is "realistic," only in the sense that its *ingredients* are given. Every work of art is like a gastronomic recipe produced in the kitchen: the dish itself is as distinct from the sum of its listed ingredients as a living human being is from the various inventories of his body: anatomic, nervous, chemical, etc. Why? Because the dish depends upon vital conditions, certain relations, as much as do all the generic factors of physiology in a human individual. A badly produced food recipe is a robot dish. So is a badly produced concatenation of technical gimmicks conceived as a movie plot; it becomes a more or less atrocious robot movie whether or not it is nominally about robots, or mechanical men.

We must examine this point carefully. For me, a robot is symbolic of a merely contrived and trivial movie, no matter what its demonstrated technical resources, or a bad national government, no matter what the efficiency of method by which it maintains internal social order and economic prosperity. For me, a documentary tends to be a robot film because of its passive imitation of retinally received appearances and the great intellectual limits it sets upon its own planned shape and range through this same attitude toward reality. Lately, a film theorist with a leftist background, Jay Leyda, has gone so far as to extoll and explain "the compilation film." His book* is simply an application to film of complex research methods giving order to whatever statistics about the world may be transferred onto photographic and voice records; it is an earnestly filmic sort of

---

* *Films Beget Films: A Study of the Compilation Film*, New York: Hill & Wang, 1971.

encyclopedism. But it makes film technique an aspect of technology, not art, because its true function pertains to sociology and its scientific subdivisions—say, racial and religious psychologies—not in the least to art; and not, I would add, even to high intelligence.

Documentarist ambitions, even if ingeniously well informed, must halt at a certain stabilized level of world intelligence. The level is logically fixed by gauging it to a special audience's intelligence, which means, further, that its facts, its truth, its moral virtue, have all been rendered objective by imposing on them certain strict collective measures. One doesn't have to see a specific documentary film devoted to drug addiction, its statistics and experimental cures; one can imagine one. All it can do, at the best, is to generalize a given set of case histories by testing their factuality and judging their typicality so as to put all this knowledge in a form that persons of very modest education, teen-agers and adults, can understand. To fiddle around with *too much* technique might be self-defeating, for something might result strongly suggesting the pleasant rewards of drugtaking: what is now called the psychedelic experience. This experience—telescoped by 2001—is simply the artificial experience of inner space; that is, the chemically simulated reflection of the "magnitude" attributed to outer space.

Quite aside from the problem of social health and sanity—whose reality cannot be denied—the technological transformation of a compilation film about drugs into a fantasy film about drugs points to a subjectification that parallels the effects of the drug itself on its addicts: see a movie titled *Revolution* and notice the avenues that open up; see one titled *The Trip* and notice how those avenues, in the name of comic-strip fiction, were indeed opened up. Then there is the considerable number of

"A-head" or "acid" films, one significantly called *Head* and including *Performance* and *Gimme Shelter*. Not by chance is the rock star, Mick Jagger, in both the last-named; it is just that *Performance* is sophisticated Pop fiction, a weirdo, and *Gimme Shelter* a "documentary" that displays the double face of rock ecstasy and drug ecstasy, and how sinister the underside of both faces may be. In the latter, a mortal knifing takes place before the camera as a climax to the chaotic end of the Altamont performance.

From the viewpoint of the human individual, choice eventually and inevitably presents itself in all cases of drug addiction. The "good" effects which are superlative and the "bad" effects which may be equally superlative offer simultaneous attractive and repulsive forces within a single order. Instantly, one notices that precisely this is a general characteristic of human experience and in art works supplies a major plot-energizer. Many, many sensations in the world besides those due to drugs offer antithetical and difficult consequences that evoke the world, literally, as a moral labyrinth. The identical structure is true of all initiation rites, whose moral psychology and moral purpose span vast periods of time, however the form of the rites may have changed, however symbolic they may have become. Drugs, in fact, have often been associated with religious mysteries, and in pagan times provided a mechanism of direct access to ecstasy and allegedly to the god himself.

A drug, however, is but one subjectivizing mechanism and may have nothing to do with artistic creation. Even when a drug and such creation have been combined in certain individuals who produced works growing out of drug-taking (such as Poe and Rimbaud, Coleridge and de Quincey), the combination appears as a rarity and is held suspect for obvious reasons. My only purpose in bringing up drug addiction as a film subject is to show that a drug is simply a physiological toxin with a subjectivizing structure that aligns it as logically and naturally with imaginative inspiration, its pleasures and works, as with medical correction and its works. All sorts of psychopathology have the same socially alienating, privately aggrandizing nature; that is, lunatics and withdrawal cases, while objectively "undesirable" because socially embarrassing and as a rule humanly pitiful, are still persons who assert a certain subjectivity as a personal decision entailing private advantages. I need not expatiate on the evidence by which lunacy is associated with the scientific imagination as well as with asylums, and how much power lunacy has had to inspire poets and other artists. In the film world, Robert Wiene's *The Cabinet of Dr. Caligari* remains as a little classic to compare with the Poësque fantasies of madness—madness as a rational strategy no less than a great poetic enrichment.

Where, now, does my theory emerge? Not from the clouds of a quandary but from the sole clear brightness of a quintessence. The true psychedelic structure, if we orient it to film, *has nothing to do with drugs.* The drug experience—take even Cocteau's romance with opium-smoking—provides only a chemical metaphor for the natural operation of the imagination, or mental creativity, as a wonder and delight of visual dynamics and its sequential patterns. With a drug as the *only* animator of internal space, the mind is too passive; it is in a helpless state of dream and cannot act of its own accord. In art, the mind *must* act of its own accord. I am not trying to give an ornamental glamour to my film theory: this matter is one of accurate, and quite basic, distinctions. We can look to surrealist experience in general, to Samuel Taylor Coleridge's *Kubla Khan* and Arthur Rimbaud's

Season in Hell as equally archetypal. These works are very close to the filmic operation, and for reasons historically relevant.

Photography, by which I mean still photography, had the great shock of novelty and seemed as much a scientific as a quasi-artistic achievement. There was a vast restimulation, however, on the emergence of the cinematograph, in that the previous static field that photography produced was replaced by a dynamic field. However extraordinary seemed this new automatic mode of "recording history," it was soon suggested to the sensitive (as Élie Faure's classic essay illustrated) that the possibilities of cinema were "endless" in both spatial and temporal senses. A romanticism inheres in the first responses to any great discovery; and because of the cinematograph's immediate popularity, both its fact-finding and its romance-building held a large dose of naïveté. The circus wonder of the new visual invention very soon had this "realistic" and "reportorial" medium reproducing stage magicians' acts both fragmentarily and in the form of *Arabian Nights* fairy tales. Georges Méliès' *A Trip to the Moon,* a standard item of the archives today, was explicitly a Folies Bergère parody of scientific exploration and of course it utilized crude filmic illusions. Also there were absurd if valiant attempts to provide a sort of visual journalism in which sensational international events, such as the revolt of the sailors on the battleship *Potemkin* (the subject of Eisenstein's film), were "reconstructed."

It is good never to lose sight of these historic elements. Obviously, to the aesthetically minded, the one thing that early film magic lacked was the true spontaneity of a creative medium. It slavishly aped two kinds of "given" reality: magic acts and everyday sights—the more commonplace the latter, the better. This dual personality of a medium simply reflected its mass function; it was something new to amuse the world public and it defined the first step toward television. Faure's concept of an illimitably photographable space and illimitably photographable time, going forward as well as backward into human history, was simply the "magic act" of cinema on the most spectacular scale imaginable. If a Parisian laborer or housewife of 1905 could have seen one day's television programs with time out only for meals, he or she would have thought him/her self in the ultimate paradise of entertainment, commercials and all. Yet the implications of Faure's visionariness were contrary to the true nature of cinema as an imaginative instrument. It was only the rosiest, richest possible brand of banality that Faure "prophetically" foretold. Today, one must admit, there is a film antiquarianism. If archaic film fantasies are cherished as period camp, it means that élitist subjectification has been at work during the decades; audience response has creatively isolated the charm of poetry in these same naïve film fantasies.

Gathering due speed, the dynamic field of the film took its inevitable evolutionary course by occupying the technical provinces of the stage and the novel and cultivating them in workmanlike manner. At first, the patent vulgarity of the new medium fended off creative genius despite occasional inspired notice by connoisseurs. The very first apprehension of the seriousness of film was of the surreal type because it was clear that a serious and richly potential instrument was being treated like a toy. The magic carpet tricks of early cinema held the poetry of the fairy tale, as we know, but not merely as a commodity to entertain children from eight to eighty. After all, many an old "entertainment" film appears to us today, whatever period charm it may have, as strikingly robotlike both in plot and performer movement.

The dada/surrealist sensibility appeared in film even before its official formulation in art circles. This was true even though surrealist precursors such as Erik Satie and Alfred Jarry had been operating in other art forms before an epochal elision between film and avant-garde ballet took place in the classic avant-garde film *Entr'acte*, made by René Clair to show audiences between the acts of a modern Swedish ballet, *Relâche*. The expected scandal, of course, took place at the première. It was interesting to note this dada/surrealist tradition being revived as recently as 1958 when *Dom* (a brief work by two Polish film-makers) made a calculated and sophisticated parody of primitive film movement by varying speeds as well as skip editing and by treating life as a sort of animated collage of archaic hieroglyphs, partly taken from old movies.

It was no casual joke but thoroughly inevitable and right that serious artists, Marcel Duchamp and Man Ray, should appear as performers in *Entr'acte*. Certainly, Duchamp was soon to give up the art in which he had already distinguished himself, Cubist painting, while Man Ray had already made a film with abstract light forms dubbed ray-o-grams, and would proceed to make surrealist films, one of them, *Les Mystères du Château du Dé*, anticipating the love game of the much later, avant-garde oriented film *Last Year at Marienbad* by the novelist Alain Robbe-Grillet and the film director Alain Resnais. In the 'twenties, that decade of film's coming of age, the artist appeared as partly performing clown, partly performing madman, in specific revolt against the bourgeois establishment that was surely evolving the popular commercial film—evolving, that is, a mirror reflection of modern civilization that would, in fictional terms, be set at an average intelligence level, just as the documentary film, in parallel evolution, was already setting itself at the corresponding level.

If we take head-on the issue of madness as a state describing a type of human mental/physical behavior, we simply isolate in all the arts the thing known as passional obsession, typically libidinal and typically criminal, typically dreamlike and typically mortal. We see it in the already mentioned Poe-influenced *Caligari* (1919) as well as in the archaic French serial admired by the Surrealists, *Les Vampires* (1915), which showed gang warfare in nightmarish style and provided, with anonymously black-sheathed figures of male and female criminals, a cast of Freudian dream symbols. There is no question but that art tends to rationalize madness, to systematize the most extravagant and dangerous passions, especially erotic passions. Part of the "art madness," we must note, is the conscious assertion by the artist himself of nonresponsibility to anything but the imaginative workings of his own brain. Essentially, this is behind the theater-of-cruelty rationale of the *revolté* Antonin Artaud, in that the artist's subjective independence, carried to its ultimate, could only be interpreted as an act hostile to common human interests, those very interests studiously ignored by the artist.

Purely conventional art, on the contrary, tends to reflect (that is, imitate) the forces of spatial and temporal order that rationally hold all excess (especially individualistic excess) in restraint. The thing that defeats even this highly systematic effort of the establishment is its own willful if unconsciously motivated sabotage by the modern fantasy film of time/space exploration already much discussed here. This exploration must be under the control of robots, else it would get out of hand and lead to some of the catastrophes which Kubrick kept out of 2001 but which occupy less psychedelically inflected films of the same type, films that show those far-space misfirings corresponding to ordinary lunacy, natural disasters and power failure on Earth.

The science-fiction genre, in or out of film, is destined (with a fate now much realized) to cope with that combined spatial megalomania and spatial paranoia that I define as mankind's oldest known sort of self-harassment. It is in Bowman's story in *2001* and in K.'s story as told in Welles's *The Trial*, both films being in different ways "horrible examples" of human and imaginative failure. The only really effective antidote for such failures must come from individual genius and authentic imagination. Coleridge's *Kubla Khan* is alignable with the Surrealist films *Un Chien Andalou, L'Âge d'Or* and others simply because all these art expressions proved that the most extravagant and illogical visions (things perhaps quite chaotic in other versions) can be controlled and produce a harmonious effect *if completely subjectivized by expert craftsmen who are left free to do their work.* The very title of a Man Ray film, *Emak Bakia,* is much to the point here: the two Basque words of the title mean "Leave me alone."

Possibly it is appropriate at this point to mention that the work ritual of an artist, in its intensity and selfish exclusion, approaches madness—is, at least, one of the passional obsessions. A film that is properly put together is therefore, frame by frame, a series of mentally put together physical steps appearing as images *that in toto do not pre-exist;* as soon as film-making becomes a mirror for physical steps that patently do pre-exist, it is *improperly* put together and can only partially succeed as a creative act. That the fiction plots of naturalistic novels or the ineptly termed social novels are planned to give the illusion of human behavior as it literally happens in the objective world is, when not a transparent artifice, a silly documentarist pretension. If Flaubert, because he heard about a woman's suicide in a French town, proceeded to contrive a silken mosaic of words, phrases, sentences and paragraphs, something with a story line and hence a "novel," inspired by that suicide, it was only to state, when asked about the lady's true identity, "Moi, je suis Madame Bovary." Try imagining Shakespeare giving a like answer to the same question concerning Lady Macbeth, Cordelia or Cleopatra, and you will gain some sense of the progress made in the conscious subjectification of the art process during the past four centuries.

Film, it can arguably be said, first arrived in the form of the still photograph as an easy way of imitating the imitation of painting—that is, reproducing the optical image of external objects as they struck the retina, while from the still photograph, the moving photograph developed to extend this triumph-minded rivalry of the camera with the brush, to the camera's advantage, by adding something that the brush could only suggest— as indeed brushes proceeded to suggest by imitating the blur given moving objects by the still camera: Futurist painting and the time implications of Cubism's multiple-view arrangements. Such painting styles were stages in the process of art's conscious subjectification and led logically to the ultimate subjectification now known as action painting, from which even the geometric layout of earlier abstract art disappeared, as if it seemed too much related to architecture and the "city plan" of the objective world.

The reader must not think that I am propagandizing for extreme abstractness and that my film theory as a world force is thus a plea for an art so cryptic as to be incommunicable to all but an élite few. First of all, I must affirm here the definition of aesthetic pleasure as finally and necessarily produced by an intuitive, not a rational, type of recognition. Music by itself is an art of total abstraction insofar as its resemblance to all sounds that are not musically organized is accidental and irrelevant. Of course, it is the musical sense that causes us to detect harmonies, melodies, arias in "accidental" or unconsciously musical sounds. The charm and power of music constitute a mystery: the same mystery as that cast by certain color combinations, their shapes and proportions. But the identifiable image, the identifiable human situation, the traditional patterns of human drama—none of these is excluded from the operation of a world film theory as I conceive it.

It is best to proceed, since I mention tradition and the mechanical act of simple identification, by italicizing what I specified above when citing Flaubert's remark about himself and his heroine Madame Bovary. After all, obviously defined abstraction in any visual medium offers no problem of identification with objects, with anything external to the work. Apparently, naturalistic and rational orders, orders using "mirror images" of the preexistent, such as classical painting from its beginnings in the West to the Renaissance and nineteenth-century academic painting, are "subjectivized" not merely because they are illusions of objects and objective space—not the external world itself and what fills it—but because they have the particular identifying mark, true of all genuine art, of style. It is *style alone* which separates imitated human situations in art from human situations as they exist in the world. Idle fancy or dreaming, or a drug, can purvey a certain quality to what is registered of the external world, but it will not purvey style to it unless somehow, however "intuitively," the conscious mind devises a plan for it and keeps that plan under control. The above expression "imitated human situations" is therefore not quite accurate. Art style may have elements of imitation, untransformed mirror imagery. This sort of degenerate style is what doomed academic painting and caused the twentieth-century revolt of the visual arts.

It is why, for example, photography was originally identified as an inexpensive version of painting (the portrait memento) and an inexpensive version of reality (the common memorandum). Probably it was part of the professional paranoia of the academy, thus a "professional strategy," to imagine that photographic likeness could be achieved by a machine as well as by brush and pencil. If a still photograph impresses us with its composition, its general plastic feeling and particular design, that is because someone trained in optical observation has, in a "decisive moment," abstracted from the stream of his optical consciousness some passing aspect that fortuitously made an appealing, satisfying plastic form. When, moreover, a still photographer frames off an aspect of inanimate nature, such as a countryside, the result is artistic and creative to the extent that his technical mechanism, the camera, and his intelligent eye have combined their resources to produce—to *extract* as it were—a distinguished image that was inherent in pre-existing nature but that stayed there concealed and inarticulate till thus consciously disclosed.

It is doubtless unoriginal to say that art is not *imitation* but *emulation*. Still, to say so is to touch upon key matters here. The nuance of highly stylized art, literary or visual, is that of a much heightened, indeed psychedelically gauged recognition of precisely the real, the "preexistent." If we take Oscar Wilde's vivacious, incredibly witty farce *The Importance of Being Earnest*, or novels by the mature Henry James—say *The Golden Bowl* or *The Ambassadors*—we find the delight of what it is perfectly just, I think, to call a great psychedelic experience;

which is to say: *style* is nothing if not a consciousness-expanding mechanism that is, and always was, in competition with drugs. James in *The Golden Bowl* creates a mesmerically overwrought verbal pattern of a type situation in human drama in which, as a greatly conscientious artist, he has included dialogue—a perpetually practiced conversational idiom—to match the careful and elaborate nuances of his third-person narrative. Part of the spell is the very simplicity of this conversational idiom, the fact that as vocabulary it is amazingly limited, and yet, as a feeling pattern, as music, is so prodigiously scrupulous, so downright extraordinary, so incredibly manipulated. Finally we must grant that this dialogue, fashioned with a supreme craftsmanship, exists solely to mirror the truth of perfectly comprehensible, perfectly ordinal human thoughts and emotions. James's prose is a moving picture of common things viewed most uncommonly. Remember that James considered ethical decency and moral purity things possible for human beings to attain even if at the price of great effort, perhaps suffering. Therefore no effort of the artist was too costly to ascertain the reality of this possibility by demonstrating it in imaginative form.

This point is essential to the theory of any art. Whatever the objective field of the work proper—pages of printed words, an oblong of canvas, a reel of film—it must be submitted to the laws of its *space proper* and has no subservience to *space improper*: to, that is, the laws of our objective planetary space, such as the law of gravity and the vacuum outside the stratosphere. I do not thus hint at any destructive opposition. The energy of one set of laws does not seek to imitate another, much less reproduce another, any more than to destroy it, but to be *coordinated* with other laws and their energy. What is the thing called "illusion of reality"? It is only the witness's, the spectator's consent that one type of formal dynamics, the "artificial" type which is art's, be accepted for that prevailing (and departmentalized by science) in the real world. True, when at times we speak of hallucinations, we may refer to a momentary quandary in the witness, when technically he cannot tell if his vision, or his hearing, the artificial (that is, one proceeding from technical means, like that of a film image); supernatural (that is, one created by divine or demonic force); or simply real: a normal material object rather than a sheer image or "object" of air, perhaps a mirror image. Thus my definition of the world's robot-nature, essentially the computer-nature, is that it is both an image and an actual object of *confusion*—confusion about *all reality* in the complete spectator: the world's misled witness.

The artificiality of art is the opposite of the robot's artificiality. That is why the robot is a sort of devil image, pseudo-divine, its presence and activity a concentration of superstitious awe, fear, at once a symbol of megalomania and paranoia. Much has been said here about the robot-hero and the fantasy art enclosing him: Dr. Caligari's somnambulist is as much a robot-hero as the mechano-mythological beings that popular movies offer us as denizens of some other planet. It is well to note that he is animated and directed by a "lunatic," that is, by some sort of creator with a lunatic dream—even as Dr. Frankenstein who produced a live monster from a legally certified corpse. It is no news that such robot men are—from the viewpoint of a huge part of the world's film audiences—symbolic vehicles, and that what they symbolize is lust: erotic violence and the violence contingent on it. The "Golem" legend already mentioned is that of, as I said, the hero who is tribal savior; so his violence, while it may frighten women who fear being raped, is actually a political violence.

Thus, when I say that the robot-nature, at bottom, means confusion, I imply paranoia but also passion; I imply sex as well as politics. I imply art, non-art and anti-art. It remains to be seen just where the *popular confusion* lies, just where the *élite art* . . . To Salvador Dali, who collaborated with Luis Buñuel on the famous *Un Chien Andalou,* we owe an important insight into these affairs. Dali himself called it the paranoiac-critical method, and he expressed its portent epigrammatically when he said: "The only difference between myself and a madman is that I am not mad." The same thing could have been said by Poe, Baudelaire and Rimbaud or any artist who obsessively explores the extremes of passion and "supernatural" vision. The relation of Surrealists to both madness and manic behavior, as well as to the supernatural, is matter for exact analysis and bears decisively on the present argument.

The space in which a lunatic lives, and which tacitly he "sees" in some sort of objective way, is obviously related to dream space and drug space no less than to magic-carpet, or fairy-tale, space. It is space, as it were, unfettered from true dynamic laws, from the limitations of specifically human and planetary existence. It is, in general, perilously "unstable" space. Only *film* can make stable space out of this peculiar instability through visual means. Other arts hint it, approximate it; film shows it. We know how easily art has produced formulas to deny "limited" physical laws by manipulating what is known, in a word, as illusion; in art, it is voluntary illusion, while in pathological experience it is involuntary, and known as hallucination. What the Surrealists did when they took over the new field of film for their activities was simply to manipulate what technically might be called mad hallucinations as if they were normal actualities; not illusions, but realities; realities, I mean, *only as human activities*, not realities as also external space and the material world.

Hence the lack of a manic style in the form of such human actions as occur in *Un Chien Andalou*. There is something sober and studied about the step-by-step of the film's irrational plot, which has deliberations and rest points quite untypical of the Pop style of melodramatic action based on crime and lust. And yet there is no tiptoeing about as in horror and crime mysteries, where persons move in the dark, quietly, on their grisly errands, and so on. As to pace and nervous reaction, *Un Chien Andalou* moves rather like a bad but not uninteresting day in the life of a high-keyed housewife. Its most important image of emotional violence, not surprisingly, relates to woman's paranoiac fear of rape. This is when suddenly we see a woman cowering against a wall, very agitated because (as the camera duly but not abruptly reveals) two men are approaching her, each dragging behind him, attached by ropes, a grand piano on which lies the corpse of a donkey.

The excitement of the action melodrama of film has been long celebrated and overcelebrated. It is headlong —that is, it hurls itself into real space, the world, not altogether sure of just what paths it can find, just what paths it may best utilize. Here is one thread of the confusion of which I speak. The action of the film melodrama is predominantly in the "chase" mold: someone pursues, someone escapes—someone seeks, someone hides; both may be shooting, or somehow fighting it out, seeking to survive and triumph. The conventional climax is often a doubly deadend catastrophe, a climactic smashup that abruptly ends the affair with violent accident and very possibly death. The excitement it evokes— something shared, we should note, with a certain equality by spectators and participants—is that of the "game" but converted, in this world of crime melodrama, into the "game of life and death."

The above paragraph is only a much simplified statement of what the antique tragic melodrama (the original music-plus-action, song-and-dance thing) has been historically changed into by the movies. Once, its chief significance was that it involved man's responsibility to the gods, who set him lawful example and punished his departure from it. As we know, of course, this function of a divine justice, operating like a real lawcourt even in the Theater of Dionysos, was signally ironic, owing to the myths that attributed to the gods themselves the crimes for which humans and demigods were punished by the Highest Authorities. Hence there arose the "Euripidean" irony that the gods were simply arbitrary and self-willed; as they are, indeed, in the Trojan War portrayed in *The Iliad*, when they take the side of this or that human participant because of some previous personal commitment or family tie, so that the gods themselves were part of the old tribal pattern of the blood feud.

Not altogether in passing, we should note the "madness" of the old tragic heroes—Oedipus goes temporarily mad and mutilates himself on learning his guilt; Orestes experiences a kind of madness when, having murdered his mother and her lover, he is pursued by the Furies, and Hercules is made mad and slays his own children. Madness has no such status in modern times. Now the hardest (i.e., the least plausible) thing to establish for a hero is "tragic guilt." Neurotic guilt, yes. Passional and hysterical guilt. But not tragic guilt. The principal guilt of our times, you see, is *confusion*. It is the ensign worn by Kafka's protagonist, K., and he deserves it because his richest guilt, when all is said and done, is that he has voluntarily as well as involuntarily submitted himself to a system which is an objective quandary, a path of perpetual indecisiveness; he has not resorted to the subjective paths open to creative individuals, but bowed the knee to the world's incoherent dictation. K. is the paradoxical hero *par excellence,* because it took a true creator, Kafka, to think up the negative subjective irony of his positive objective situation. This world-wide confusion is a sort of public health situation, a question of moral ecology, and the principal "medicine" for the megalomania and paranoia it breeds universally in groups and individuals is not just communicated, disseminated, by the popular media: this "medicine" *is* the popular media—TV and the movies above all!

part iii

CRISIS AND TRIUMPH

8

THE DUAL WORLD OF ART AND REALITY

Despite the note on which I've ended the previous section, this book's purpose and my own greatest dream remains a very positive world theory. A precise, an indelible world theory. Not a robotlike, technically overproduced, confused and confusing theory, but simply a true one. Creativity is not a medicine of any kind, a corrective, a panacea for whatever ills. It is part of health itself. It is the tissue of health. That is where the paradox of a contemporary writer such as Thomas Mann, who repeatedly connects art with disease and morbid illusion, must be carefully studied and read for its true symbolism. The theory of disease, in relation to art, must be inspected and cleared up. The virtually timeless concept of therapeutics, for example, historically crossbreeds physical with mental ills and hence has bisected itself into a department of mental medicine and one of physical medicine. The result, of course, is that these departments find themselves curiously overlapping. So with sanity and insanity; so with the real and mythic super-structures of social and economic health.

Just when we think health and disease are much too facilely connected in rhetoric, we look more closely at the subject of the rhetoric, its physical and sometimes mental data, only to decide that, however we partition off elements of health and disease, in any particular area of the body personal or the body social, they become at some point vague and confused, they overlap and mock the desire of the investigator that they be clearly defined, that they keep, as it were, to their assigned territories. Perhaps this is the lesson of Thomas Mann's fiction: it is self-conscious creativity. It is an art myth. And its myth is that art itself includes disease the way life does, the way life includes all sorts of death and perhaps, hope-fully, resurrection. This inherent paradoxical structure of life and art's creativity is what ordinary men find the hardest to accept—which is one reason why doctors are still regarded as miracle workers.

Still, when we drastically generalize about any sub-ject, we will soon arrive at the sphere where the claims of the physical body, that having measurable weight, come first because they look easiest to define; certainly, their problems are, technically, the easiest to handle. So it would seem! And so it seemed when the chief problem of far-space flight, next to propulsive power (the power required of a very heavy body to cover very great dis-tances), became just the opposite. It was the problem of relative weightlessness at rest, so that the astronauts, pas-sengers of that "very heavy body," could anchor them-selves on the Moon, whose gravity is much less than the Earth's.

The chief limitation of the documentary view of film-making—a limitation, it seems to me, profound and fatal —is that it treats our inevitable subject, the world, as if it were only this given, this vast engineering feat of which I spoke above, that feat of which space travel and the "conquest" of other planetary worlds is the latest contingent phase. The only climate it defines is that in which the human *body* lives and thrives. Actually, every art, due to its specific viewpoint, has a subject different from something so general. Film, like the other arts, is about the climate in which the human *soul* lives. This climate includes material aspects, of course, yet the very existence of all that we call illusion, imagination, creative works that have a meaning beyond their specific physical properties and the report of those properties by retinal observation—all this testifies that there *is* another world; truly, by metaphor, this other world is a shadow of the physical world but has totally different laws of behavior insofar as its shape, the manipulations it involves, the ways in which it rests and moves, become stable *or* unstable; all such elements set it apart from the real world, whose link with it is a mere family resemblance. These same two worlds, conceived as separate organic bodies, are as independent yet related, as if they were brothers living on opposite sides of the Earth.

This is something I wish very much I could put in terms immediate and simple for everyone to grasp, including documentarists and those with theories counter to mine. Maybe, in the final sentence of the above paragraph, I have succeeded. Anyway, something more concrete would be to take a film such as Vittorio de Sica's *Bicycle Thief*, whose surfaces, if seen as social documentation, comprise only a pathos story with a political moral: the humble worker, in bad times when his trade has failed him, and unsupported by unionism, may be sorely beset and perhaps utterly balked by his supposed guardians, the state (mainly the police) and the church. The modern institution of the welfare agency might rescue him from his dilemma (here the tool of his economic support, a bicycle, is stolen and he can neither recover it nor buy another) but such a force of succor and restitution is absent; nor is the help of the trade union of any utility. The worker (who uses his bicycle to paste up posters around Rome) is so desperate—finding that all the church offers is banal spiritual consolation—as to resort to a fortuneteller who, if she cannot divine the location of his stolen bicycle, may at least be able to tell him whether or not he will recover it. Her reply is enigmatic; the worker is baffled by it; and while he does thereafter find the bicycle thief, he never gets back the bicycle.

This might be called the external, socially underwritten and documentary shape of *Bicycle Thief*. But just what I have reported of it above would be dreadfully flat, and filmically only "decorative," if the story did not have a specific plot that defines it as a soul experience; that is, a finely worked-out peripetal pattern of a sudden revelation of personal guilt, by which the bicycle's owner, yielding to the impulse to become himself a bicycle thief as the only answer to his dilemma, is immediately caught —and then forgiven on the spot by the bicycle's owner, so that he goes free. There is, you see, no economic solution—in fact, the economic plot is instantly dissolved in the moral plot because the moral plot *does* have a solution: stealing private property is a universal crime and even the virtuous, the heretofore "innocent," may be driven to it by misfortune.

One subtlety by which we may value the power of what is symbolic, especially in the form of visionary thought, is that the fortuneteller to whom the worker applies in this film delivers in riddle the nature of the situation by which he will achieve his moral enlightenment. For he will regain his bicycle, she says, "either right away or not at all." Instantly, on emerging into the street, he sees the bicycle thief (*without* the machine on which he glimpsed him peddling away), chases and finally catches him but cannot have him arrested, for lack of material evidence. Later, in stealing the bicycle which he sees unattended by a street doorway, *he* becomes a bicycle thief. He does not regain his bicycle at all since he does not immediately regain it from the original thief. But he causes another bicycle owner to regain his bicycle by stealing it. The worker himself, caught and forgiven, has *regained* nothing but he has *gained* something else: his soul.

At first sight, it might seem hard to determine just the way in which prime authorship can be attributed to de Sica, the director, for the film was based on a novel by Bartolini as adapted by de Sica's sensitive collaborator, the script writer Zavattini. The film action is simply unfolded, without any tricky effects, but while so simply felt, it is also very subtly felt, and only de Sica's filmic imagination could have made its modest, sober narrative the very impressive thing it turns out to be. How did he do this? Simply by tenderly realizing how much the repetition of stealing a bicycle would mean to the subjective interior feelings of the original bicycle's owner if *he* became a *thief*. The worker has wished to arrest the man he felt morally certain that he recognized as the thief. When the situation is turned round, when he is the thief, and another the property owner, he sees that the difference is something that took place in a property owner's heart; it does not matter that now this man has *his* bicycle back while the man we already know, the worker, still lacks his. What matters is that the worker, in his own heart, can now forgive the original bicycle thief.

When first I wrote of this film in much the same vein as here, I did not become aware of any special theoretic value. But now that the occasion of film theory is before me, *Bicycle Thief* seems rich with value of its own and with valual reference to other films of similar subject matter. Another film by de Sica, almost as fine, was *Shoe Shine*, which concerns two growing boys of Rome who, caught being foils of a black market racket, are sent to reform school. In the school, their friendship pact made void by separation, and seemingly ruined by intervention, they experience a drama of personal jealousy so intense that, finally, both having escaped, they quarrel and one accidentally kills the other. Perhaps de Sica moralized a bit too much on the documentary side by emphasizing the social and institutional conditions that force the two boys into their moral trap and its showdown. But surely, speaking humanly rather than sociologically, it is the pure nature of the boys' emotional commitment to each other, their passionate response and its tragic outcome, that really matter; in other words, it is the dramatic design of the interpersonal relationship that charges *Shoe Shine* with its higher human meaning, its larger aesthetic form, not the tacit, morally rather naïve, social commentary. Two other boys, suffering the same accidental fate, the same human indignities, might have responded quite differently; indeed, we see many other young inmates who suggest a very contrasting human caliber. De Sica chose the pair that displayed a particular, and particularly meaningful, *subjectification* of the common reform-school conditions in which the boys find themselves; it was owing to this specific subjectification that his own subjectivity prompted him to make the film.

The very fact is striking, I think, and sheds here special illumination, that de Sica belonged to the postwar Neo-Realist school of film-making that took on a pronounced social-documentary complexion. One beautifully wrought film, *Forbidden Christ* (1952), has been virtually forgotten because, while it invited (with its local postwar theme about Partisans who resisted the occupying Germans) a routine Neo-Realist treatment, its maker, the novelist Curzio Malaparte, brought so intensely subjective a calculation to its story, yielding no place at all to documentary fact-fondling, that it seemed, set beside works of similar outlook, rather too personal and tightly formed, too much committed to its "Christ" theme of self-sacrifice, even too "arty," to be welcomed by advanced public opinion. Yet, as plot-particular as it is, as amazingly ingenious and competent as coming from a novelist suddenly turned film director, the work is perfectly plausible and surely very genuine. It does not cheat the realities of its social environment nor does it cheapen its theme by facile melodramatics. Malaparte's quite sincere and successful film is a sad illustration of how an imperviously intent artistic subjectivity may alienate even those equipped to appreciate true values because it declines to pay the expected eye-service to the politically oriented film cults of the moment.

Roberto Rossellini was another distinguished Neo-Realist director, so undisputed that he may be considered the movement's prime initiator. The identity of still another Italian director, making as it were a belated concession to the predominance of the Neo-Realist school, is even more to my present point. This is Luchino Visconti, who came to films from the Italian stage, so that his luxurious sensibility may be termed operatic in timbre. More traditionally Italianate, more sensual and demonstrative in technical expletiveness, he was interested in "overwhelming" audiences, in reaching down deep through emotional agitations. His film manner tended to be lush, and of course expensive, so that some of his films (especially the ill-fated *Senso*) now seem headed for utter oblivion.

But the fact that in 1948 he made *La Terra Trema,*
doomed (at least for the foreign market) because it was
so long, demonstrated that filmic subjectivity, even when
wayward and luxuriously mannered, could discipline itself and express more than one style. Only a deplorably
cut version of this film achieved what is called commercial distribution in the United States, and even so, only
film buffs welcomed it with any clamor. Visconti is, of
course, the author of two fairly recent films, *The
Damned* (only partially successful) and *Death in Ven-
ice* (almost wholly successful), which patently separate
their maker from any suspicion of surviving Neo-Realist
ambitions. *La Terra Trema* is like a tour-de-force, therefore, in being an austerely naked account of the life crisis
of peasants brought about by the threatening economic
forces of our time. One can the more liberally and indifferently grant that documentary buffs simply loved *La
Terra Trema* when one considers that a man with a
gifted theatrical instinct, a man with true subjectivity,
made it what it is, and that a documentary theory did
not.

Ready sanction of this opinion comes from the first
film from Visconti to win an international success, *Rocco
and His Brothers,* which could easily have stemmed from
his study of the peasant temperament in *La Terra
Trema.* It treats the disintegration of a displaced peasant family coming from southern Italy, where their farm
has failed, to "make good" in Milan. The main portraits
are of the two eldest sons, both grown and natural males,
but one, who becomes a professional prizefighter, "bad,"
the other "good," or morally true-blue, who eventually
follows his brother into the ring. Visconti's intimate
touch is never banal or just vulgar. The bane of commercial cutting (aggravated by the film's foreign language) at first made it look out of shape in spots, super-

ficially summary, but the complete version restores its authority. The mother is beautifully characterized by Katina Paxinou, an actress likely, through training and temperament, to look "theatrical" as a peasant woman, but one who, for that very reason probably, Visconti could deal with to the right ends. Surely, Alain Delon, as the stalwart son who succeeds in the prize ring where his brother fails, is made to look as little like a popular juvenile lead as possible.

I would never call *Rocco and His Brothers* a model film of any kind, but certainly, for its dramatic impact and deft technical ways, it remains impressive and memorable. The lurid plot, taken by Visconti in stride, includes a gang rape of especial ugliness, a gruelingly prolonged fist fight between the two brothers, and climactically the black sheep's murder of the little whore with whom he is carnally obsessed, and who has been the technical cause of all the trouble because she *really* loves the "good" son. Visconti is nothing if not audacious; so when, to top all this with anticlimax, he has the wretched black sheep, having committed the murder, come home to mother and brother during a party celebrating his brother's winning a championship bout, and provoke a literally screaming scene of family vituperation and recrimination so that everything seems to collapse, one has to admire the director's gift for building up emotional power and then—with perfect dignity—exploding it in one's face.

In behalf of my theory, I note eagerly that the sole human subject here, documentarily defined, is that of an Italian peasant family trying to achieve middle-class comfort. Obviously, this theme would mean nothing, and might well have been an offensive bore, without the particular theatrical gifts Visconti brought to making a film of it. These gifts, however imperfect at times, are his own property: *they are subjective.* And the force of this film depended on its exact frame-by-frame composition as much as on the script and the actors. Someone—in fact an *author*—had to be in control of the end-product and relentlessly vigilant. This is the law even of the Marxist-dialectic theory of Eisenstein, Pudovkin, and those other early film masters of Russia. What do the studied, almost pedantic aesthetics of Eisenstein's carefully choreographed action mean in *Ivan the Terrible* but a formal principle, an artistic order, for Marxist, Anarchist or any other sort of leftist film-maker? Fine pictures, moving pictures, of leftist revolutionary inspiration have also come, so to speak, from satellite-based film-makers.

I would pick out, as the best of these, the Hungarian film-maker, Miklos Jancso, three of whose films have been seen in the United States as of this moment: *The Round Up*, *The Red and the White* and *Winter Wind*. Perhaps the finest, because the tensest and leanest in form, is *The Round Up*. Actually, concerning the roundup of armed rebels placed in an isolated prison camp, the film has a most remarkable physique, a dramatic use of open space and constriction, of rigid outwardness and elastic inwardness, of opposed forces suspended yet always "working," with the simple rhythmic plot ending in a grand, collective gesture of tragedy. The action of *The Red and the White* is looser, more in the open spaces of field warfare, with many guerrilla brushes, dashing squadrons of horsemen and picturesque incidents, so that its dramatic line tends to get lost in the facile familiarities of the War Movie and the Horse Opera. Still, it is scenically striking and composed by a true film craftsman. *Winter Wind*, on the other hand, is a magnificently crafted portrait of both an individual hero and the plot-situation which his profound anarchist temperament creates about him. In other words, it makes a beautiful image of the violently subjectivized, powerful individual operating on those around him who form the collective objectivity. All are conspirators of deadly intent but the strongest one, the film's protagonist, is too mysterious and arbitrary a quantity—as if he were already a tyrant of some kind—so that finally, despite the aura of magic about his established identity, he is suddenly, at the decision of a committee, liquidated with a certain pomp.

One of Jancso's most artistic filmic inventions is in *Winter Wind* and it may be—this "bodyguard camera"— the most vivid proof of my theory of film as totally subjective imagery. It is merely that the direction of the camera's gaze is always as if itself watchful, ever circulating in the given spaces of the film's restricted scene (the conspirators' headquarters in a country villa and the adjoining countryside), hesitating, scrutinizing, only to move on quickly, ever turning, as if stealthily, like a person sworn to a coming action, and guarding *its* safety as well as *his* life. We, the audience, are aware that a habit of the protagonist (with whom of course the plot and the camera are the most concerned) is never, on strict principle, to allow anyone to get behind him since it might be a traitor who will kill him; thus he must be always alert, on the move. Those of us filmically sensitized are due to realize that what the camera is doing is imitating the hero's movements as if it, too, wanted nobody behind it, wanted always to have the world in front of it, as if it were indeed the hero's bodyguard. This is why the film begins to seem veritably like a dance, a complicated choreography of watched and watcher, of persons entering and leaving the visual range as if in circles. This is why, at times, one may be moved to wonder what happens to these men—and these women who are present, theoretically, to serve the men sexually— when they are *not* watching, thinking, plotting . . .

when they are supposed to rest, sleep, make love, *just live . . .*

Every filmic device, such as this one of Jancso's, is sufficient to the need thereof, and offers itself in the conscious guise of a "device" only if that guise is first required by actors aware of the function of the action in which they participate; that is, the device must first represent the shape and identity of a subjective motive, else it will look imposed, unnatural, a piece of camera show-off. This applies to every kind of film, whether irrational and fantastic in action, whether an "impossible dream" or quite ordinarily plausible, realistic, "representational." This allows, then, for the most extraordinary things to have filmic representation without seeming abnormal or "mad." A key is set; a style is initiated, developed; a mood takes form and dominates. My reasoning is called "circular" but here it happens to be authoritative: anything is permitted to the imagination, and seems logical, if it is something the imagination can literally put together and offer as an organic-seeming form. We are on territory whose peculiar legitimacy the Surrealists intuited, and of which the erotically compulsive male who goes berserk from frustration, in *L'Âge d'Or,* is the hero.

The whole point of this film by Luis Buñuel is that a purely subjective, or mental, order is established from the outset by assuming that the frustrated libido—a man and a woman making love on open ground are pulled apart and the man arrested and taken away—will precipitate itself on a career of action mixing mental fantasy with physical deeds, while at no moment will it be actually distinct whether the protagonist's manic behavior is in his mind or in the objective physical world. In *L'Âge d'Or* we see that, as for physical action, what takes place after the love-obsessed male is arrested and he escapes his detainers, rushing then to his mistress's home, is all quite "possible," however "implausible" or "unconventional." He wants to make love to his mistress and apparently will commit any act, however basely rude or absurd, however violent, in order to do so, and in revenge on others for balking him. That this hero is also characterized as profoundly infantile simply lends a color of human credibility to his outrageousness: he slaps the face of his mistress's mother when she accidentally spills a drink on him and he is infuriated into protest when the polite necessity of listening to a little concert interrupts his preliminary love gestures in a garden nook. Restrained by the party guests, at whom he throws things, he finally hurls out a window all the furniture of a bedroom where he is locked. With calculatingly cutting irony, the music to which the guests have been expected to listen is love music by Richard Wagner. Buñuel thus agreed with the Surrealists that the artistic superstructures of sexuality, as sponsored by the bourgeois élite, represent a substitute for the true libido, whose great cause is dogmatically taken up by this film's erotic "madman."

The Surrealists did not imagine that such things as take place in *L'Âge d'Or* and *Un Chien Andalou* either did or should take place in the physical world. Yet it was all important to show that they *might*, that they *could*, take place there, and if they *did*, they were certainly justifiable. The anti-art which the logic of their situation dictated the Surrealists should espouse, in opposition to the art they disdained, did not necessarily mean that they themselves did anything (even when their imagination was at its wildest) except exploit *the mental order*. In also creating a kind of social ritual, the Surrealists, performing quasi-irrational acts as if they were today's Happenings, were in the identical position of sadists who find an erotic creed, a bible, in Sade and indulge in light sadomasochistic pastimes, but never actually commit any of the criminal acts of which Sade perpetually wrote in his books. Some people do commit crimes they read of in books, but this fact does not prove that, with those same books unread, the crimes would not at some time have been committed anyway. Murder, like love, issues not from the written word, but from the human heart.

Once the Surrealist painter Roberto Matta, before an audience in Paris, let himself be branded with a hot iron as a sacrificial act of Surrealist faith. But such a physically experienced ordeal has been rare, if not unique, in Surrealist annals. As a rule, the Surrealists' antics did not go beyond the "mass" demonstrations of today when believers in a cause chant slogans, make symbolic gestures and may (like the hero of *L'Âge d'Or*) propel themselves into more or less literal acts of violence. *L'Âge d'Or* itself offers us a profane glimpse of Jesus as the nobly suffering, and supposedly satiated, leader of the dreadful orgy in de Sade's *120 Days of Sodom*. As an interpretation of Christ, this is, of course, a conceit. What it actually does, as an image displaced from one context to another, is to let sadism (and incidentally surrealism) profit by stamping it with the sacred nature of ritual. However important or unimportant Christ may be today as the central figure of a universal religion, anthropology can display him as but one of innumerable beings, in diverse religions and cults, who have been ritually—perhaps physically, perhaps only in form—sacrificed by his own group or an enemy.

One of the really significant things all Surrealist endeavor pointed out (and still points out whenever a surreal film classic be shown) is that, in service to positive mental and emotional drive, the ultimate commitment be made in a *form* of some sort. When in 1958 the film *Dom*, made by two Poles, Jan Lenica and Walerian Borowczyk, won the grand prize at the First International Experimental Film Festival in Brussels, many observers were shocked because *Dom*, treating even live action as animation, was constructed like a Surrealist toy; as a film, it lacked the force generated by the Dali-Buñuel collaboration, while also it lacked the poetry and the stature of Cocteau's original avant-garde film, *The Blood of a Poet*. It seemed a contrivance, a conceit. In a way, it was just that. Yet the filmic principles by which it was created were ingenious and perfectly sound. It startled if only because it was aesthetically pure in a day when the experimentalists of the avant-garde ranks were growing very careless about form and regarded the poetic quality as something bestowed automatically on any young film-maker who had wanted to write poetry but somehow, instead, started making films.

In this book, I have insisted on subjectivity as my primary focus in order to counteract the widely prevalent allegiance of film-makers to so-called objective reality, while, if truly defined, their real occupation would be data distribution, fact fondling and injustice collecting, yielding us superficial and fragmentary glimpses of the world. Such a world, naturally and through accidents, is caught equally well in a state of dishevelment or "normal" orderliness. So a subjectivity which is merely passive, blindly egotistic and arrogant, thinks as elementarily and futilely (so far as art goes) as a street demonstration which presses into vocal slogans and a few banners and picket signs the message of the cause or group represented. Rudimentary signals like those can be expanded into documentary films by recording them with a film camera, but they cannot become works of any real power or particular meaning, certainly not works of art.

If their enthusiasts believe in them as art or even as a meaningful anti-art, they are mistaking pious social sentiments, on right or left, for artistic objects. Works of art attain their authenticity, as I have said, by translating important subjectivities into equally important objectivities. Yet if the subjective begin by being mostly *wishful thinking*, no amount of laborious objectification will convert it into a work of art.

It has been arresting in the past few years, when the destiny of Andy Warhol has got around to finding him eligible for museum retrospective shows and classifying his works with the world of art, to hear him characterized as a "dandy" as if in echo of the way a famous predecessor, Marcel Duchamp, was often characterized. What ought to be emphasized is the immense difference between Warhol and his predecessor. Duchamp gave up the profession of painting after demonstrating that he was indeed a ranking professional: a cubist painter. Thereafter, he joined with the Dadaists and the Surrealists in making "objects" and "ready-mades" while, privately, he devoted himself to chess. Warhol more or less consciously gave up the idea of art, however, just when he began taking himself seriously as a professional; that is, one who makes a livelihood and a public reputation by producing art objects—perhaps I should add, original art objects. Prior to that, he had been earning a living by doing derivative ink sketches for books, phonograph albums, fashion pages and a shoe manufacturer; in short, by working in commercial illustration. When, around 1960, the Pop Art movement began showing itself in force as a sort of commercial-minded Neo-Dada school, Warhol resurfaced as one who produced easel works by various quasi-photographic and stamping methods. It was only that, like Duchamp, indeed as if he were mimicking him, Warhol ceased doing things with his hands or emulating in any way the traditional plastic effects of art instruments; not pen, pencil, brush or even the paint can's spurt, pour and splatter, were of use to him. Not only did he substitute for these creative instruments the methods of mass production by imprinting, he also eschewed any modern abstract composition of forms—and in fact he dumped any kind of art composition aside from convenient "framing." Effects of grandeur were obtained by empty space, mechanical dilation and repetition of image.

He had turned, in brief, to a type of interior decoration, except that this decorativeness, for some mysterious reason, appeared in the shape of easel and mural works. Naturally, then, he became more of a factory supervisor and idea man than an artist (he dogmatically repudiated being an artist), and when he began making films in 1963, he duly became more an entrepreneur and stage manager than a film-maker. Hence, if he could be termed a dandy and be said to have elegance, his dandyism and elegance were rather those of a bohemian Beau Brummel than an aristocratic Marcel Duchamp. If he declined to do his own work, delegating that labor to assistants, he could justly be compared to the gentleman who is so wealthy (and such a dandy) that he employs a valet to dress him, and keep him at top presentability. Warhol may be an imitation Duchamp, but if so, he is one with an unintended vengeance. The shallowest person has his deepness, I suppose, but malice (even the most devious sort) is something I'd very reluctantly attribute to Warhol.

Even the élite public, which in general "supports" the arts, spend most of their time making money or speculating with it, so that it has little—less and less, I should say, as time passes—creative subjectivity to allot to tastemaking. It has been much easier, with the advent of Pop

Art, to let the professional makers of the art themselves, rather than the professional taste-makers concerned with the art (the critics), make up their minds for the collectors: it's actually economical, a way of eliminating the "middle man." The Dada-Surrealists succeeded beyond their wildest dreams and in a style which the originators and their disciples, if still alive, would repudiate as modern vulgarization. But then, the great bourgeois who became the patrons of modern art, from Impressionism to Abstract Expressionism, had always been compromised by their special position as arbiters of taste. Once, remember, there were, rather than critic-connoisseurs, princely and priestly connoisseurs. The great collectors of our present age, beginning in the late nineteenth century, had advisers beside them, as Isabella Stewart Gardner had Bernard Berenson, or else, like the formidable Albert Barnes or Peggy Guggenheim, they were individualists with an egotistic desire to rely on themselves. But all the collector-connoisseurs I have named are, in 1972, pretty much old hat, unavoidably old hat. This type, even more than the professional critics in the same age group, have become remote because they behold a breed of collector less demanding, less intellectual, less qualified than themselves, engaged in making Pop Art the newest avant-garde—as thinly as that avant-garde has been spread with the passing of time. Perhaps a bit of minimal art, a bit of color-field painting, can be added to *their* collections—but not a Tom Wesselmann, a Roy Lichtenstein or an Andy Warhol!

A very good reason for this lies in the fact that spatial paranoia is something affecting everyone, although as a symptom of moral disaffection and emotional upset, it is less apparent than temporal paranoia as manifest in an age of instant communication and speed-up in physical travel. It is viable to argue, I think, that minimal art means, in a strong and significant if not total sense, *minimal effort* and *minimal skill*. One color-field painter may be subtler than another in adducing mood and thereby gaining artistic stature. Yet when it comes to Pop Art as inspired by comic strip and wallpaper and advertising art, values are not so ambiguous or difficult to assess. Warhol abstains from direct contact with true art processes the way an agoraphobiac shuns large, open spaces, a claustrophobiac small, enclosed spaces. Warhol's robot film camera is an excellent gauge by which to measure the general analogy.

It is as if Warhol "the artist" were playing possum, or like the chameleon, protecting himself by remaining perfectly still and relying on his environment to efface him. However, Warhol's sort of self-effacement is not altogether a publicity maneuver, a way of acting the shy cynosure to help attract crowds; nor is it merely a social reflex derived from compulsive personal shyness. It is also a pseudo-aesthetic strategy. On his film camera, at first, Warhol imposed both a marathon persistence and a proportionately obvious deadness of pan. He wanted a very limited surface, a still image, or an image with minimal movement, to carry the burden of the message. Above all, he did not want to change anything the camera eye could see, or to tell anyone in front of the camera to do anything, except (for instance) kiss . . . and just go on kissing . . . This was artificially to impose on film an outgrown primitive function which at one time had been overcome by commercial film in two ways: by magic tricks and headlong (usually comically headlong) action and speed-up movement. In the midst of this device, stop-motion (the freeze) appeared as a magic trick of its own—see René Clair's *Crazy Ray*. Relevantly, filmmaking began to sustain the interpretive, the expressive and dramatizing devices as a natural result of its ambitiousness, its desire to compete with the established spectacles of the stage. Yet this energizing faculty—something inherent in a specific medium—has lost caste with the gradual rise of the false ideal of truth-telling (rather than tale-telling) as the film camera's supreme faculty. In their way the Surrealists represented a revolt against the same ideal as well as against its opposite: the faculty of the camera to conceal reality with entertaining tricks and the mere exciting illusion of space-covering—something that issued in film as science fiction from *Trip to the Moon* through *Destination Moon* to *2001: A Space Odyssey*, which seeks to look *beyond* the "conquest" of the Moon. In contrast to Cocteau's use of film tricks in *The Blood of a Poet*, *L'Âge d'Or* and *Un Chien Andalou* never make us aware of the pyrotechnic faculties of the camera: the only subjectivity in these Surrealist films is that of the poetic imagination, the mind itself; the cachet lies altogether in the peculiar, emotionally weighted message of which the film happens to be the chosen vehicle. Yes, here the film is a "reporter"! But what it reports is, purely and simply, mental activity, the internal translated as directly as possible into a limited film vocabulary.

Warhol's school has reverted to old-fashioned storytelling partly through the acquisition of a new surrogate assistant, Paul Morrissey, so that at this point Warholism in the film has progressed to the 'twenties in terms of film technique engaged in relating "plots." Often the small budget of such a film makes it look like television drama, taped or live. The plots themselves happen to be camp plots; that is, various sorts of parody based on the delusion-of-grandeur milieu (with its conscious aesthetic of the Ridiculous) from which the Warhol Studio has drawn its cast of actors. This automatic technical progress toward "art" is made, of course, not in the service of anything that could be called art, but rather in the service of the time-honored commercial creed of providing popular entertainment for the sake of box office. This is no guess or speculation, but the publicly announced aim of the Warhol Studio, so that Warholism is simply competing, on a small scale, with all commercial film-making. The role of mind and imagination is deliberately set at a minimum so that the "subjectivity" attained by Warholism and related types of independent film-making is strictly limited to naïve story-telling, naïve playing up to the fun and adventurism of that very large public for which the comic strip, more or less sophisticated, is the principal norm: a norm that spans, of course, television as well as film.

When the Surrealists simulated hysteria—which they did consciously and explicitly as one of their proud boasts—they managed the simulation through inventive images, astonishing images, images meant to reach the libido and the unconscious; thus, the strangeness and the high pitch found in both Surrealist painting and Surrealist film. Salvador Dali, with his theory of the paranoiac-critical method, was well aware of the paranoiac function of dreams as revealed through fantastic organisms inhabiting immense, as if perilous, spaces—spaces that seem, as in dreams, self-transforming, unpredictable and thus unstable. Most important, in Dali's case, is that his images are drawn and painted with photographic finesse of detail no matter how normal or abnormal they are. Dali made organic distortion and retinal distortion a kind of visual pun, thus opening the way for his assiduous exploitation of complex trompe-l'oeil effects. The trompe-l'oeil (fool-the-eye) pun supplies movement through the instability of shifting from one sense of a given volume or configuration to another. Dali's painted world, consequently, is full of things that seem photographically exact, thus "real" in the realistic sense, and yet organically monstrous if we should take them for anything other than sheer optical illusion; usually they seem to be pseudo-organisms or simple trompe-l'oeils.

Dali's is a kind of multiple exposure, visible in still imagery, but weighted with changeful illusion as well as a content mixing dreads and desires: the familiar ambivalence of value typical of actual dreams; the exposure of one given configuration would be attractive, another unattractive; such a technical identification is itself disturbing, like good and evil qualities (that is, moral instability) in the same person. At the same time, there is a necessity about the feeling of disturbance, which, in augmenting desire, augments the figure of desired satisfaction. Under the constraints of emotional experience and compulsive mental fantasy, people in general tend to grow hysterical—they have hallucinations, they develop phobias, manias and schizoid tendencies; they may end with a double personality. Moreover, they may commit crimes or cut themselves off from others and withdraw to an inner life. They may become, in short, "lunatics" of one kind or another. I have already discussed these human types and experiences as they appear in creative filmmaking, which, in the act of subjecting these types to scrutiny, subject them to control. However, the point about so singular a phenomenon as Warholism is that it has reduced to a minimum whatever may be achieved by creative film through the avenues opened up by mental aberrations, their development and their control. This "minimum" is quite arbitrarily established, as if the true authority about, say, weirdos and withdrawn persons were a film nonpoet such as Warhol, or the maker of *Titicut Follies* (a black-bile documentary about the criminally insane), and not Ingmar Bergman, who *is* a film poet.

The Warholist film camera is the catatonic film camera: the camera that literally *does least* for whatever it photographs. Thus, so far as imitating reality through a medium goes, Warholism makes the passive film camera itself into a catatonic individual, very slow to move, unresponsive to invitation: a direct surrogate for the actual catatonic human being. Here is the film art of Warhol *in extremis*. For the sake of making money—as with the exquisitely titled *Trash*—his camera, under the direct tutelage of Paul Morrissey, has functioned like a gossip columnist from *The Village Voice*, approximating as nearly as possible, in groovy prose, the human adventures to be found in deepdown New York bohemia, where Home Relief, pot and promiscuous sex constitute the agony and the ecstasy, the drama and the dross of life's daily round. Yet the gossip-columnist camera is a mere figure of speech. Actually we have the personnel of Superstar bohemia striving to imitate the old-fashioned underworld life as brought up to date in the minds of the contemporary middle class fond of "dirty movies" and of members of the mod cult who are devoted to the aesthetics of the Ridiculous.

It should surprise nobody that Warhol's opposite is to be found in today's underground film, and that the result should look symmetrical as viewed in terms of my thesis that spatial paranoia is one of the film medium's compulsive, automatically formulated "theories." In fact, the opposition goes straight down the line as if Stan Brakhage and Andy Warhol were two halves of a whole. Brakhage, after a rather experimental beginning with idyllic poetry on film and a prophetic item of the hippie life style named *Desistfilm*, continued with the film camera as an agent of movement—film taken in a moving

vehicle or with the camera swinging from side to side
—and then moved on to fantasies that steadily grew more
abstract-decorative till his work (getting longer and
longer, more and more circular in feeling) reached the
point where great stretches of film looked like so many
parts of a pulsing Jackson Pollock painting drifting in
space. A tour de force, *Sirius Remembered,* plainly takes
up the spatial metaphor by viewing an unmoved corpse
of a dog in a field with shots covering the four seasons,
and then complexly recovering and recovering the same
footage, so that we have the abstraction of a dead dog
varied and repeated in terms of camera movement and
several viewpoints, changing colors, textures, etc., the result (which might have been lyric or symphonic) being
in my opinion a monotonously overexpanded rhythmic
cycle of film shots on a strictly limited theme. Thus do
some film-makers mistake sheer compulsion for development and complexity of consciousness. Such a thing as
Sirius Remembered, even done more sensitively and
cleanly than it was, would have been modest in value.
As it stands, it seems a preparation for the even more
manic style illustrated in Brakhage's ensuing epic, *Dog
Star Man.*

The main action of this film is apparently a man and
his dog engaged in climbing a hill. But the hill (with
man and dog) is really the cosmos in both the microcosmic and macrocosmic senses; again I add that I do
not interpret: this was the film-maker's stated aim. However, the rate by which images change—the general "film
time"—is from nervous to manic. If a startling, perhaps
beautiful, image or gesture emerges, it is immediately
swallowed up by the pace. If Brakhage were dealing
with still imagery, one would have a sensation of hopelessly confused multiple exposure. Hence this is a paranoia oriented more to time than to space, while space

too is involved, owing to the microcosmic/macrocosmic plan: from the smallest possible (ultimate destination of the centripetal) to the largest possible (ultimate destination of the centrifugal). In Brakhage's film work this is palpably a studio fiction; not, as in 2001, a pseudo-interplanetary fiction to correspond with the actual plan of journeys to the Moon and (hopefully) beyond.

What makes Warholism and Brakhagism peculiarly "subjective" are the respective harnesses of time/space paranoia of which they are made, as if they were time/space suits for the film camera: one a strait jacket, the other an automatic-massage outfit. Why does Brakhage seem to exploit a perpetual motion, Warhol a perpetual nonmotion, insofar as their respective products be things "made" within the camera, on the film roll and controlled by arbitrarily modulated speeds? The respective Warhol and Brakhage motives seem to me to be contrasting psychological pictures, of which the film is the medium, exploiting certain nervous/emotional responses to life. These responses are not objectified, dishonestly, through the usual formulas of commercial film, but honestly, according to each film-maker's private constitution. To some extent, this is a definition of what all underground/avant-garde film is today.

The film camera becomes the vehicle of an offbeat response that is technically *pre*oriented; preoriented, that is, in some abstract way. Thus what we have, and what we are expected to value, is the medium rather than the message; or, as McLuhan's airtight jargon has it, we must honor the medium *as* the message. Of course this is ipso facto an evaluation, and so McLuhan's coquettish denial of a value judgment secreted in his "descriptive" analysis is absurd and irresponsible *unless* he admits that *that public for which his analysis is true* is itself absurd, irresponsible and innocent of value judgment. I readily admit that the film medium, as the film message, is the delusion of an uncomputable number of active young independent film-makers in love with doing spontaneous variations on mere laboratory processes. But I add that this absorbing occupation is usually followed without the least thought that the true test of mind and imagination is the intensity, variety and interest the subjective instruments called mind and imagination may impart to human drama as a comprehensive project—a project with truly wide and deep scope, a project about the *total* of human life. Such an art ideal is largely regarded today as impossibly old hat. The contrary ideal of experimental film in 1972 is but one of the corrupt, morbid and arrogant vanities that the now-dated obsession with abstract art has left us as its irksome heritage. Here is a technological hallucination, a technological vanity, which finds its chance medium in the film camera. The technological hallucination is a magic sign against the race's paranoia that grips so many of us in so many ways, through so many media. Still, in any ultimate, true and valuable sense, this magic underground strategy will fail as a "cure." It is only a stopgap measure, like freezing wages and prices in an economic crisis. It is hugely, transparently tentative: inconclusive. At its very best, it is only the occupational therapy of cultural dropouts.

I think the time/space syndrome of the experimentalists may be formulated thus: the hysteria of the phobic (Warhol) *paralyzes;* the hysteria of the manic (Brakhage) *precipitates.* Their twin distinction, spreading its influences in the smaller film world, is to have eschewed the commercial megalomania that provides the regular moral reflex to paranoid sensation as it grips the modern world and of course provides megalomanias of its own. Commercial megalomania leads to thinking in such conscious group terms as have given us the superspace spectacle as modeled by 2001. The underground competition in this vast public field of psychic response must operate on a much smaller scale. But it would be a great mistake to conclude that the new stylists in avant-garde film are either allergic to commercial types of interest or "hate" them in the way the Dada-Surrealists did. There is a very good reason why Pop Art should be called Pop Art.

Popular art hides its eccentricities. It's only that in emulating and competing with outright commercial art, an organization such as the Warhol Studio leans toward, and superexploits, whatever is already offbeat, pathologically tinted, desperate, voyeuristic and sexually obsessive in the common public psyche . . . that psyche which still gloats over Superman and Flash Gordon exploits, pathological violence and sexual extremism (all still much seen in banal commercial films). Warhol once declared that a new film about a futuristic, robotized world (artistic rating: Grade C) was his "favorite movie." His slant is not unique. You will find a number of Undergrounders setting cheap, far-out commercial thrillers above the serious intentions of the modern art film. This, I concede, is Neo-Dadaism, if by that term is meant Dadaism with a considerable difference. One difference is provided by the ascendancy of *camp* as a new value.

That camp has become a very elastic, ambiguous style and a valual category is testified by its suddenly "taking" as part of ordinary speech idiom when only ten years ago it was decidedly sectarian-élite. Camp means parody, but a parody of various sorts and differing intentions. Commercial film's extreme robot-fantasies, in which the traditional human being is pitted against an elaborate mock-duplicate that is part dummy, part machine, are assuredly campy. But one of the aesthetic problems of camp is how large it really bulks as humor, satire and parody. The radical avant-garde, no matter of what incidental persuasion, tends to dispense with subtleties, gradations, definitions and so on, and to rely on pointing and voting to establish its "new" values. This tour de force of radicalism is one of its dangers—it is dangerous to its longevity, for one thing, and it tends on another score to make the avant-garde more of a minority, thus more desperately besieged, more a weapon of guerrilla warfare. The Pop strategy has been to borrow strength from the world of the comic book, as if the robotism, the human simplism, of that weirdly unfunny world could be "taken over" the way the territory of a large gang is taken over by a small gang using cannier, more resourceful tactics.

But doubtless that is another megalomaniac dream— *the little film world's dream!* Warhol may already have become rich on it. I doubt that anyone else has, or will. It *is* a theory. But it is not a theory of film art, or even just film; it is the sort of theory that used to be called a get-rich-quick scheme. One may politely recall the fast buck of timeless legend. Commercial studios, large or small, perpetually have it on their minds. And of course the little commercial studios that are turning out porno films faster and faster—films to which some in the Underground bear family resemblance—regard the buck, fast or slow, as something divine. As always, the film industry continues to turn out its megalo-paranoid myths dealing with man's perilous position in the time/space universe. In this universe, interplanetary war becomes a monstrous first cousin to total planetary war: it's a mere matter of extending the objective field of vision and pretending an ESP concerning "things to come."

To play on the world's paranoiac emotions, on its enshrined megalomanias, seems so simple and obvious that it's doubtful such an activity can be honored by imputing to it a "theory." Superstition would be a much better word to describe the cornerstone of both its logic and its imagination. But momentarily I should like to leave the field of technique and contrast two different yet related responses of the myth-film faculty for situating human destiny in time and space. I refer, of course, to filmic vision where the imagination is employed through fiction to make as total a statement as possible about human nature. This means that I do not refer to the cozy strategies of TV newscasting by which—as Marshall McLuhan has faultlessly put it—"We are there" and "They are here." This is the myth of speed communication through eye and ear as "instantaneous."

The two films I have in mind are vastly different, *The Tenth Victim* and *Antonio das Mortes*. As they are to be used in behalf of my theory, I had first better dispose of the TV newscast as a "radical" theory of film. From the momentary glimpse of a spot-witnessing camera to solemn editorial comment, in which the thinking reporter thinks for our benefit, the TV newscast is a banality, and for many watchers, I daresay, a trivial enough entertainment to fill in between more important occupations. Yet to others, this watching of the world in its woes and its passing triumphs is a veritable passion. Justifiably, I think, one may wonder what such a passion means, how great its moral and its aesthetic values, and thus what importance we can attach to the phenomenon (the TV institution) that arouses it. To heed McLuhan on this subject, one would think that neither aesthetic nor moral values were involved, nor any arguments that might challenge the rhetorical weight he gives it, and that this state of things is due to some self-evident majesty—as if the TV newscast were a giant step forward for civilization in its historic desire to perfect itself!

McLuhan's rhetoric (recently WABC devoted a full-

page advertisement to it in the New York *Times*) devolves entirely on a tacit and most disputable assumption: TV as a purely technological phenomenon, we
are to understand, is so important that it is beyond valual
computation, so it would be pointless even to try to discuss its values. It is as if television were not just a scientific invention that utilized certain electrical factors in
the atmosphere surrounding the Earth to facilitate the
transmission of news—not just an up in the technics of
journalism, but rather a vital change within our planet's
complex of spheric conditions, conditions which somehow eliminated, made "technically impossible," all other
forms of communication, all things such as bookprint
and the stage spectacle and music independent of electric circuitry: music, that is, played before one's eyes
in a hall. Naturally "the medium is the message" if the
watcher/hearer is indifferent to whether he witnesses
Stokowski rehearsing an orchestra or a Women's Lib
demonstration on Fifth Avenue, American soldiers looking wretched in Vietnam or an American audience laughing at a TV Special.

Such a passion for witnessing the sights and sounds of
anything geographically distant, no matter what, cannot
possibly have aesthetic and moral values nor ratings as
to same; it can only be a *technique* plus a *mystique*—
that is, a matter of absolute faith in the performance of
an extraordinary machine. I refer once more to the computer, which is likewise "programmed." Even so, unless
one is already one of the faithful, a convert to this universal pseudo-religion, we must remark that, to so operate,
television must be assumed to have no competition of
value; at least, all other competitive forms would be un-
real, the vanities of decadent backsliders who will soon,
as a breed, die out anyway. Ironically, I can add that
such has been, rather than a truth, simply the delusion

of all universal religions in the past: the wish-fulfillment dream that enough passionate faith in a "church," or absolute creed, will convert all resisters, all enemies, bring all the human sheep, at last, safe into the fold.

Whether the headquarters of this church are at NBC, ABC or CBS, it is absurd to think that it exists except as a technological lunacy or the victim of the deepest poker-faced satire to come along for quite a while. The mistake devolves altogether on a misconception of the nature of unity—to which the term unification bears a necessary structural resemblance. Even when unity is a given condition, it is not always apparent, save perhaps in hints, in various indications that in themselves are to be tested. A blue sky is not, or very seldom, a uniform blue; besides, a uniform blue is merely one part of the blue portion of the spectrum. What, then, confers unity on a work of art? Surely not the mere imitation of the world of appearances, and the less so, the more variegated the prospected world is: the world in sight, the world with which one wishes to deal, to understand and depict. Therefore unity in any respect—logical or aesthetic, elementary or complex—must be attained by unification, or the act of being united. Science and politics have had to intuit and then master this principle of organic usage. For its own part, art must do the same— which is why science and politics were first called "arts."

The other evening I was watching the "Eyewitness News" team perform on ABC and was rather startled to have them flash on one of the various ceremonies denoting the celebration of the Women's Liberation movement, which had set aside a day on which to make itself unanimously felt throughout New York City. One of the chief newscasters announced, with as impersonal a mien as possible, that today "Eyewitness News" had been the recipient of something I think he termed the Old

Hat award from the Women's Lib organizations; this was explained by switching in the customary way to their man in the field, who had a microphone to the lips of a lady who accused "Eyewitness News" of a disrespectful, actually frivolous attitude toward Women's Lib—the ladies had gotten this impression of old, she said, so two weeks had been devoted to critically listening, without let-up, to ABC's newscasts just to learn if their impression could have been exaggerated. No, she reported, it was *not* exaggerated! The frivolous attitude of the nearly all-male team was as reprehensible as ever. Pressed for specification, the lady being interviewed complained, quite truly, that "Eyewitness News" tended to make jokes of, or put joking intonations into, all references to Women's Lib activities. "Of course," she added ruefully, "you joke about everything."

I can understand how shocked the loyal gentlemen must have been at a blow in this particular spot. For that blow was against the very heart of their stock-in-trade—their *style*, their witty presentation, their debonair way of transmitting the worst and the best of news, the grimmest things and the gayest; in fact, it was their talent for performing that had earned them, according to their best means of belief, the last Emmy Award. For this award, the stations had submitted a selected newscast, whole or in part, on which the standard and the style of newscasting was to be judged. ABC had won and what they had won with, I recall, ended with the weather forecast bit, which in this case closed with the only female member of the team, Melba Tolliver, joining their regular weather man, Tex Antoine, at his map of the United States and asking him, with a rather hysterical giggle, where Texas was . . .

This in turn reminded me that during Mr. Antoine's last vacation, various members of the team at "Eyewitness News" were enlisted to fill in for him, and that each time, they did so with comically paraded ineptitude, as if the only thing to do in the absence of the lone, true and supreme exemplar was to make of weather prediction a mild sort of clown act. Without difficulty, I think, one detects the working of a formula—the exact formula which won them that Emmy and which it would take a lot of fem lib, indeed, to make them lose faith in. Everyone who watches "Eyewitness News" must know the content of the formula. In a word, it is entertainment. The theater of reality demands its acts, who see, just as does the theater of fiction.

To study the various phases of the way all kinds of news are presented on this station is to learn the secret of a style. What can one term this style? "Debonair familiarity" would probably do justice to it. And a good part of this quality depends on the personalities of the various members of the team: their ease of delivery, their informality, the inflections of those sitting in a comfortable chair lightly or seriously chatting with you, rather than of those burdened with the office of communicating disasters, tragedies, murders, scandals, political events and the war scene as well as robberies, rapes, fires, demonstrations, strikes, prison riots and the latest from the ecological fronts. Can't one imagine the heroic emotion felt by the male members of "Eyewitness News" when one of them has to report, not just that they have been hit below the belt by a ladies' organization but that they have just received from that organization an award, then having to go on, with face as straight as possible, to explain the *meaning* of the award?

All those varieties of unification, however stylish, that derive from paranoid states must be dismissed, I think, as aesthetically inconsiderable if not also offensively inept. The mere act of communication that is electric circuitry, according to McLuhan, is an act of unification. It is not merely that he exaggerates. If we have to grant his point technically, we need not grant it any other way. In fact, it is *only* as technical that we *can* grant it. As a myth of "world unity," it is simply the greatest fake imaginable. The newscast plus the soap opera plus the comedy special plus the old-time movie, and so on, constitute an anthology of anything if not everything, and as such is not a true unification except by the most rudimentary mechanics. One might interpolate: "But isn't your conclusion childishly obvious? Who could possibly maintain otherwise?"

There will be those to maintain otherwise so long as Establishment practices in all fields decline to recognize the paranoid state of their daily fears and instead keep on "in the faith" and invent ever-renewed strategies to convince themselves and others that there are quick and easy solutions to those fears. This is the explanation of the blend of fact and fiction on TV and what has made that blend outstrip the movies as an entertainment medium. The reduced scale of the domestic TV screen is compensated for by the charged flattery of having it in one's living room or bedroom. A viewer's tacit psychology is that while, here on Earth, great and earnest political bodies are perpetually engaged in the task of solving human and natural problems on a global scale, equally committed and durable forces (the so-called Space Program) are engaged in another conquest "out there": solving the difficulties of human passage through interplanetary space.

The time/space metaphor came ready-made to science fiction and now serves the same old historic purpose as military conquest and colonization did in olden times. The creation of a foreign war, like the subjugation of a foreign people, was for long a nation's most serviceable weapon in displacing emphasis from ugly and insoluble problems at home toward seemingly soluble, yet hardly beautiful, problems abroad. The most seemingly soluble problem abroad, you see, was apt to be a decisive military victory for our side and a decisive military defeat for theirs. A war which is not won or lost, like the Vietnam War, but seems to be in perpetual motion, is quite as bad as the worst avant-garde movie whose antics-in-a-vacuum never seem to end: both may well have perpetual motion built into them. True, even a twenty-four-hour movie ends, at least formally, and even the United States' longest war may end, formally, some day. However, I doubt its conclusion, even if it be over by the time this book is in print, will mean an end to wartime hysteria. If there is one achievement of modern peace, it is surely and insidiously this: all of us on Earth have been taught to abide in, even take pleasure in, wartime hysteria. What then could this peculiarly, peacefully consolidated "wartime hysteria" be? It is only time/space paranoia *temporarily stabilized* . . . And now for our true films and my final argument.

9

THEORY OF FILM
Objectified Mind

From that first Five Year Plan of the newly established Soviet Union to the recent price/wage freeze of our own knockabout democracy, the United States of America, the powers of our planet's upper political air have more or less daringly speculated with the future—theoretically, with everyone's future as decided by national boundary lines, and constantly (if more theoretically still) with the race's future. Yet the international repercussions of President Nixon's economic move were instantaneous and not advantageous to the U.S.A. in worldwide terms. Viewed as a long-range strategy, as well as a drastic stopgap measure, the said freeze might work out, but at the moment of this writing the United States and the world must remain in an anxious state of speculation. To speculate with futures—that is a stock-market practice, an economic factor. But every theatrical venture, including movies, is something of the same. From buying a million-dollar lottery ticket for three dollars to making the safest, most cautious stock market purchase, we live in a present which invests in the future and which psychologically, and of course morally, is involved with the tactic of *programming*.

What could the category of science fiction, equally well known to comic strips, the movies and TV, actually mean in terms of theory, if we dare to make that theory an aesthetic one? Now just what—mechanically, descriptively, analytically—is science fiction? It means that the human imagination has devoted itself to the dream of scientific invention as man's chief hope of self-improvement, which includes the improvement of the environment, an important qualification now that atomic radiation, atmospheric and other elemental pollutions have made man's comfortable survival more of a problem than ever. The scientific imagination has usually been devoted to the invention of useful machines—which surely do not have to be catalogued—while the irony of this same fruitful devotion is that every invention, as it multiplies and becomes common, brings in its train a series of drawbacks and even disasters. It isn't just that, while volcanoes may stay dormant and floods are but seasonal, railroad trains, airplanes and automobiles are regularly wrecked and thousands of human lives lost thereby, but also that the consequences of the most peaceful and enjoyable mechanical proliferation—take automobiles and industrial furnaces—tend to be lethal by causing a high rate of air pollution, with the result that special economic agencies must be set up to fight such pollution.

Or, in the world of human health, take the medical discovery of cigarette smoking as conducive to lung cancer, so that one of the simplest boon discoveries of the human mind—the chemical pleasure to be derived from smoking the dried and processed leaves of the tobacco plant—acquires in practice a positive hazard and sets up a new moral tension in addicted cigarette smokers. Well, to think like this is, in a way, to bring human existence down to its most typical material problems, one of whose dangers is that one suddenly gets the sense of floundering helplessly amid platitudes: death and disease are two huge statistical facts that cannot be eliminated from human life or, quite logically therefore, from human consciousness. The point is just not to note them descriptively, in passing, but to *do something* about them.

Quite so! The question would necessarily be: What to do? All responders to it, earnest and otherwise, could not be expected to do the same thing. Variety is the spice of life—and, to give an edge to that blunt platitude, let me add without ado (though at the risk of offending pun-haters) that, to film-makers, it is also the splice of life. Perhaps, in the foregoing pages, I have said enough that is deleterious, ironic and skeptical about the machine as a mass myth, but the special delusion I wish so eagerly to strike down forever is the enslavement of the film camera as one more, maybe the most potent, of those dubious and dangerous machines which are supposed to outlive or transcend their destructive faculty and become man's most constructive friends—and if in the form of television (one might think from what one hears) his *best* friend. Yet how, it might occur to some to ask, is the film camera to be considered at all a *destructive* machine?

The answer is that, in its exploitation of all kinds of horror and terror, all megalomanias and paranoias, on the planes of the latest news and the most daring science fiction, both as deadpan reporter and something inflamed with weird imaginations, the TV film camera daily reinforces, succors and encourages—indeed, flatters—the mental/emotional wreck of our era's Collective Man. At one end of his shattered personality, Collective Man believes that God has all the answers; at the other, that computers and other complex machines—space suits, for instance—have all the answers. Neither belief, as we Earthlings have learned to our sorrow through the centuries, is anything but an immensely puffed-up delusion. Even if it be conceded that nobody has the answers, to go forward merely exploiting the paranoiac states induced by this yawning gap in human and divine intelligence is a very sad, greatly humiliating, error.

What I deplore so much, owing to my sensitivity to the film medium, is that the film now appears as the leading instrument chosen to exploit this lamentable human condition: this abject submission to the terrors of our failure and our deluded, if "joyous," escapes from these same terrors. The very worst of the escapes, whose popularity cannot be underrated, is that everything can, and does, appear in the mask of *entertainment*. Ah, but there are entertainments and entertainments! Entertainments can differ vastly on aesthetic grounds and have moral implications that set each other wide apart —far outside, at times, the magic of "electric circuitry." I think it must be declared and believed that McLuhan's theory of the absolute victory of electric circuitry as a concept utilized by television and the movies is the most cruel indictment ever made of the historic foolishness of man. And if McLuhan's lurking irony is as highly developed spiritually as I think it is, he knows the same of that indictment.

What makes the whole idea of popular entertainment and its dazzlements so foolish, so delusive—so "chimerical" in a really vain and stupid sense? Answer: exactly its pretension that it refers to an abiding illusion of the masses—to an illusion, that is, in the least significant sense of being an illusion. When an illusion is based on the least, has the *least* genuine stability, the *least* imaginative reference and moral virtue, when it is an utterly fake myth of unity, a kind of drug that works on everyone, requiring the least active cooperation from the taker, the least verifiable inclusion of the witness, *then* has the ultimate nadir of "communication" been reached. That the world is brought into the living room by the television set: insofar as this fact is not a commonplace, it is the chief figure of the applauded deception of electric circuitry and is closely related to limiting "belief" to that most elementary of all communication signals: *the label.*

It seems apt to take a cue from the way a certain label has affected art communication: I mean the label on a can of Campbell's Soup. It tells you the kind of soup inside the can, but here its communicability abruptly ceases unless we live in the foolish mythland of the devout consumer. It is a small bit of literary statistical information, is it not? Your experience of eating the soup inside the can then tells you something about the signal—a particular signal, the one on this particular can. A relevant word on this hypersensitive subject: the same thing is true of Warhol's film camera. It is no more than a brand name and wishes (or at least has wished for several years) to tell you as little as possible beyond what you already know or expect of the product it announces. Hence as the art of the film, Warhol's camera fulfills, as nearly as possible, a robot's function. It is, as I have said, deadpan—why not deadcan, indeed, since finished film reels also come in cans? Warhol's camera leaves the interpretation of the imagery to the objects it photographs, so that the emergent film is a special-information documentary.

With art, on the other hand, no matter what the medium, the situation is quite the contrary. Art brings everything internal—in analogy with the soup can, whatever is inside to be consumed—*to the surface,* with the result that *only the label* matters. Yet it matters, then, a great deal. Art is nothing but "label" as the text following a book's title is only a continuation of that title to the very end. The book or the painting, having a title and a signature, is simply the extension of an initial signal closed in its own field of reference. So the substance of a work of art is what one might call altogether a deep shallowness; an outside which, *in extenso,* is likewise an inside. What is present is conveyed by extending the label—that is, reading the book—and is therefore an act of total consumption.

A painting is variably sized and generally less than an inch deep; a page of print is even thinner. Yet because of the message to be read on this mere "surface," a painting or a novel is both incalculably deep and wide. In the arts, nourishment is found, the finest cuisine appreciated, by consuming the self-evident to its very last morsel. In art, the container and the thing contained are *one.* Yet to add that, in such a case, the form is also the content ("the medium is the message") would be false. There is a novel form, novelistic genres, but no one novel is just the same as another because the messages of novels, if not always the styles (even by the same author), differ radically. The film is a definite medium, but each use of it has, theoretically, a different message. If the use of the film is simplistic and robotlike, while the message may have a certain interest of its own, perhaps even theatrical interest, a fatal split necessarily occurs. There result, as it were, related fragments of a theater spectacle in the photography form, but not *a film.* In the same sense, a bad play, mechanically put together, splits itself off from whatever good scenes, good lines or good performers it may contain.

An unexposed film roll is exactly like the tin container of a can of food. Exposed (for example, affixed with an articulate label), all is revealed: the contents are created by the "label," or the images appearing on the sensitized, processed roll. As I have been saying, although technically the sensitized film surface is passive, the camera, or technical instrument of film, has *not* remained passive, but assumed a decisive part in creating the nature of the label. In a validly creative film, the spectacle before the camera is invented, not "given," but part of the spectacle we finally see on the screen is invented within *the camera* and *the laboratory,* so that the camera too is a performer, a collaborator, in the resultant product. What, then, has it "photographed"? It has photographed a psychology of creativity, so that the exposed film roll is now to be termed *objectified mind.* When the camera is not asked to perform beyond grinding away in the mechanical act of exposing the roll within it, it becomes a robot incarnate. Every second of a turning film roll, frame by frame, is therefore a unit in a creative crisis. The total time/space composition must be a responsible montage: a perpetual adding of image to image and sound to sound. In this respect, film-making is first and last both dance and music.

The whole point about man's self-creation is also the whole point about film's self-creation: one goes as far as possible toward transmuting and reshaping the given materials. This is the direct opposite of simply adding the given materials together (even when the addition, as with electric circuitry, is a scientific stunt). All that stuff leads to minimal film or minimal television, not maximal film. My theory is a theory of *maximal film.* This is the chief reason why it is valuable to discuss, as I shall now, films whose themes are self-conscious of the conditions under which man labors to create himself—that is, to build, in the most meaningful sense, a world for him to inhabit. First, it must be built *psychologically*—I mean filmically—and then *socially,* in terms of total objectivity.

Life tends to turn things around: people are more comfortable with a simple "accomplished fact" than a created object, a formal thing. Yet film as only propaganda for a Utopia is wish-fulfillment film, not true film. The arts can be programmatic, even propagandistic, but should not be so in a literal, direct form, a form depending upon objective "proof." That is always premature. To say that life is imitation is more correct than to say that art is imitation; a kind of inspired self-imitation, worked for unselfishly by individuals. Civilized life *is* this. Art, through mind, provides the models; life, through mind, imitates them. In this sense, art is the purification of the so-called media. Life is not the thing to be copied; mind is. In copying mind, life becomes an art.

The time/space paranoia to which I have devoted so much attention is simply the intensified aspect of the Zeitgeist of creative responsibility. This responsibility, however, must be seized in its sincerely profound dimension, not left in the inane, smug and superficial dimension where the commercial arts place it. This responsibility—this creative survival of man—is usually placed in the sphere of facile bedazzlement because the popular arts wish to flatter and lull the human conscience; to displace attention from its sense of real danger to its sense of false reassurance. The best way to do this is to represent everything—but everything!—in infinite masks of the entertainment idea: a sort of "house of mirrors" into which reality, so to speak, has been historically smuggled. Life at its worst and best must be simply one endless, absolutely continuous source of diversion—the perfect vaudeville act or TV Special. Which is why the genuine fright occasioned a portion of the radio public, many years ago, by that fictitious newscast stunt of Orson Welles ("The War of the Worlds") showed how science fiction with its terrors can be fake realism. Taken seriously, as reality, it means a supreme planetary crisis; taken as fiction, a few minutes or a few hours later, its effect is turned inside out. Oh, yes, this is theater! But, even like so much camp, it is theater for morons.

There is high-class theater for morons; by which I mean high-class camp to be appreciated by those who care for that sort of thing. Often it's a matter of mood and circumstance; often it's a sign of the desperation, the frank escape-gesture, felt, at times, by the soberest of us. An excellent example in the science-fiction genre—infinitely more imaginative than Welles's juvenile piece of tomfoolery—is the next film to be discussed: *The Tenth Victim*. Its technique is conventional film style of the snappy narrative kind but transposed, imaginatively, to the bizarre comic book world of science fiction, where we are taken, once again, to a planetary future where the computer idea, if not the computer robot, reigns supreme. The film's substance, I think, is wittier and more sophisticated than one has a right to expect. *The Tenth Victim* takes a tongue-in-cheek view of those utopian expectations of the human outlook made ambivalent by our omnipresent but submerged dread of a new atomic war. Regardless of the price paid meanwhile, the race (according to *The Tenth Victim*) has reached a point where what fashionably is to be called the war problem has been solved by what resembles rational ingenuity. Does it look absurd all the same? It does. But that is part of the flashy trick. According to a theory of psychic compensation, it is logical to suppose that man's internecine hatred, of which wars are presumed to be the savage animal expression, can be channelized by allowing individuals "legally" to hunt one another down with guns at appointed intervals.

Personal numbers, divided into those of aggressors and defendants, are drawn simultaneously by a computer, day after day, in the lottery manner. When your number comes up, you're both, as hunter and hunted, on your own. You can defend yourself of course by shooting down your pursuer or otherwise disposing of him. So, in effect, we would have a legalized, universally practiced but deadly series of private duels taking place continuously all over a generally peaceful planet, from which all collective wars have been eliminated. Even so, you see, the innocent bystander is endangered and, as always, will have to take care of himself. Far be it from my intention to imply that this superior piece of comic-book joking is in any wise morally in earnest. On the contrary, it is the "excellent example" which I call it because it has a slyly satiric, not crudely naïve, style of camp. When, in the opening sequence, the heroine—Ursula Andress —as the hunted gets her man, the hunter, she finally does so with a dramatic strategy. Dodging into an oddball "dayclub" where seemingly she is a performer, she comes out in her number and plugs him with what I recall as a firing tit. Proceeding to cut off the corpse's necktie, she proudly displays it to witnesses; thus she is like the hunter who wins the fox's tail, or rather, since the situation is turnabout, the fox who has won her hunter's tail: the female as triumphant castrator.

But that's only a beginning. The plot glides them into a situation where Miss Andress is the hunter and her computer-chosen victim is no other than Marcello Mastroianni, so that we have a variation on the old theme of male and female spies out to do each other in and meanwhile falling fatally in love. More or less! Love in this rather speculative future world, where sexual comfort stations have been installed, is put in question along with that other now-statutory thing, war, so there ensues a spectacular struggle between the sexes with some very tricky reversals of fortunes and tactics. Nor is love the only "questionable" survival. In line with the sadism of comic books (sly, arch or just vulgar) man has become dangerously (read "thrillingly") robotized. This new society that has so cleverly exiled collective war has had to institute a few drawbacks to one's remaining human in the old sentimental sense; for instance, cherishing one's parents in their old age is forbidden. Science fiction in its moral visionariness does not hesitate to penalize the advances of a scientifically planned society, whether bitterly satiric and pessimistic like 1984 (when the individual per se is the despised victim); gloriously, irresponsibly psychedelic like 2001; or, as in *The Tenth Victim*, brazenly cynical, fantastic, relying on sugared-up nightmare logic. O ye olde irony of the Electric Circuitry going on and on and on . . . to the point where, if you love your two old parents the way Mastroianni does in this film, you'll keep them (perfectly happy, of course, because they have a TV set) behind an automatic sliding door that pretends to be an immovable wall! You see, in Mastroianni's revised society, old people are *de trop*, an economic burden and legally to be eliminated. How? I should think that a painless private gas chamber would do nicely.

Offenders in this domain, like sentimental-son Mastroianni, are arrested. For there are no bones made about the fact that, whatever Peace may have achieved in this future world, its citizens live under strict dictatorship. The beautifullest of the film's sharp little, flip little ironies turns out to be that Mastroianni, betrayed by his own wife through jealousy of Miss Andress, has a typical home where it is remarked that nowadays the coveted "first editions" are not—of all obsolete things!—those fabled Shakespeare folios but simply rare comic books.

This touch both celebrates and apologizes for any idiocy of the imagination or the moral sense the story may be thought to contain. Carefully assessing this excellent example, we find that all it does is utilize science-fiction gimmicks toward concocting the same old spy-melodrama stuff in superslick form: sex, suspense, surprises, reversals, anticlimaxes and scads and scads of shooting.

What is space in *The Tenth Victim*, what is time? Both are computerized into the hidden, everlasting hazard that faces one at every turn, and which, to escape, to end up in the arms of romance (as happens here), one has to be both especially canny and especially blessed: fate's exceptionally wise and lucky favorite. Thus is time/space paranoia translated for the large public these days into old-fashioned, vulgarized ritual, from which one emerges victorious after moderate suffering. The old movie serial was built on this model and numerous campy Pop-cult films, nominally tongue in cheek, have revived this supposedly dead "art form." *Modesty Blaise*, *Planet of the Apes* and *Barbarella* are among the recent, less subtle "excellent" examples of this form. All such films offer models for the childish mass brain to feed on—the mass brain whose daily menu is television.

That it is possible to be more sensible and realistic, even more intellectual, about the modern world's psychic paranoia (central cause: the atom bomb) was demonstrated, not altogether chancily, by the gifted Japanese director Akira Kurosawa. The film was called, in the U.S.A., *I Live in Fear*, and although available for distribution in the 'fifties, it seemed to exhibitors so radically depressing (it has no sex-romancing whatever) that it was not put on commercial screens till the 'sixties, when it went into oblivion with even less flash than a meteor burning out on striking the earth's atmosphere. In 1960, however, I included in my book *The Three Faces of the*

Film a brief essay on this film titled "The Atomophobe: a New Culture Hero." In conclusion, I remarked that probably this rashly termed "culture hero" (beautifully played by Toshiro Mifune) was "our century's first *truly serious* worrier." I don't see how, even as late as today, that literal description could be disputed.

The worrier (a prosperous manufacturer) is a hero because his actions are directly predicated on his deepest mental convictions, his deepest emotional base. Fearful, indeed certain, of an all-out atomic war in the future, he has minutely calculated that the safest place on Earth to be, when such a catastrophe arrives, is Brazil. So convinced, he immediately makes plans for moving his wife and family of sons and daughters (as well as a mistress and their child) to that fancied haven. Given his nature and the presumed facts, there is no other logical course. Therefore he does not mind that the proposed emigration means uprooting from home and country, the sale of his thriving factory and so on. However, his legitimate family, to a unit, does mind—especially his wife, who naturally is jealous of his mistress and appalled that he wishes to consider her part of "the family."

Hence, the family goes to law to have the patriarch declared incompetent if not insane; and incompetent, in spite of his eloquent defense of the reasonableness of his position, is what a specially appointed board of three arbiters declares him. At this blow, he is reduced from head of his family to being its outcast, embarrassing, tolerated dependent, while the management of his factory and financial affairs passes to his older son. Now it is that he becomes a true culture hero since, by his own lights, *he* is sane and *the world* is mad. Yes, he has attained artistic vision: *the world has been totally subjectivized.* Technically, judged from the outside, he is a psychopathic nut; from the inside, he is not only wise but a savior of the race, and it is as such that he proceeds to martyrize himself—after a spate of humiliated brooding —by burning down his factory in the forlorn hope that its loss may compel his family to emigrate with him to Brazil.

Inevitably, his act has the opposite effect. It is now possible to declare him legally insane and he is duly put away after a scene in which his stricken family and even his workers denounce him. A tremendously effective touch ends the film. One member of the board that has condemned him has never been certain that its judgment was right, and this sympathetic man takes occasion to visit the ruined patriarch in his solitary cell, where he sits reading calmly. At first the "madman" takes no notice of his visitor; he seems withdrawn, unreachable. Then, of his own accord, he lifts his eyes from his book and asks his visitor, "By the way, what happened to the Earth?" Getting no answer from the shocked man, the patriarch rises and goes to his window, through whose frosted glass the image of the sun blazes. "There!" he cries. "You see, it's burning up!"

This culture hero is simply the "mad artist" who has achieved total identity with his vision. We must thoroughly understand the moral of all this. Here is not merely a speculative study of what can happen to a paranoid individual in an atomic age. The nice part, the great part, is that, viewing the question in terms of my theory, one does not have to be an extreme paranoiac to "achieve total identity with one's vision." One can also and otherwise do this simply by making a good film, a really *subjective* film. The culture hero of *I Live in Fear* subjectified time and space into capsulated catastrophes, and so he had to take the objective consequences. Yet *aesthetically* he succeeded. *His* is the viewpoint of this work of art. However authentic as an imaginative concept (surely it *is* authentic) his vision is but one plot, one response, one style in which a world condition may be conceived and acted upon. It is obviously not the most popular, the most practiced. No! By no means! The fashionable thing, for a long time now, has been to project a "brave new world" which seems to warn against the doom of the ultimate fascist state and its robotized society while getting as many cheap, common thrills as possible out of the naked, sadomasochistic spectacle of this worldwide human disaster as if it were a hoax. *Vide* that stop-press thriller, Kubrick's *A Clockwork Orange*. Or think of *Jesus Christ Superstar* which would have us make a clown show of Jesus' agony just to prove, apparently, that even Christians can groove with grimness, when timely, and make a new rock out of the Rock of Ages, meanwhile bringing the Christ into line with Mick Jagger et al. and the tradition of zany film comics.

Truffaut's transposition of a typically vulgar sad-new-world project (surely as glum as *I Live in Fear* but also cheaply, simplistically sentimental) was *Fahrenheit 451*, the utterly monotonous image of a future society where books have been rigidly banned because they are flammables in a milieu which otherwise has been modishly rendered inflammable. Naturally, a contrary remnant of bookworms ("culture heroes") seclude the tabooed articles and get hunted down and burned up with their treasured cache. Truffaut's film is an extraordinary instance of how paranoia, once an "artist" puts his mind to it, can be converted systematically into a deadpan bore, with all the sugar coating forming the inside, the contents, and the contents proper, the style and the imaginative vision, forming a cruelly bitter icing meant to pass, one presumes, for worldly wit and wisdom—or, at any rate, for "straight entertainment."

Not that moral hysteria (taken by film melodrama in

stride) is not a widely prevalent, perfectly authentic human condition. The issue is what one makes of this hysteria. All kinds of controls may be applied to moral hysteria from the outside—the most elementary being, one might add, the strait jacket, and so on (up the medical incline) to the private sanctity and mysterious offices of the mental clinic. But this is social hygiene in the looser, more casual sense. As an emergency measure, or simply a way of regimentation under a dictatorship, it has the crudity of concentration-camp tactics. It is like converting filial cherishing, as in *The Tenth Victim*, into an undesirable sort of moral hysteria. Actually the whole world may be considered hysterical, with the shrewder set of "lunatics" dominating and imposing sanctions on the stupider, or simply more passive, set. For example, who is really "sane" in George Orwell's *1984* as a film? Who is really "human" in Kubrick's and Clarke's *2001*? Who, if any, are the "culture heroes" in *Fahrenheit 451*?

Victim and victimizer become as one through some tour de force of fate. Their origins and intentions remain swathed in doubts and compulsive, opaque acts of persecution, which may well (as in a revolution) become mutual, promiscuous, retroactive. This is an acknowledged world of time and space over which there can be nothing but mechanical controls or a drug-induced state of absolute self-deception, where the split between "subjective illusion" and "objective fact" is a yawning, incalculable gulf; or else, on the contrary, a case of fatally imperceived overlap. One condition is as deadly and hopeless as the other. All space "out there" means nothing unless it has limits as limits are defined by the existence of a comprehensive, efficient organization of parts, so that grasping any smallest part means you are also grasping the whole. This operation cannot be achieved unless there is a concrete theory, that is, an adequate image, in the mind of the operator. And in turn this means that *all space* is, actually, "in here" not "out there."

Bowman, the surviving cosmonaut of 2001, who seeks the conquest of the solar system and so goes "all out" for it, is making a primary mistake, and to all intents and purposes has the hopelessly incoherent, unmanageable consciousness of someone under the influence of a drug. He not only is *not* really out there, he is also not really in here because he's "subjective" in the useless, indefinable and uncreative sense. He's a voluntary victim of the phony, science-fiction syndrome of outer-space control. Thus he deserves to lose every foot of the psychedelic space he so obviously, spectacularly gains by courtesy of laboratory tricks. Indeed, he seems actually to lose it—which is the proper moral, if not the proper art.

It would be a mistake for the reader to suppose that, all this time, I have been plugging a theory of film which means that superior motion pictures must be painstakingly intellectual and philosophically, no less than morally, conscious; that every film, accordingly, must be rated as a construct of some deep and refined ideological system. Not so! Film does not interrelate ideas among themselves as in a closed world. No, it is logic which does that; science, philosophy and didactic ethics which do that. Which is why 2001 issued as an irresponsible hybrid. Film, however, does interrelate images as the various aspects and interactions among material objects, one of these being the way human beings are affected by "ideas" and act in accordance with them. Thus, film literally photographs the life of the mind as the mind converts images into ideas, gives them a role in the motor reflexes and makes them participate in the grand designs of the imagination. Necessarily film does this in a double sense because the human beings we see in a film exist, properly speaking, in some creator's mind—I do not say in God's mind; I do say in a creator's mind—so that the process by which we see ideas governing human motions and emotions is literally through the mind of a beholder who is engaged specifically in putting his own consciousness onto film.

Every theory requires, perhaps, a perfect illustration—in the case of an art theory, the best illustration may not mean the best work of art or even the best class of works, but the work must bear a particular lucidity and be, in this rareness, second to none. For its main purpose is to illustrate a type of generality, to form a vivid, tightly graspable pattern which it shares with things better and things not so good. I could choose a small film such as Jean Genet's *Un Chant d'Amour*, put together with the highest theoretical purpose of simply portraying homosexual aesthetics among male prisoners. It has no film gloss at all; it does have style atmosphere. It reveals the strategies of frustrated desire, the voyeurist ritual of the corridor guard, outright ritual masturbation as a dance, and the union of two lovers in the open fields—a facet of the action which we cannot identify as fact or fancy owing to Genet's perfect grasp of film's subjectivity. The action here (as in all film) is primarily mental, so that when the two prisoners seem liberated in open country, chase one another and finally make love, it may be only in the imagination of one or both, or it may mean an actual escape, transient or lasting. The point is that there is no break between the reality of this possibly fantasized little escapade and the unquestionably physical rituals of masturbation, a kiss achieved through blowing cigarette smoke through a wall and a sadistic love gesture of the guard toward a cell inmate:

first he lashes him with a belt, then rams his revolver into his submissively open mouth. He does not pull the trigger: it is only a symbolic act.

But citing this brief film is useful in an introductory sense, for exactly at the point where the imaginary *might* take over and convert the true prospect of space in Genet's film (the prison cells and the corridor outside them) into the illusive prospect of open country where two lovers are free to make love—right at this point, I think, we can identify the kind of space that film always and necessarily creates. This is not external space reaching into an infinite, but cosmic space identifying itself in every millimeter of the reel as consistent and the same, whatever images it may carry as features of the action. If a sense of unity abides among variegated things, there is no issue of "unification." Cosmic space such as this may be, in the Einsteinian sense, relativist space, but by no means is it necessary to make this correspondence since the validity of a film theory cannot be defined thus.

Cosmic space, or, as I would put it, *filmic* space, means being everywhere at once, or that "place" where the viewpoint is the same as the vanishing point; the most inward, the same as the most outward. Perchance the reader will now remark: "But that is McLuhan's idea!—that is the 'you are there' and 'they are here' of electric circuitry via television." Heaven forbid! I mention such a reaction as a possibility; I greatly hope it is not true of my readers. As I've iterated in these pages, this wonder of interchange between thereness and hereness is work which must occur creatively in someone's intent imagination, someone's mind; it is never conferred by a sum of external events that might be considered by a TV station as significant enough to represent the "news"! Yes, that is what *McLuhan* means, or says he means; it is precisely the opposite of what I mean! As for television in a creative capacity, it has already developed a special sense of space and style of acting, something adapted to intimacy and the small-scale screen. But first the theory of television art must be put thoroughly into practice and offered the spectator. The miracle depends not in the least on electric circuitry as a technical phenomenon, a means of communication; it depends entirely on what message the electricity is circulating and the form that articulates it.

As I say, then, passage through true cosmic, or filmic, space is not physical, but an illusion of the physical: it is *pure* illusion. As also I have said, filmic time is only so long as a film takes to run: it is literally its "running time." This aesthetic time of film is therefore the same as musical time. For, although there are tempos within one musical work, the work exists as an entirety all at once; one part, strictly speaking, is simultaneous with another because the whole cannot be considered separately from its parts, or vice versa. Every image in a film is simultaneously present in the same way, so that passage from image to image is simply a rhythmic and formal matter; it has nothing to do, except by coincidence, with the specific density of objects in the physical world, the manner or the rate at which they may actually be moving.

The world of the imagination, where film participates like any other art, is weightless in that it may assume either weightlessness or any weight at any time. Any single frame (that is, any instant plucked from the flow of action in a film) automatically assumes a certain "plastic" weight, a thing of related rest and movement, depth of shadow and brightness of highlight, balanced stability and instability; this quality of a frame is both something in itself and relates to the frame preceding and the frame succeeding it. This is why violent impact, like a blow struck, a falling object or an automobile collision, is not the same in a film as in life (whether experienced subjectively or objectively). Even if we are not in the collision, for example, but only witness it, it is never the same, for on film such a violent impact is variously manipulated, and in any case we know, if in the movie house, that we are seeing, not material objects, but only their mirror images. We react to the idea of a collision, not to a collision.

True, our experience of the physical world creates what is called kinaesthetic sympathy when we are merely watching, participating only through the eyes and ears. Yet the actual laws governing, for example, a dancer, laws of which the dancer himself is aware while dancing, do not apply in turn to the spectator; the latter can only know these laws by analogy (that is, by a certain optic/mental/nervous operation of his own), but when a dancer is transposed to film, when, during a leap for instance, he may be made to float, seem not even to touch the ground, then he himself is made to participate in the cosmic or filmic space of which I speak. The late avant-garde film-maker Maya Deren made a film exactly to illustrate the way film may transform actual space into cosmic space, *A Study in Choreography for Camera*, where the quality of the dancer and his dance changes as much owing to his suddenly changed environment as because of the changes of his steps.

I have been drawing my lines very fine, theoretically, but this is in order to define essential details of the theory as such. To illustrate and climax this theory, I choose Glauber Rocha's film *Antonio das Mortes*, because it deals directly with its narrative structure and takes its filmic space simply, as if in analogy with real space, without manipulations that create spatial and temporal illusions through filmic devices; as, for example, those of Deren I've just mentioned. While there is nothing supernatural (or, of course, superplanetary) about the action itself, *Antonio das Mortes* is full of ritual figures representing transcendent, concentrated, typical and perennial human forces; at once, it is a magic battle and a sacred rite, the story of a hero-savior's death and the reversal and dissolution of the triumph of evil, the force that puts the hero to death. The title role is that of the Dragon (here in plausible human form) who manages to conquer the Dragon Slayer, his appointed killer, only to become the Dragon Slayer, supplanting him and turning against his (the Dragon's) sponsors and annihilating them.

Rocha's film work came out of a new film movement, independent and socially committed, that arose during recent years in Brazil, so that the apparent throwback of this film to folk ritual and outdated traditions was made as an allegory of continued oppression and persecution of the people and the latter's eventual triumph after suffering. Ultimately and unfortunately, Rocha found it impossible to make more films in Brazil. The figure in *Antonio das Mortes* that would be the Dragon Slayer in the medieval tradition of Europe is rather, as here transposed to the figure of the traditional outlaw of Brazil, the *cangaceiro,* the sort of folk hero that Robin Hood was in European mythic tradition: the romantic rebel (sentimental and the people's possession) who robbed only through necessity, who helped the poor, loved freedom and was doomed to be a perpetual fugitive. Essentially, in strictly modern perspective, he is the idolized guerrilla chief, the revolutionary leader, and one suspects that the legend of a Che Guevara is related to the downfall, in this film, of the heroic *cangaceiro,* the peasants' champion.

His triumphant opponent, who gives him a fatal wound of which he eventually dies, is Antonio das Mortes, the professional killer hired to suppress a revolt on a great Brazilian estate by killing its leader in a personal duel, which turns out to be (though professionally Antonio carries a gun) a sword match. As an actual contemporary type, such men as Antonio das Mortes, while presumably dying out, are unofficial policemen, hired to "arrest" professional gunmen who themselves have been hired to intervene in political elections by creating disorder and actually killing rival candidates. Rocha has simplified the actual situation by mythifying and ritualizing the human types and their actions as if he were dealing with a morality play and its allegorical heroes and villains.

The cast is as typed as the figures of the Commedia dell'Arte: the Colonel (the estate-owner), his Mistress (a sensual blonde), the Police Chief, the Teacher. All these are carnal free-livers who intrigue among themselves and are rivals for the Mistress, who actually hates her lord and master, finally, in a fit of crazed brutality, killing him herself. These, representing a shabby provincial establishment, are of course the movie's villains. On the other side, composing the leaders of the peasants' revolt, are the *cangaceiro* himself, a picturesque, naïvely exalted, swaggering young man, a female Saint and a solemn sort of black witch doctor: all these typify forces in Brazil arraigned against the oppressors. They represent a mystic cult not so much in reality as in the mind of the auteur director, Rocha, who sees in the young *cangaceiro* a hero inspired to espouse the religious unity of the peasants, represented by a "front" made up of the followers of the female Catholic Saint and the black male Mystic.

One of Rocha's most impressive feats in *Antonio das*

Mortes is to have located the power of the peasant revolt squarely in ritual sensibility, a deeply rooted belief in dancing and singing as sacred potencies. This is emphasized by the local picturesqueness of the costumes, poor but improvised for show, as if for a feast-day celebration that puts on view a people's most precious possessions. The background of the duel between the *cangaceiro* and the professional killer is the mass of ecstatic peasants as an articulate chorus, reacting as an audience and also part of the spectacle. Their movements are choreographed to music and song, and so with the duel itself, as though it were not real but symbolic, part of a dance rite. This element gives ancient majesty to the duel, to its fatal outcome (in which the revolt seems doomed) and to the ensuing peripety.

Victorious, the evil killer Antonio becomes converted as he gravitates toward the mourning figure of the Saint, who (as she gives vent to her sorrow over the dying *cangaceiro*) virtually assumes the role of the Virgin Mary in the Pietà. Finally, main force, in the form of a squadron of hired gunmen, arrives on the scene and proceeds to mow down the followers of the Saint and the black Mystic in a gunfight where the victims have no defense. Then the transfigured Antonio appears as their chief opponent and conquers them, shot for shot, almost single-handedly. The turmoil has already precipitated the inner-directed destruction of the oppressors, who have started quarreling over the Colonel's mistress during the pathetically humble funeral procession of the dead landowner.

The final scenes of the film—during which several men, including a priest, roll around on the ground trying to rape the Mistress—are virtually an allegoric put-on of the way modern theater groups stage Happenings in the street. The style here is part Theatre of the Ridiculous, part Living Theatre straight stuff: crude, bold, silly, deliberately scandalous. The windup—when nearly everyone on both sides lies dead with the exception of the converted Antonio, the Saint and the Mystic—is like the desolate center of a town in an old-fashioned, period American western, when nearly everybody but the hero and his sweetheart are strewn around, inert, with bullets in them.

Now the Saint and the black Mystic appear riding the same horse and carrying a banner. They are allegoric symbols alive and triumphant at a scene of human devastation. As for Antonio, taking his solitary departure along a modern highway with adjacent gas station, he seems like those good-bad conquerors in certain western movies who erase themselves, solo, by fading into the distance. Surely, *Antonio das Mortes* is not the most original or brilliant film of recent times; its present importance for this book, however, is that it is both recent and authentic, and as authentic has its own brilliance and originality. It has obeyed the theory which I think is at the heart of film, that determines its relevance and the high mark of its relevance. In this it is like such complex films as Carné's *Children of Paradise* and Renoir's *The Rules of the Game,* such simple films as Eisenstein's *Potemkin* and Genet's *Un Chant d'Amour.*

As literature be important, it is built word by word, phrase by phrase, sentence by sentence, and so on; film likewise, to be important, is built frame by frame, action by action, scene by scene. This can be done with relative intuitiveness and relative consciousness, but even with the intuitive dominating, behind it must be (as behind the conscious) a governing concept, an idea of true unification which results in that tangible/intangible thing called style atmosphere. It is a matter of subjective germination entirely, mental germination of the subject's profoundest feelings. Only this factor knows instinctively what to choose from a given medium that will best suit its specific purposes and realize those purposes. Only by this process can the cosmic time/space of true film be created. Each art is but the portrait of an idea which takes a chosen time, a chosen space in which to state itself. Film is the portrait of an optic, or optic/aural idea.

Since, of all the arts, film most closely resembles the real world, its idea may be said to appear in the disguise of the real world. There would not be a disguise, however, if the things we see on a film screen really happened in the real world; then, what we see would be the naked truth, however fragmentary, ambiguous, involuntarily distorted and inadequate. Documentary film (unhappily I think) aspires to this same ideal of "the naked truth"—but not so, true film; not art film. If the naked truth were enough, why film it? If the naked truth of acts and speech were enough, why the works known as films and books? Self-evidently, that nakedness is not enough. Still, the arts do not rival reality as things within reality rival each other (causing war, hate, despair, profound unhappiness); rather, the arts play a game with reality in which the rivalry is entirely ritual or symbolic, so that defeat or victory is also symbolic. Always life remains, not death. Just as life, not death, remains at the end of *Antonio das Mortes*.

Again I emphasize that it is Rocha's simplicity with respect to this basic theory of film that makes his work loom so importantly at the final stage of this argument. The mise-en-scène he has created with this film is an actual background, an arid, rocky, sparsely vegetated portion of Brazil that hardly qualifies as a land of plenty. Yet obviously it is as much the ultimate ground of social destiny as the Garden of Eden. In a sense, it *is* the biblical Garden made desertlike as a symbol of man's desperate situation in the modern world. It is full of local color, which makes it particular, yet it is vividly scenic, "theatrical," so as to collaborate with Rocha's idea of a universal struggle and its conditions. There are few films in which, as here, the background has so much functional importance. In Rocha's film, the somewhat ragged richness, the cactusy decorativeness, the shady air, the dialectic of plainness, poorness, grayness with fine texture, insidious color, vitality of form, contribute to balancing the play of struggling forces, rival forces, so that an air of plastic justice possesses the film: style atmosphere pervades it.

There is a wonderful shot of the fine open face of the youthfully bearded *cangaceiro*, a peasant type, yet humanly typical, a sort of Ideal Man who suggests both Jesus and the mythic Saint George. His arching, splendid sombrero, silver-studded, turned up sharply in front and peculiar to the mixed culture of Brazil, is like both a halo and a helmet; his eyes are the eyes of a fighter and a dreamer, his full, well-formed lips have the faintest of defiant curls, his somewhat unkempt hair flows on his shoulders like an angel's. A shining openness lives in this image, yet something darkened too. It is utterly, humanly, grandly itself. But the figure of its opponent, Antonio das Mortes, is just the opposite. Antonio is taller, powerful, gross; his heavy black beard covers his expression, except for the eyes which are hungrily dark, level, determined. His brimmed hat is turned down like a gangster's; his alertness, his decisiveness, is also like a gangster's. He is the incarnate, essentially guilty, force of the professional killer: the enemy of mankind. His conversion under the spell cast by the grieving female Saint is entirely plausible because he is a man without a spiritual center. Everything in him is really only around him: *he is totally armed outside*. But through this armor the human heart cries out—and finds its call answered. He is really very much like the grossly misled conception of bad films, films by those who think the film screen is a passive mirror, something that reflects horror and happiness as if they were the same, essentially shapeless things, as if deeds of wanton killing were here to stay and could provide as much entertainment as any other phenomenon. I wish this wrong and very injurious conception of film could be converted, as was Antonio das Mortes, by the sight of the true truth, by the true theory of film. The true theory of film is simply the photograph of what man's mind can bring of goodness and grace, aesthetically whole and victorious, to the spectacle of the world. Sprocket by sprocket, this is the chain of film's being. It will last as long as mind and art last. If film-makers cooperate . . .

So, film-makers, I make an *envoi:* Hold to the sprocket holes of the images dictated to you by your own voices, your personal and peculiar voices, and no other voices. This is your hope, and of course my theory. The shadow of an airplane climbs the Empire State Building . . . I saw that from my window the other day while I took a turn about my room in a moment of recess from the typewriter on which these pages are being written. As I saw then, you could have seen—seen *that it can happen in the world too* . . . this wonderful shadow existence of the film . . . The all-important thing is that it should happen, consequentially, decisively, in *you,* this climbing shadow of a thing making a design and a mystery, a miracle that is yet a fact. Because, insofar as you make a film of such a thing, it *does* happen in you. And then you make it happen in a film camera just by opening a lens inward at the same time you open it outward. All images on the film screen, you understand, belong to the mind. The actual lens is only the mind's surrogate lens. And this has to be improved on by the most exacting process in which the work is mentally reformulated, image by image, so that only what the mind wants is there: all else has been eliminated. The film work is the most faithfully objectified portrait of the brain—that is, the brain's content, not its form—yet invented by man.

Only by *being* and *being* and *being* . . . can anything truly become: truly arrive. And this is especially true of art because it can so often, in many of its forms, be mistaken for imitation of the world; art is so "classically" the mirror for objective things, pre-existing things, completed things. Think how photography, and then its supreme development, cinematography, were born into this time situation of our planet as into a yawning trap. Film came at a moment when, owing to science, the truth of philosophy and social morals and politics bore more than ever the literal, the matter-of-fact, look! Film became the fool of fortune presiding suddenly over the empire of delusions that many people still call facts. I have referred to the mass brain, the public brain, as if it were an object, something to be isolated and inspected and inventoried. In a way, surely, it is such a thing. Yet, being preoccupied with two vast delusions, *time* the inflexible circle and *space* the expandable box (both mythically external and at times dangerously incalculable), the mass brain tends to feel both persecuted and pleasured, indiscriminately so, and remains, to this day, confused by these chimeras.

What an ally, then, did film seem to be for the mass brain when it arrived! Surely, film could be utilized for every contingency in which cowardly human complacency found need for self-deception, for coddling its pet megalomanias and feeding, even while seeming to allay, its crowding paranoias. Thus, film joined all the other technological gimmicks which science could supply and which are given such open play in the deluge of commercials that interrupt TV programs. All commercials, whatever the real usefulness and special superiorities of the products being advertised, are another variety of science fiction—as I think all of us who really care to think about the subject already know. With all the huge problems besetting us planetary dwellers, one is apt to take for granted the ignoble smugness, the balmy blindness and the profuse frivolity that help make life look, according to the movies and their TV cousin, only a species of harmless entertainment.

But this book, in striving to define a film theory belonging to the world, has perforce not taken such things for granted and has tried, in fact, to indict harmless entertainment and robotlike scientific progress as the enemies of truth and art. Against the gruesome array of optical gimmicks today, there is only one true champion (one Saint George) of film theory in particular or art theory in general: *the truly creative act.* If we look carefully at the mass of our data, we find, where one true filmic guide may exist, a hundred thousand false filmic leads; for one genuine filmic statement, a million plagiarisms of "reality" are waiting on film reels to be rerun. It is because of film's insidious power as optical evidence —it is always *that*—that I insist here on the true power of that evidence. This power rests not at all with what it can tell us about the nature of the material universe— that thing "out there" that both surrounds and pervades us—and the puzzle of eternity that lies in the circle of every watch, each tower clock and punch-in time system. Laboratory documents, science files, newspapers and all sorts of computer systems can tell us about those aspects. It is the function of film (as other than a mere assist to such documentation) to be artistically and intellectually creative in its own right: to provide us with a unique image of what it is to think with the imagination, to add to the world's objects something else specifically and exclusively created by man. The destiny of film, and its only possible greatness, is to photograph this mental process; indeed, millimeter by millimeter, *to be* this mental process, to produce the organism of this induplicable and supreme object . . . the work of art that is a total optic/aural subject rendered precisely as a total optic/aural object.

INDEX